Americans without Law

Americans without Law

The Racial Boundaries of Citizenship

Mark S. Weiner

NEW YORK UNIVERSITY PRESS

New York and London

NEW YORK UNIVERSITY PRESS
New York and London
www.nyupress.org

Library of Congress Cataloging-in-Publication Data
Weiner, Mark Stuart.
Americans without law : the racial boundaries of citizenship /
Mark S. Weiner.
p. cm.
Includes bibliographical references and index.
ISBN–13: 978–0-8147–9364–0 (cloth : alk. paper)
ISBN–10: 0–8147–9364–9 (cloth : alk. paper)
1. Minorities—Government policy—United States.   2. Minorities—
Legal status, laws, etc.—United States.   3. Minorities—United
States—Politics and government.   4. United States—Race relations.
5. United States—Politics and government.   I. Title.
E184.A1W344   2006
323.17309—dc22   2005032447

New York University Press books are printed on acid-free paper,
and their binding materials are chosen for strength and durability.

Manufactured in the United States of America
10 9 8 7 6 5 4 3 2

For Stephanie
Only, Always

Contents

Preface

This book contributes to the literature on American conceptions of race and citizenship from the perspective of the cultural history of law. My aim is to depict a specific language through which the racial character of civic belonging in the United States was understood from the late-nineteenth through the mid-twentieth century, a way of speaking and thinking that I call "juridical racialism." In sketching the contours of this civic language, I seek to highlight not only its role in the transformation of what historian David A. Hollinger has called "the circle of we," but also its place within changing elite views of the relation between the individual self and the expanding apparatus of the liberal state. In addition, I wish to offer a window onto how the rise of the concept of culture associated with anthropologist Franz Boas entered U.S. constitutional law and influenced American conceptions of national identity.

Americans without Law addresses students and scholars in American studies, political science, history, law, and related fields in the humanities and social sciences. Although it appears after the publication of my book *Black Trials: Citizenship from the Beginnings of Slavery to the End of Caste* (Alfred A. Knopf, 2004), it is, in fact, my first book-length study. Readers of both works may discern the affinity between juridical racialism and my treatment of the concept of a "people of law" in *Black Trials*, and indeed the research undertaken for this first book lay the conceptual foundations for the second. At the same time, this study takes a more expansive and theoretically generalizable approach to issues of citizenship by placing the history of juridical racialism in a comparative racial frame, as well as by exploring issues of subjectivity, state formation, and modernization.

I wish to thank the Social Science History Association for awarding the manuscript of *Americans without Law* the President's Book Award of 2000, an honor I will always treasure. I also wish to thank Dean Stuart

L. Deutsch of Rutgers School of Law-Newark, who provided the assistance of the Dean's Research Fund so that I might prepare the manuscript for publication; my colleagues at Rutgers, particularly my fellow legal historian Gregory Mark; a group of exceptional senior scholars in American studies, legal history, and law and society who supported this project through their intellectual and personal generosity, especially Jean-Christophe Agnew, Rogers M. Smith, William E. Nelson, Robert W. Gordon, William E. Forbath, John Brigham, and Christine B. Harrington; the librarians and library staff of Yale University, the Houghton Library at Harvard University, the Library of Congress, the New York Zoological Society, and the National Archives; my friends Mitchell A. Orenstein, Thomas Hilbink, and Mark Atwood Lawrence, who gave early encouragement to my work; and Adam Goldman and Monica Moore for heroic editorial assistance at the final hour. This book is dedicated to my wife, Stephanie Kuduk Weiner, for all her love.

Introduction

"[T]o imagine a language," wrote the philosopher Ludwig Wittgenstein, is "to imagine a form of life."[1] This book examines how one aspect of our national life, the racial limits of American civic belonging, was imagined and brought into being through a culturally potent and institutionally productive language of law. I call that language "juridical racialism," and I believe it was a basic feature of the history of American citizenship in the late-nineteenth and early-twentieth centuries, though it has gone largely unexamined and unnamed until now. Juridical racialism was a civic rhetoric that fused the concepts of race and law into a single idea—in which the two concepts were mutually constitutive—and that drew its principles from prominent contemporary social scientific theories of human variation, especially those associated with the developing field of anthropology. Juridical racialism was present throughout public discourse in the wake of the Civil War, much as public language is now saturated with principles of economic rationality, and its legacy persists within controversies about the use of American power to advance democracy abroad. By considering the role this powerful rhetorical amalgam played in political debates and Supreme Court decisions about the civic status of four minority groups in four successive historical periods, I seek to reveal not only its significance for the history of American citizenship, a task that opens a window onto the influence of the modern concept of culture in American law, but also its centrality to the linked history of American state development—a story, in turn, based on a transformation in conceptions and practices of the self. At root, I argue, juridical racialism was a historically significant discourse of modernization that enabled the United States to manage its civic boundaries in ways that furthered national economic growth.

In the chapters that follow, I examine the role juridical racialism played in debates about the civic status of Native Americans in the 1880s,

Puerto Ricans and Filipinos in the 1900s, Asian immigrants in the 1920s, and black Americans in the 1940s and 1950s. Each chapter is divided into two parts. The first part explores the life and work of a public thinker who followed a particular mode of racial or anthropological thought and, accordingly, promoted a specific juridical-racial vision of the group whose status is at issue in the chapter. The second part considers how the racial views the thinker advanced were mirrored in the jurisprudence of Supreme Court decisions that affected, and in most cases diminished, the civic standing of the group. In chapter 1, I examine John Wesley Powell, founder of the Bureau of American Ethnology and advocate of the principle of unilinear social evolution, alongside legal decisions supporting the constitutionality of the Dawes Act, which subdivided native lands during the assimilationist era of U.S. Indian policy. In chapter 2, I discuss Senator Henry Cabot Lodge, progressive exponent of American imperialism and student of the Teutonic origins thesis of American government (a school of thought that lay at the boundary of legal history and anthropology), alongside one of the *Insular Cases* (1901–1904), which defined the civic status of the territories the United States acquired through the Spanish-American War.[2] In chapter 3, I consider Madison Grant, popular champion of racial eugenics as well as a virulent, racialist theory of European and American history, and *Takao Ozawa v. United States* (1922), which lay the basis for the exclusion of Japanese immigrants under the Immigration Act of 1924.[3] And in chapter 4, I examine Gunnar Myrdal, author of *An American Dilemma* (1944), a thinker broadly influenced by the psychological and anti-essentialist principles of the Boasian culture-and-personality school of anthropology, alongside the midcentury desegregation case of *Brown v. Board of Education* (1954).[4]

Over the course of these chapters, I develop four related arguments. The first argument is that juridical racialism formed a distinct tradition in the rhetoric of American citizenship in which racial groups were characterized in terms of legal categories and in which law was described through the lens of racial difference, a rhetoric in which race and law were mutually constitutive. Most important, in the rhetorical tradition of juridical racialism, minority groups were characterized in terms of their relative legal capacity—their ability or inability to uphold legality as a general ideal and to follow specific forms of legal behavior—and this characterization served to justify a group's place in the circle of national civic life. As I will explain, juridical racialism drew its intellectual authority and rhetorical tropes from prominent contemporary theories of human variation in the social sciences, especially anthropology, a relation to the professional disciplines that marks it as a historically specific and distinct expression of the tendency of many national communities to describe outsiders as peoples without law. While juridical racialism was implicated in the public perception and civic status of most racial minorities in the United States, not all its rhetorical manifestations were equally important. Those I examine in this study were significant for the role they played in furthering state and economic modernization at critical junctures in national history. Moreover, while juridical racialism has been an active ideological presence among a range of institutional actors, it has been especially salient among the groups I consider here: academics and intellectuals, as a framework to understand human variation; political officials, as a tool with which to advance generally exclusionary policies of citizenship; and the judiciary, as an underlying structure of jurisprudence in constitutional and statutory adjudication.

The second argument of this study is that the character of juridical racialism changed radically as a result of the development of the modern concept of culture. Because juridical racialism has mirrored contemporaneous social-scientific theories of human variation, its history involves the story of an intellectual revolution. In the social sciences, that revolution took place when the modern culture concept, originally advanced by Franz Boas, displaced modes of understanding human difference associated with nineteenth-century ethnology and the intellectual fields and frameworks against which anthropology set itself as it grew into its own as a professional discipline. These included most prominently theories of unilinear social evolution, in which all societies are classified according to a single continuum of upward historical progress, and those of racial essentialism, which attribute cultural differences to somatic inheritance. The success of Boas and his students in their campaign against these now rejected views effected a decisive break with the social-scientific past. The history of juridical racialism involves a parallel discontinuity, in which forms of juridical racialism that drew on pre-Boasian notions of race, and thus helped justify the exclusion of minority groups from full civic belonging, were displaced over the course of the twentieth century by a culturalist juridical-racial framework that furthered racially inclusive civic ends. In this respect, the story of juridical racialism illustrates one way in which the modern concept of culture helped transform American civic life along the politically progressive lines its advocates envisioned; indeed, as

I indicate in chapter 4, under the influence of the concept of culture, the tradition of juridical racialism came largely to a close.

The final two arguments that structure this study approach juridical racialism in terms of continuity rather than change. Most important, the rhetoric of juridical racialism was a discourse of modernization that, in all its forms and stages, advanced the constitutional authority of the federal government in ways that furthered national economic growth. Each of the following chapters describes how a rhetoric of juridical racialism was used to manage the civic status of a particular minority group whose fate was tied to one of the era's central dilemmas of political economy, which was resolved through the judicial reaffirmation or expansion of federal power. In chapter 1, I consider how juridical racialism enabled the more effective exploitation of Indian land in the late-nineteenth century, in a process Karl Marx ironically called "primitive accumulation," by laying the legal foundation for the Indian plenary power doctrine.[5] In chapter 2, I examine how juridical racial thought helped secure better access to overseas markets in the early-twentieth century through its role in the development of the doctrine of territorial incorporation. In chapter 3, juridical racialism served the goal of stabilizing domestic labor markets in the 1920s by restricting Asian immigration to the United States on the basis of national plenary immigration authority. And in chapter 4, in the wake of the Boasian revolution, juridical racialism helped facilitate the expansion of postwar consumer society by supporting the cause of southern desegregation, which was made possible by the expansion of federal power over the states under the Fourteenth Amendment and the Commerce Clause. In each instance, juridical racial rhetoric formed a conceptual link between national civic identity, American state development, and material, economic progress.

In each instance, moreover, the development of federal power facilitated by juridical racial thought was linked to a distinct mode of personal being centered on individual subjection to the idea and institutions of the state. I illustrate this bond, the final framework that structures this book, through interpretation and presentation of individual biographies and the conceptions and practices of the self it reveals—a bond for which the rise of the culture concept represents, once more, not a break but a culmination. Each anthropological thinker I examine was an anti-traditionalist modernizer at the level of both society and the human person, an individual who attempted not only to further the progressive advancement of social and economic life, but also to transform his own personal being according to the needs of the new world he envisioned. Each inscribed the social dynamics and institutional imperatives of modernity into the deepest regions of his own self, structuring his life according to those masculine attributes of "infinitely competent responsibility and self-cohering discipline" characteristic of modern legal identity.[6] John Wesley Powell, navigating the Colorado River with only one arm, mapping the territory; Henry Cabot Lodge, moving from the passive world of historical scholarship to the staunch, forward-looking advocacy of imperialism; Madison Grant, hunter, misogynist, steel-willed Nordic explorer; Gunnar Myrdal, hard-driving prophet of modernization—all were men of stern, rigid discipline, fired by ambition, who lived in their own experience an ideal of modern legal order. Through a process of conscious self-fashioning, they "[drew] together and indistinguishably absorb[ed] the diversity of existence that is being in law," thereby forming the cultural site in which was lodged the very existence of the legal order and of the state.[7]

The remainder of this introduction provides a context for the chapters that follow. I first discuss the origin and nature of juridical racialism in greater detail, in doing so also placing this study in a broad scholarly context. I argue that juridical racialism developed in the mid-nineteenth century from a general ideological tendency of nations to characterize outsiders in legal terms, a tendency buttressed by the philosophical origins of western principles of legality, and I characterize its study as part of a larger effort to classify the basic conceptual units of American civic identity. I also describe juridical racialism as having served as a medium, in sociological terms, for national boundary maintenance and intersystem adjustment, binding together varying social and institutional spheres of American life as they adapted to new material circumstances and exigencies. Second, I discuss the history of anthropological and other approaches to human variation, especially the rise of the modern concept of culture associated with Franz Boas and his students. Specifically, I describe the conflict between the Boasian culture concept and those theories of human difference it displaced as the field of anthropology grew into a fully professional discipline. This discussion proceeds in part as a sketch of Boas himself, anticipating the biographical features of chapters 1–4. Finally, I discuss the interpretive perspective and method that guides my analysis, specifically as it concerns the historical relation between law and the social sciences. In particular, I explain how my approach departs from the view of law and social science fostered by sociological jurisprudence, and how it instead is driven by an interdisciplinary model of legal history influenced by the field of cultural anthropology and grounded in narrative.

Nations are based on myths. The "imagined community" of the United States is like that of any other nation in being grounded in often tacit beliefs about the meaning and purpose of the state—beliefs that determine who can and cannot achieve full civic belonging, or citizenship.[8] (I use the terms "citizenship" and "civic belonging" interchangeably in this book to indicate that citizenship is not simply a narrow legal matter of rights but also one of identity and cultural acceptance.) In the United States, as in many other nations, for example, full citizenship long was limited to men, who were thought uniquely to possess those traits necessary for republican government, a principle both enshrined in state and national laws, such as those limiting the franchise, and manifest across a range of social behaviors and cultural values. Juridical racialism was one such language of national identity, one component of the imaginative history of American nationhood. In this respect, this study contributes to a recent body of work in political science investigating the various forms of ascriptive, anti-liberal hierarchy that have underlain statutory and judicial constructions of citizenship in the United States—work based on the notable claim, developed by Rogers M. Smith, that "civic myths" are manifest especially in narrative form.[9] Similarly, the study of juridical racialism advances the more general historical project outlined by Fredric Jameson, who has called on scholars to identify each of the "minimal 'units'" of social and political discourse he calls "ideologemes." According to Jameson, scholars should direct their work toward "the identification of ideologeme[s], and, in many cases, of [their] initial naming," and he further observes that such minimal ideological units have the peculiar quality of being "susceptible to both a conceptual description and a narrative manifestation all at once."[10]

Citizenship, it is worth emphasizing, has generated an extensive scholarly literature over the past generation, and there are no signs this interest will diminish.[11] In political science and law, history and philosophy, literature and cultural studies, scholars have explored the subject in ever-greater range and detail. This scholarship has been eclectic in its methods and motivations, but it tends to be bound together by a concern for the status of minority groups within conceptions of American civic identity, especially the groups David A. Hollinger has termed "ethno-racial blocs."[12] Such scholarly attention to race is hardly surprising. As Edmund

S. Morgan revealed thirty years ago, the fundamental ideas upon which the United States was founded were created under conditions of African chattel slavery, and the nation has been grappling ever since with the consequences of that original sin.[13] More immediately, the memory of the Civil Rights Movement and the rise of one of its academic legacies of the 1980s, the intellectual and political banner of multiculturalism, brought fresh interest to the ways in which racial minorities have been drawn inside or excluded from the "circle of we."[14] Whatever the cause, the status of racial minorities in civic life has become one of the driving themes of contemporary academic discourse. This book contributes to that conversation from the perspective of legal scholarship, but with a difference. Like most scholarship about race, law, and citizenship, this book is concerned with the way legal institutions drew the boundaries of the American nation, with which groups were excluded, or included, and when and how. As a study of civic rhetoric, however, whose historical approach is influenced by principles of anthropology that trace ultimately to linguistics, its final concern lies not with the law but rather with the idea of law, and not with race but rather with its conceptualization, and with how the mutual constitution of those two principles formed a widely used, productive language of American identity. It contributes to the study of race and citizenship through what might be called a cultural history of jurisprudence.

The tradition of juridical racialism in American civic life is not sui generis.[15] The mutual constitution of the idea of race and the concept of law is implicit in the life of most nations. Groups achieve a feeling of solidarity in part through the exclusion of outsiders, typically justified by the belief that those excluded lack some essential normative quality that members of the group share, for instance racial descent or observance of a particular religion. A commitment to shared legal ideals is an especially powerful criterion for defining community boundaries, all the more so when the community is coterminous with the geographic boundaries of a nation state. In Durkheimian terms, law is a morally integrative force that holds complex societies together through its expression and formation of collective values.[16] As a historical matter, then, it comes as no surprise that the founding of national and other collective identities on shared legal commitment has deep roots in the West, tracing back at least to the ancient Israelites, who were transformed from a collection of seminomadic tribes into a people and, ultimately, a nation, through their acceptance of the law brought from Mt. Sinai—an acceptance that made them, classically, a "people of law."[17] While Christian thinkers would later draw on the theology of Paul to distinguish between a people of law and a "people of grace," the Christian community that grew from Judaism continues to be based on a shared vision of law, one proclaimed in the Old Testament but transformed and superseded by the New Testament. This long-standing disposition to define group identity in legal terms, moreover, has equally expressed itself in its mirror image. In Western literature, the characterization of outsiders, especially from primitive societies, as lacking the capacity for law extends at least to Homer. In Odysseus's encounter with the Cyclops, in a passage that has an important place in the history of critical theory, Homer describes the one-eyed beast his hero will defeat as "lawless" (notably, the defeat will come through a trick of Odysseus's own self-abnegation).[18]

The tendency of groups and nations to describe outsiders with what might be called broadly ethno-legal rhetoric—to distinguish it for a moment from its more particular form of juridical racialism—also derives from the historical development of the idea of law itself. For modern law in the West was founded on a series of conceptual oppositions. Most important, modern law has been seen as the antithesis of the primitive phenomenon of myth, the collective stories that express the cosmology of a society and justify its forms and institutions. Law has been defined, especially, as a form of governance that is the obverse of myth, and on that basis has been lauded for the transparent rationality it poises against myth's hidden logic of symbol and pattern. But as socio-legal scholar Peter Fitzpatrick argues, this view misperceives the historical development of Western legal thought and the contemporary legal order, for modern law in fact is saturated by myth in the very "theory of its being": the vision of law as the transcendence of myth and its qualities.[19] The mythology of modern law, that is, the collective story by which it is justified, is its proclaimed opposition to myth. Western legal thought thus defines law not in exclusively positive terms—not, that is, in terms of the substantive qualities and contributions of modern legality in and of itself—but rather in terms of what it is not. These patterned oppositions include the association of law with human civilization in contrast to the proximity of myth to nature; the universality of law in contrast to myth's social particularity; law's internal development and facilitation of a community's economic growth in contrast to myth's static timelessness; law's function as the basis of modernity in contrast to myth's association with savagery; and the fixed geographic attachment of societies based on law in contrast to the ceaseless nomadic movement of myth-based communities.

The political roots of the negative identity of law, moreover, endowed it with a distinct racial character. For, as Fitzpatrick further argues, the philosophical contrast that lies at the foundation of modern conceptions of legality was grounded in the world-historical force of European colonialism. In this setting, law established its identity by repeatedly opposing itself to racial groups that were said to manifest the absence of its qualities, dark-skinned peoples lacking the personal attributes central to legal civilization. These far-flung, often primitive communities gave material form to the ideas against which western law was established, and they physically marked "the outer limits, the intractable 'other' against which Enlightenment [legality] . . . [gave] its own project a palpable content." Notably, in this materialization of conceptual antitheses, the figure of the American Indian played a historically central role. For in developing his deeply influential argument that the existence of the state constitutes a transfer of power to a "mortal god," Thomas Hobbes claimed this abdication arose from a particular "negative necessity": without the state, "there would be a reversion to 'the condition of war', to a chaotic pre-creation"—one embodied in the life of native peoples in America.[20] That ethno-legal formulation has been common ("in the beginning," John Locke would similarly note, "all the World was America"), a standard feature not only of colonial discourse about distant peoples written from the centers of metropolitan power but also of elite and popular legal thought.[21] The tendency of national groups to use legal categories to describe outsiders, then, the historic foundation of juridical racialism, draws on the discursive tradition of Western law itself, which from its inception has been associated with principles of racial opposition.

While ethno-legal rhetoric is a general and long-standing phenomenon, juridical racialism is historically specific and modern. The mutual constitution of race and law assumed a qualitatively new status with the gradual emergence of professional social scientific disciplines in the United States, especially in the wake of the Civil War. The emergence of modern social science transformed the mutual constitution of race and law by placing it within a new matrix of social and governmental authority. Ethno-legal rhetoric became juridical racialism through the institutionalization and professionalization of knowledge in the service of the state, becoming at once more elaborately developed, frequently invoked, and ideologically significant. I address this social and institutional context more specifically over the course of the chapters that follow, and I pay special attention to the relation of juridical racialism to the emerging discipline of anthropology. For since its distant origins, first spurred by European contact with primitive peoples in the sixteenth century, anthropology has concerned itself with the causes and character of human variation, with what would become known as differences of race. In its attention to race, indeed, anthropology provided the foundation for much modern intellectual life by developing powerful frameworks for cultural and phenotypic classification. Historically, it has been the preeminent intellectual field dedicated to portraying and understanding peoples who are different. As it grew into its own as a professional discipline in the second half of the nineteenth century, then, anthropology provided a powerful institutional locus for the juridical-racial expression of the ethno-legal impulse. It offered the primary body of knowledge and analysis from which the civic vocabulary of juridical racialism was constructed through a cultural operation of Lévi-Straussian *bricolage*.[22]

Through its connection with anthropology and those related fields dedicated to the study of human difference, juridical racialism came to serve an especially vital, dynamic role in the community it helped define. Rather than simply a set of ideas individuals might use to understand their national identity or that philosophers might employ to develop arguments about the nature of law and society, juridical racialism became a discourse actively constituting social, political, and psychological life. Most immediately, as a framework for knowledge, juridical racialism supported and was inseparable from those emerging social science institutions central to the liberal state. More important, juridical racialism played a role in mediating and coordinating distinct loci of social power and supporting the operation of the United States as what sociologists call an internally differentiated social system.[23] It helped maintain the boundary between inside and outside, a basic element of the life of all systems—in the case of juridical racialism, the racial boundary of American citizenship—and, in maintaining that boundary, provided a pattern of values that facilitated the integration of the linked spheres of politics, culture, and personality as they responded to the pressures of a changing material environment. More than a theory about who should or should not belong to the nation and claim its rights or an unspoken principle underlying feelings of community solidarity, juridical racialism furthered the achievement of national economic purposes by providing an ideological circuit through which politics, culture, and the self were brought into alignment. It is a supplementary goal of this book to portray that process. As I explain further below, this goal can be achieved most effectively with a particular interpretive perspective and historical method.

Because juridical racialism is bound to the field of anthropology, it shares its history. In this book, I am concerned specifically with the relation of juridical racialism to that branch of social science first developed in the United States as "culture historicism" and known today as cultural anthropology (as distinct from the other main branch of the discipline, physical anthropology, and the subfields of linguistic anthropology and archeology).[24] Closely tied with the practice of ethnography, cultural anthropology is devoted to developing integrated observations of individual societies and forging holistic theories of human variation and social experience in its material and symbolic dimensions. The history of juridical racialism intersects specifically with the most significant innovation in the field, the development of the modern concept of culture or "culture concept," because juridical racial vocabulary partook of modes of thought advocates of the culture concept sought to displace. Juridical racialism, that is, was bound to the theories of human difference that formed the ground from which modern anthropology grew. Indeed, while it was the growing professionalization of the social sciences, and anthropology in particular, that prompted the transformation of ethno-legal rhetoric into the more specific discourse of juridical racialism, the full professionalization of anthropology that was achieved with the ascendancy of the culture concept marked the decline of juridical racialism as a tradition. The history of juridical racialism thus can be appreciated best from the perspective of the world it helped create, that of modern culturalist thought; moreover, as I suggest in my discussion of methodology, the development of the culture concept was a "condition of possibility" necessary for discerning the existence of juridical racialism as an ideological phenomenon.

As Raymond Williams has noted, the word "culture" has a tangled, hotly contested past.[25] To understand the modern professional definition, it is helpful, first, to consider two prominent approaches to the term from nineteenth-century England: those of poet and critic Matthew Arnold and early anthropologist Sir Edward Burnett Tylor.[26] In *Culture and Anarchy* (1869), Arnold posed the term "culture" against the word "civilization." For Arnold, civilization denoted the routinized, everyday social experience of expanding capitalism, whereas culture represented the literary and philosophical traditions of the West. Culture, wrote Arnold, was "the study and pursuit of perfection . . . the best which has been thought and said in the world."[27] This definition limited culture to the high arts, literature, and philosophy, and was a humanist principle employed as a tool of social critique. Alongside the Arnoldian view stood that of Tylor. As a Quaker, Tylor was prevented from pursuing a university degree, but family means enabled him to pursue his studies independently, and after traveling in Mexico in the 1850s, his interests turned especially to cultural variation. In *Primitive Culture* (1871), Tylor sought to explain differences in past and present human societies by developing a doctrine of progressive social evolution. His definition of culture was more expansive than Arnold's. For Tylor, culture included the "complex whole which includes knowledge, belief, art, morals, law, custom, and any other capabilities and habits acquired by man as a member of society."[28] Yet, as historian George W. Stocking, Jr. notes, Tylor's definition of culture was unitary. In the framework of *Primitive Culture*, there was a single phenomenon known as "culture" (never "cultures" in the plural), which developed along an evolutionary historical path that all societies shared.

Early approaches to culture also typically were intimately linked to the idea of race. Like the story of culture, the history of race is complex, and any brief treatment must rely on simplification. Its appearance as a scientific category emerged first in the early eighteenth century with Carolus Linnaeus's *Systema Naturae* (1735), which divided human beings into four distinct categories or types, *Homo Europaeus*, *Homo Asiasticus*, *Homo Afer*, and *Homo Americanus*, a classification further elaborated by Johann Friedrich Blumenbach in "On the Natural Variety of Mankind" (1775), which established the Caucasian, Mongolian, Ethiopian, American, and Malay division of the human family still roughly in use today.[29] There is no need here to detail the subsequent history of the racial idea, except to indicate that in the wake of these powerful classification schemes, until the rise of modern anthropology, race and culture were thought to be inseparable.[30] According to the widespread if often unspoken view, the social and cultural characteristics of human groups were manifestations of an essential part of their collective being, frequently of a set of in-born and inherited characteristics. The complexity of a society's technology, the beauty and sensitivity of its art, the nature of its kinship structures, the complexity of its language, the severity of its taboos, the form of its religion and, most meaningfully for this book, the state of its law, all were seen to arise from the inner nature of the group. What we today call culture was not so much a symbolic framework in which individuals grew and learned to behave, the "software" for the "hardware" of the human brain; instead, it expressed the upwelling of intrinsic group character. Culture was race made manifest.

The modern understanding of culture differs from these older theories in two important ways. First, it is pluralistic. In contemporary anthropology, there is no single culture of the best that has been thought and said, as there was for Arnold, nor is there a unilinear historical sequence through which culture advances, as there was for Tylor and others. Today, there are not one but many cultures, each with its own unique history and identity. These cultures, moreover, are viewed in a relativistic frame. Not only do they stand outside a transcendent evolutionary scheme, but they also can be known and understood only on their own individual terms, according to their own self-contained systems of meaning. Second, the modern understanding of culture differs from older uses of the term in that culture today is severed from race. The human social variation that was the spur for the development of modern anthropology is no longer viewed as the manifestation of in-born racial essences. Societies are seen instead as built on mutable, learned systems of meaning, and these symbolic systems—cultures—are seen as the basis of human difference.[31] Culture is historical and radically contingent, no longer the upwelling of a racial spirit. When the term is used at all (for it is highly contested), race is a purely physical attribute and holds no explanatory power for cultural life. This definitional transformation was one of the single most important developments in the history not only of anthropology but also of the social sciences, and among the many thinkers who brought it about, the most significant was Franz Boas.[32]

Born in 1858 in Westphalia, Germany, Boas was raised in the town of Minden, on the banks of the river Weser.[33] His family was Jewish, though not religiously observant, and sympathetic to the failed revolution of 1848 and its universalist values of liberal political rights. Boas's mother maintained particularly close ties with German liberal democrats, including Carl Schurz, while her sister Sophie married the physician and reformer Abraham Jacobi. As a youth, Boas was drawn to the natural and physical sciences, and after completing studies in physics, he became a professor of geography at the University of Berlin. In 1883, he visited Baffin Island in the Arctic to continue studies of water begun as a doctoral student and to undertake a cartographic analysis. The trip marked the start of a formative intellectual change. Struck by the warmth and hospitality of Eskimo society, Boas became increasingly interested in general questions of human variation and the history of particular social groups. After studying a band of Pacific Northwest Indians visiting Berlin in 1885, he sailed for British Columbia to undertake fieldwork among the Kwakiutl, famed for the institution of potlatch. In 1887, he emigrated to the United States, settling in New York City to help edit the journal *Science*, and taught at the newly established Clark University from 1889 to 1892. He became a professor of anthropology at Columbia University in 1899, an institutional affiliation he maintained until his death in 1942, garnering numerous professional awards, serving as president of the American Anthropological Association and the American Association for the Advancement of Science, and teaching generations of students who became prominent and influential in their own right.

For the purposes of this study, Boas's ideas can be grouped into two broadly related areas, the first political, the second scientific; in both, they were the principles of a modernizer. In the realm of political life, Boas was an anti-racist, and as a principled man of the left, he viewed scientific knowledge about race as a basis for progressive social reform. Boas's anti-racist commitment was guided in part by his family connection to the liberal ideals of the 1848 revolution. More personally, it was driven by his own experiences as a Jew in Bismark's Germany. During his college years, Boas fought several fencing duels over anti-Semitic remarks, and he bore prominent scars on his face from those encounters. Boas brought his sensitivity to racial prejudice with him to the United States, and after his appointment at Columbia, he dedicated himself to an unremitting public attack on individuals and groups espousing Anglo-Saxon supremacy (his death came, fittingly, at the Columbia Faculty Club amid a heated debate on the continuing need to combat racism).[34] He was particularly devoted to the cause of black Americans and spoke on numerous occasions to black organizations and universities, emphasizing the importance of learning African history as an incentive to black achievement.[35] Similarly, he dedicated himself to combating the American nativist movement, working to discredit the intellectual premises underpinning the activities of groups such as the Immigration Restriction League.[36]

This liberal commitment was reflected in Boas's anthropological work as well. In the late nineteenth century, anthropology was torn between its amateur heritage and its future status as a professional discipline.[37] Boas was a partisan of the scientific professionals, demanding that the field be guided by detailed, first-hand observation; systematic physical measurement; the careful compilation of languages; and skepticism toward speculative theorizing. For Boas, professionalism also entailed abandoning the grand, Victorian schemes of social evolution and attributions of cultural difference to race. He asked anthropologists instead to examine each society they encountered on its own terms and refrain from judgments of value in order to understand the society's symbolic intricacies, which he identified as the primary object of scientific study. In this respect, the divergence between race and culture was for Boas not only a conceptual matter, but also an institutional one—the intellectual basis for the future of anthropology as a professional field. This claim of divergence, expressed most famously in *The Mind of Primitive Man* (1911), brought him into conflict with a number of prominent anthropologists and racial thinkers over the course of his life, particularly several who appear in this book: John Wesley Powell, the social developmentalist examined in chapter 1; Daniel Garrison Brinton, president of the American Association for the Advancement of Science, who appears briefly in chapter 2 as an advocate of white racial supremacy and an academic ally of Henry Cabot Lodge (against whose mode of history Boasian anthropology also defined itself); and Madison Grant, eugenicist standard-bearer for theories advancing the "racial basis of European history" and a subject of chapter 3.[38]

It was Boas who won these scientific battles, transforming both the social sciences and American civic life. The history of juridical racialism illuminates that transformation in anticipated and unexpected ways. For the story of juridical racialism indicates, first, one of the specific means by which the Boasian split of culture from race widened the "circle of we": not simply through the widely heralded achievement of fostering increased tolerance of human difference by relativizing cultural value (a principle advanced especially by Boas's students Ruth Benedict and Margaret Mead and taught to generations of undergraduates), but more particularly through encouraging new rubrics for thinking about the nature of race in relation to the concept of law—rubrics, as this book shows, that were absorbed into the law itself.[39] The story of juridical racialism thus can help cultivate a fresh appreciation of this important transformation in modern American life. In addition, the story of juridical racialism suggests how the civic metamorphosis engendered in part by the culture concept might be understood as a surface change that masked a deeper continuity. When viewed from the standpoint not of anthropology as a discipline but rather of juridical racialism as a discursive tradition, the culture concept can be seen as having furthered postwar economic progress, the modern state, and modernizing conceptions of the self. Indeed, it did so in ways consistent with the social scientific approaches to difference it displaced. Against the backdrop of pre-Boasian juridical racialism, the culture concept appears as an avatar of the larger historical principles of material development, state modernization, and social systemic equilibrium.

As a civic language in which race and law were mutually constitutive, and which was present at once in anthropological analysis, political discourse, and legal doctrine, juridical racialism can best be understood within an interdisciplinary historical framework, in particular one whose methods are influenced not only by legal and historical scholarship but also by modern cultural anthropology and literary theory. Because this approach substantially departs from, though it does not reject, a significant branch of legal history—that concerned with the relation between law and the social sciences, and specifically the use of social scientific evidence in judicial decision-making—it is important to state my theoretical and methodological commitments from the start.

The implicit origin of most scholarship about the relation between law and social science might be said to lie nearly one hundred years ago in the Supreme Court decision of *Muller v. Oregon* (1908).[40] *Muller* concerned a maximum hours law enacted to protect women working in laundries and factories and was but one of many such worker protection regulations in place across the United States at the time. In the wake of the Supreme Court's decision in *Lochner v. New York* (1905), which held a law limiting the working hours of bakers to be an unconstitutional violation of due process under the Fourteenth Amendment, these regulations became vulnerable to attack in federal court.[41] Accordingly, the Oregon statute was challenged by the foreman of a laundry company in Portland who had been fined after he required an employee to work beyond a ten-hour day. The law was upheld by the state high court, and the case eventually made its way to the Supreme Court of the United States. There, the cause of the state government was championed by progressive lawyer and activist, and future Supreme Court Justice, Louis D. Brandeis. Although born in the United States, Brandeis had been raised, like Franz Boas, in an atmosphere of liberal, middle-class German-Jewish political activism and high culture.[42] His family had moved to the United States partly in reaction to the failed revolution of 1848 and, tellingly, his first memory was "of his mother carrying food and coffee to the Union soldiers outside his family's home." After attending high school in Germany, Brandeis enrolled in Harvard Law School ("My uncle," he wrote, "the abolitionist, was a lawyer, and to me nothing else seemed really worth while"), and soon established an independent legal office in Boston.[43] Over years of successful practice, he came to embody the ideal of the socially progressive legal activist in much the same way Boas would in the field of anthropology.

Brandeis's approach to *Muller* would have lasting historical consequences. The Supreme Court at the time was deeply influenced by a group of jurists committed to fostering a jurisprudence of natural rights. In this "liberty of contract" tradition, statutes were scrutinized for whether they accorded with the substantive due process guarantees of the Fifth and Fourteenth Amendments. In this view, social science could hold little sway before the bar. In the early part of the twentieth century, however, natural rights jurisprudence came under sharp attack from the movement in sociological jurisprudence. Associated, among others, with Harvard Law School professor Roscoe Pound and Justice Oliver Wendell Holmes, Jr., the sociological movement in law asserted that judges should take the actual social impact of their decisions into consideration when deciding what might constitute a just result in a particular case. Moreover, sociological jurisprudes argued, judges should be guided explicitly by the light professional social science shed on legal issues. Brandeis was firmly rooted in this progressive tradition, and he brought it with him in constructing his written argument in the *Muller* case. With the aid of his sister-in-law, Josephine Goldmark, as well as other members of the National Consumers League, he chose to focus his brief on the demonstrable social impact of the Oregon legislation. His argument barely touched on legal doctrine but presented over ninety pages of social scientific material about the effect on women of long working hours, all attempting to show that the Oregon law met the "reasonableness" standard under the state's police power. The Court agreed with Brandeis, and soon the "Brandeis brief"—in which "appellate facts" drawn from social scientific studies were presented directly to the Court for its consideration—became a staple of constitutional litigation.

Significantly, the brief also became a staple of constitutional scholarship. It did so, however, not so much in immediate reaction to *Muller*, but fifty years later, in the aftermath of *Brown v. Board of Education*. Though *Brown* has been subject to substantial criticism in recent years, the decision was a *locus classicus* for the generation of legal scholars who came of age in the 1950s and 1960s.[44] As I discuss in chapter 4, footnote eleven of *Brown* made important reference to a variety of social scientific studies of the nature of racial prejudice and the effect of racially segregated schools on the "hearts and minds" of black children. In the wake of *Brown*, when the Court's citation of these studies came under attack, many scholars who supported the decision began to explain and justify the Court's actions by exploring the history of social science before the bar.[45] They looked to the Brandeis brief as an originary moment from which a line of descent could be traced to *Brown*, and in doing so forged a general framework for describing the law-social science relation. This model was based on the agenda of sociological jurisprudence embodied in Brandeis's strategy in *Muller*: that of influence through advocacy. In the model developed from this advocate's vision, social science is divided from law by an institutional fence, though the boundary can be breached when the law reaches out its hand and takes social science over the divide. Social science is linked to legal doctrine, that is, when it is directly used by courts, either for evidentiary purposes during trial or in appellate facts.[46]

There is no denying the importance of this scholarship or the assumptions on which it relies. Nevertheless, I believe the relation between law and the social sciences is richer than the model of influence suggests. By constructing a fence between social science and law that is breached only when judges actively reach over an institutional divide, the model implies that the single relation between the two fields is one of intention and causation. Law and social science are connected only through the deliberate, intentional actions of particular persons. This view poses an obstacle to a fully interdisciplinary legal history because, as Peter Goodrich explains, the purpose of an interdisciplinary study of law is not that "of juxtaposing legal knowledge with that of other, essentially separate, knowledges," or of "absorbing other disciplines or sciences into legal expertise . . . for the purposes of providing a further technical dimension of legitimation to legal discourse." Instead, it aims "at breaking down the closure of legal discourse and . . . exists to analyse the interdiscursive status of legal texts."[47] This study seeks to forward a richer account of the relation between law and social science, in part by looking toward the methods of cultural anthropology, especially symbolic anthropology. From this perspective, law and the social sciences are related not simply through intentional human use, but also at the broader level of cultural structure, in which each field manifests homologous intellectual patterns in different institutional contexts.

This interdisciplinary approach bears upon the traditional division of legal history into "internalist" and "externalist" approaches. As Robert W. Gordon writes, both approaches conceive of a "law-box" inside of which resides "whatever appears autonomous about the legal order—courts, equitable maxims, motions for summary judgment [and so on]." A scholar writing internalist history, Gordon explains, "stays as much as possible within the box of distinctive-appearing legal things; his sources are legal, and so are the basic matters he wants to describe or explain, such as changes in pleading rules, in the jurisdiction of a court, the texts assigned to beginning law students, or the doctrine of contributory negligence." An externalist legal historian, meanwhile, turns their attention to those things that exist "outside" the box, namely "'society,' the wide realm of the nonlegal, the political, economic, religious, social." Such a historian writes "about the interaction between the boxful of legal things and the wider society of which they are a part, in particular to explore the social context of law and its social effects."[48] Much legal history until the early 1970s was of the internalist type, focusing on the doctrinal development of the common law, with little reference to social and economic forces that may have affected its transformation. Today, almost all meaningful work in legal history, influenced especially by the writings and teaching of J. Willard Hurst, is written from "outside the box."[49]

While the externalist perspective undoubtedly will continue to form the core of legal history as a discipline, I believe it does not go far enough in moving beyond the limits of the internalist model in that it continues to accept the sovereignty and "self-referentiality" of the law.[50] One might say that in looking at social and historical phenomena outside the box, externalist history takes as central concerns the box and the boundaries it establishes. While acknowledging that law has its own institutional imperatives, and that there may be social facts that are distinctively legal, I believe historians ought to view law as an interwoven part of a much larger cultural field, one in which law itself plays a constitutive role. Conceptual similarities shared by disparate phenomena in that field, and not the contrast between legal and nonlegal facts, should in turn guide historical interpretation. In pursuing such an analysis, I have looked to the model provided by studies of the concept of integration in functionalist anthropology, systems theory, and symbolic anthropology. In *The Interpretation of Cultures*, Clifford Geertz draws on the work of Pitirim Sorokin to distinguish between three different elements of the integrative process. In Geertz's account, social structures are integrated according to "causal-functional" principles, culture according to "logico-meaningful" principles, and the mind according to psychodynamic principles. The scholarship on social science and law derived from sociological jurisprudence conceives of the relation between the two disciplines as a relation between two social systems, as a causal-functional link. A cultural study views the two as integrated in a logico-meaningful way, through a "unity of style" that, Geertz writes, one finds "in a Bach fugue."[51]

Rather than viewing social science as having a presence in law only when it is explicitly cited in judicial opinions, this understanding of the relation between law and social science views them as sharing a fundamental set of symbolic patterns across separate institutional contexts. Each institution maintains a distinctive causal-functional identity and yet participates in a common logico-meaningful structure, which in turn links the institutions together as part of the larger social system. Anthropological social science and law might be understood to enact the same set of basic symbolic transpositions from a fundamental dilemma or conflict, in this case perhaps between identity and nonidentity, life and death, inside and outside; or anthropologists and legal actors might be understood as thinking "equally well," as Lévi-Strauss characterizes the relation between the savage and modern minds. But in the following chapters, I merely take as fundamental the straightforward principle that juridical racialism connects anthropological social science and legal doctrine through an underlying set of assumptions shared by both, a common way of thinking. The relation of juridical racialism to law and the social sciences, like the relation of law and social science to each other, is that of a complex, repeated pattern. In this sense, this study relies upon the very interpretive principles that emerged with the rise of the modern culture concept that brought the tradition of juridical racialism to a close.

Key elements of these patterns can only be revealed by a scholarly method that includes storytelling. Like Geertz, I believe humans are "suspended in webs of significance," and that the presentation and interpretation of those webs requires special attention to method.[52] Narrative, whose determined structure gives details their symbolic resonance, best uncovers the patterns of meaning underlying juridical-racial rhetoric and the life-histories of those who employed it. Whether as a civic myth or ideologeme, juridical racialism itself found expression not only as a discrete conceptual principle but also, even most memorably, in narrative form. The following chapters thus blend traditional academic analysis with storytelling, but storytelling of a particular kind, concerned with examining the symbolic patterns that lie beyond the full understanding of individuals and so excavating and recuperating past coherent systems of meaning. In the biographies of anthropologists and jurists, and in the tropes and plots that animate both social scientific treatises and court opinions, such patterns recur and generate layers of significance and cultural power. To resolve the stark choice presented by F. W. Maitland and E. E. Evans-Pritchard between legal history, anthropology, and "nothing," such patterns are unfolded quietly, beneath the immediate surface of recounted events.[53]

1

Laws of Development,
Laws of Land

Although ethno-legal rhetoric has deep roots in the Western tradition, the discourse of juridical racialism formed in the United States only in the wake of the Civil War, when a confluence of historical developments created the ground for its emergence. Most important, the decades following the war saw the growing professionalization of a range of scientific and social scientific fields, and for anthropology, in particular, they marked what Margaret Mead called the "golden age" or "classic period" of the discipline.[1] Anthropologists active during these years helped steer their field away from its amateur roots in travel writing and collecting and toward its future as a methodologically coherent, systematic body of knowledge created by professionals who limited their ranks through formal standards of entry. These also were crucial years in American state modernization, as evidenced by the civil service reform movement and the Pendleton Act of 1883.[2] Seeking to rationalize the expanding apparatus of the state, a broad class of elites sought to replace the spoils system based on party patronage with more neutral, meritocratic procedures for the staffing of government bureaucracies. Finally, these years marked the start of the so-called Gilded Age, when modern, expansive, and extractive market relations lay the foundation for the full-scale corporate capitalism of the twentieth century and modern consumer society.[3] Scientific professionalization, state modernization, modern economic development—within this network of phenomena, ethno-legal rhetoric assumed a qualitatively new importance, complexity, and authority.

American Indians took central stage in each of these developments—those of the professions, the state, and political economy—and therefore in the emergence of juridical racialism. For the close of the Civil War and the presidency of Ulysses S. Grant inaugurated the "assimilationist era" of federal Indian policy, when the national government sought to force Indians to model their lives on Euro-American standards of behavior, especially by encouraging them to become independent agriculturalists.[4] In this context, the newly professional social sciences turned an eager eye toward Indian myths, kinship structures, forms of government, and material culture; indeed, American anthropologists first developed their comprehensive theories of society and built their professional discipline with the raw material they found in the world of native peoples. Institutionally, moreover, the late-nineteenth century witnessed the marked expansion and modernization of the Bureau of Indian Affairs, particularly with the creation of the Board of Indian Commissioners in 1869 and the increasingly specialized and expert approach taken to Indian education beginning in the early 1880s.[5] Finally, as an economic matter, the assimilationist era saw the coerced forfeiture of Indian land for government and private purposes. The assimilationist effort to destroy collective regimes of property ownership and the centrality of the tribe to Indian identity grew from the drive toward national economic expansion.[6]

In the following chapter, I consider the role juridical racialism played in the assimilationist era, focusing specifically on the period between 1883 and 1887. During these years, a legal exchange took place between Congress and the Supreme Court, the final outcome of which was the Dawes General Allotment Act, which subdivided communal Indian lands and allotted them to individual owners.[7] The Court's contributions to this dialogue were its decisions in *Ex parte Crow Dog* (1883) and *United States v. Kagama* (1886), two cases concerning the extension of federal jurisdiction over certain forms of Indian crime.[8] Together, *Crow Dog* and *Kagama* "clear[ed] the way" for the Dawes Act by forging the Indian plenary power doctrine, which grants Congress nearly complete control over the management of Indian affairs.[9] I begin my analysis, however, not with these legislative and judicial actions but with the life and work of John Wesley Powell, naturalist, geographer, and founder of the Bureau of American Ethnology. Powell constructed a developmentalist juridical racialism that drew on the anthropological writings of Lewis Henry Morgan and that would later form the conceptual and rhetorical anchor of *Crow Dog* and *Kagama*. In my analysis of Powell's work, I thus consider how a developmentalist view of race and law became constitutive of the law itself.

John Wesley Powell and the Evolution of Property

From the presidency of Andrew Jackson until roughly the start of the 1870s, U.S. policy toward native peoples centered on moving Indians west of the Mississippi, driving them onto reservations with the threat of military force.[10] This was a policy of separation, one that fortified the physical boundaries between Indians and whites. The forced removal of the Cherokee from Georgia to Oklahoma on the Trail of Tears symbolized this effort.[11] In the 1870s, however, the focus of national policy began to change. Still fresh from his military success at Vicksburg, President-elect Grant announced in 1869 a "peace policy" and a new government attitude toward the "Indian question." As Francis Paul Prucha notes, this approach to Indian affairs was less a specific statutory agenda than "a state of mind, a determination that since the old ways of dealing with the Indians had not worked, new ways which emphasized kindness and justice must be tried."[12] In this era of "conquest by kindness," Indian affairs were increasingly shaped by an uneasy but potent political alliance between Christian social reformers and western land interests, who together argued that the segregation of natives onto semisovereign reservations was both destructive to Indians themselves and inconsistent with republican political ideals. Driven by different motives, but united by a common goal, these new Indian activists directed their efforts not toward separating Indians from whites but toward acculturating them into nineteenth-century American society.[13] They hoped that this would be the age in which the "final promise" of the United States government to Indian tribes—that all indigenous peoples would "participate fully in the nation's institutions"—would at last be fulfilled.[14]

This promise was not motivated by a commitment to social or cultural pluralism.[15] Activists such as the participants in the celebrated Lake Mohonk Conference of the Friends of the Indian, the intellectual and organizational foundation for assimilationist-era reforms, were not interested in preserving Indian culture per se.[16] A small minority of whites did seek to preserve traditional native folkways or at least to slow the pace of their destruction. But most white reformers advanced an ethnocentric program of destroying traditional native societies and imposing Euro-American institutions in their place. They were humanitarians who sought to employ the civil arm of national government to annihilate the Indian way of life. Their reigning rhetorical trope was the individual, the solitary economic self. As Indian Affairs Commissioner John Oberly asserted in 1888, the

Indian must "be imbued with the exalting egotism of American civilization, so that he will say 'I' instead of 'We,' and 'This is mine,' instead of 'This is ours.'"[17] To foster such individualism, reformers attempted first and foremost to destroy the tribe as a presence in native experience. To this end, they sought the abolition of customary tribal law—the elimination of tribal jurisdiction over civil and criminal matters—and its replacement with American substantive and procedural principles. They further worked for the allotment of Indian tribal lands in severalty, the forced division of communal tribal property and its subsequent allocation to individuals. For Christian activists, those who called themselves "friends of the Indian," the result of such anti-tribal policies would be the civilization and redemption of the indigenous inhabitants of North America.[18] They would create an entirely new group of individualist selves from an inchoate corporeal mass of primitives. For western land interests, the result would be the opening of thousands of acres of property to new settlement and cultivation—and railroads.[19] Bringing modernity to the American West, in other words, manifested both Marxian and Foucaultian conceptions of the modern, for the appropriation of wealth rested on the enclosure of the ego.

The desire to resolve the Indian problem by abolishing traditional native society was hardly unique to the 1870s. The goal of assimilation had deep roots in the American past.[20] Three aspects of Indian policy in the assimilationist era, however, were specific to the late-nineteenth century. The first was the policy's comprehensive and national scope. Although assimilationist projects had been implemented by religious and governmental organizations since the seventeenth century, these had been more or less disparate or superficial actions. By contrast, the reforms of the assimilationist period were widespread and systematic, and they brought into being a series of federal programs designed to restructure the most intimate elements of native life; they employed a full range of national government capacities to tame the savage self. These programs, moreover, relied on an increasingly professional civil service that was itself increasingly guided by social scientific expertise. Forged in the midst of a movement to create a professional managerial class that would place federal administration on a scientific foundation, assimilationist policy bore the imprint of this historical origin.[21] Assimilationist reformers "looked to civil service reform as the all-encompassing panacea" as they fought for the "purification of the Indian Bureau," finding an ally especially in Carl Schurz, secretary of the interior from 1877 to 1881.[22] Finally and most important, assimilationist-era Indian policy was unique in the extent to which it was concerned with cultural-legal differences, the extent to which it attempted to assimilate native peoples socially by altering their law.[23] "If the Indians are to be advanced in civilized habits," wrote Schurz, "it is essential that they be accustomed to the government of law, with the restraints it imposes and the protection it affords."[24] "That Law is the solution of the Indian problem," wrote one advocate in the *North American Review*, "would seem to be a self-evident proposition."[25] Indian policy during the late-nineteenth century was in this respect self-reflexive, a legal project that addressed the nature of law in general.

John Wesley Powell's life, beginning in childhood, was carried forward by the modern, professional, and socio-legal commitments that also drove Indian reformers.[26] Born in 1834 near Palmyra, New York, he was raised by English Methodist parents (his father was a lay minister), who inculcated in him a deep sense of religious faith and social obligation, naming him after the Methodist preacher John Wesley.[27] The young Powell grew to manhood steeped in the Protestant vision of law, self, and society that would guide so many Indian reformers. When the Powell family moved to Ohio in the late 1830s and to what became the state of Wisconsin in the 1840s, he helped in the hard work of clearing the land and farming the prairie. As a son in a family whose prosperity and even survival depended on reliable knowledge of the environment, he developed the practical interest in natural history that became the driving force of his career. He became sensitive to ways settlers could control nature for their own purposes if they knew and lived within its limits, and he came to know and love the landscape, its rivers, contours, animals, and plants, with the heart of a man schooled in the practical affairs of land-use management. When it came time to choose a profession, Powell thus ignored his father's pleas that he enter the ministry and decided instead on a life in science. Beginning in the 1850s, he took a variety of courses at Illinois College and the Illinois Institute, as well as at Oberlin College, at the time a center of Protestant social reform and anti-slavery sentiment. Powell never received a college degree, but by participating in a number of short-term scientific projects and expeditions, he developed a reputation as an excellent naturalist and geographer—capable, intellectually independent, brimming with frontier energy, and driven by an indefatigable work ethic. He soon became a school teacher in math and science; a lyceum lecturer on geology and geography; and in 1861, the director of choncology at the new Illinois State Natural History Society, where he became a curator in 1867.

When the Civil War arrived, there was no choice of sides for Powell. From both religious training and social conviction, he was ardently anti-slavery and pro-Union. Responding to President Lincoln's call for troops in April 1861, the budding scientist put his skills to work as a topographer and military engineer in the Illinois Infantry. As Powell biographer William Culp Darrah shows, Powell developed the environmental understanding he had gained as a boy to an even higher level with the Twentieth Volunteers, coming to know on a grander scale how the human will could shape the natural world, and how detailed knowledge of it was necessary for that will to triumph.[28] If the republic were to be victorious on the battlefield, topographers had to map the landscape, engineers had to fortify cities with local materials, soldiers had to calculate the angle of artillery fire. The Union needed men with scientific and mathematical training.[29] Just as his family had cleared and farmed the Wisconsin prairie, so in the infantry Powell was required to use his natural surroundings for a human purpose, the movement, fortification, and attack of a national army at war. He did his job well, and he acted with courage. As Wallace Stegner notes, Powell "was not the kind to remain still." He entered the army as a private. Three months later, he was a second lieutenant. After another six months, having become "something of an expert on fortifications," he achieved the rank of captain and was "solidly enough established on Grant's staff at Cape Girardeau to ask as a personal favor a few days leave to go to Detroit and marry his cousin Emma Dean." Six months later, Powell "came out of the smoke and roar of Shiloh, mounted on General Wallace's horse and with his right arm smashed by a Minie ball," and he soon became commander of the artillery of the 17th Army Corps.[30] By the time he left the service, in 1865, Powell's right arm had been amputated (the hasty amputation caused him acute pain for the rest of his life), and he was ever after to be called Major Powell or simply "the Major."

Powell left the military with more than a haunting wound and an esteemed title; he left with an idea. As a military officer and engineer, he had seen what expert knowledge could accomplish with the financial and bureaucratic support of a modern state, and like the many reformers who moved from the war into government and the civil service, he became an enthusiast for large-scale scientific organization.[31] In this respect, Powell was representative of a generation of American intellectuals who experienced Civil War combat and strove to tame the energies of the American nation through centralized scientific and institutional control, just as military discipline and professionalism had created a wedge of force that smashed the Confederate rebels and drove through the landscape to the sea. Through their participation in public affairs, these war-seasoned men helped forge the "new ideal of the intellectual as scientific expert, practical administrator, and pragmatic reformer."[32] This was a movement at once institutional and subjective. At the institutional level, such intellectuals demanded the establishment of large-scale administrative systems that would create order and power from anarchic individual lives, just as Indian reformers hoped that agricultural land-owning and Protestant discipline would spark economic development from a dwindling race. At the subjective level, they demanded that individuals model themselves on the martial vision of Oliver Wendell Holmes, Jr., who ardently believed "that faith is true and adorable which leads a soldier to throw away his life in obedience to a blindly accepted duty, in a cause which he little understands, in a plan of campaign of which he has no notion, under tactics of which he does not see the use."[33]

Soon after the Confederate surrender, Powell returned to a teaching position at Illinois State Normal University. From there, he undertook a series of daring scientific explorations of the West, especially in Utah and Colorado. These were exceptional feats of surveyorship, later glorified by Stegner in *Beyond the Hundredth Meridian*.[34] Powell and his group of intrepid companions became some of the first white Americans to detail the marvels of the Grand Canyon, and they were the first to navigate their way down the full course of the Colorado River (Powell braved its rapids with only one arm).[35] Powell's initial trips were financed with private and collegiate funds, but he soon received appropriations for further western exploration from Congress, which recognized the importance of reliable knowledge about the western territories to continued settlement. Proper homesteading required maps of the land and its waters, an evaluation of its suitability for livestock and farming, and information as to whether Indians in the area would pose a threat to white families. In 1881, Powell's efforts were rewarded with his appointment as director of the United States Geological Survey (USGS).[36] Running the USGS during a crucial period of its institutional development, Powell consolidated many of its branches and helped endow it with even greater discipline and organization, advancing both of the yoked processes of state-building and professionalization. And, of course, under Powell's command, the Survey continued its steady mapping of the West. This was a colonialist science for the people, and it is largely for his topographic achievements with the USGS that Powell is remembered today.

Powell also put his vision of national scientific organization into practice as the founder and director of the Bureau of American Ethnology.[37] Chartered by Congress in 1879, the Bureau of American Ethnology, or BAE, had been charged with a mission to, in Powell's words, "prosecute work in the various branches of North American anthropology on a systematic plan, so that every important field should be cultivated."[38] The BAE was the "immediate result" of an appeal Powell made in an 1878 report to Secretary of the Interior Schurz, which gave "practical as well as academic reasons why such a program or agency would serve the people."[39] National government support of anthropology was not entirely new in the United States. Thomas Jefferson, for instance, had called on the ethnological counsel of Albert Gallatin and had directed Lewis and Clark to collect anthropological data during their exploration of the Louisiana Territory.[40] But the Bureau of American Ethnology was unique in its breadth and scope. In a period when anthropology itself was just beginning to come into its own as an autonomous field, the BAE gave it an unprecedented institutional base of support, initiating and publishing an exceptional number of studies, including Powell's foundational classification of Indian languages, the first in the United States and of continuing scientific importance, and the monumental *Handbook of North American Indians*.[41] Until the early-twentieth century, the BAE served as a scientific clearinghouse for the most significant anthropological studies in the United States. "One wonders what the history of American anthropology in the late-nineteenth century would have been like," writes one anthropologist admiringly, "if the Bureau as [Powell] conceived and directed it had never come into existence."[42]

Part of Powell's agenda for a comprehensive program for studying native peoples grew from an abiding interest in Indian languages and culture.[43] In "a very few years," he warned, "it will be impossible to study our North American Indians in their primitive condition except from recorded history. For this reason ethnologic studies in America should be pushed with the utmost vigor." In addition to this commitment to what would later be termed "salvage ethnography," Powell was also concerned with the practical administrative use of a systematic investigation of native peoples. Scientific knowledge, valuable in its own terms, would also make possible the practical management of Indian affairs and the sound settlement of the West. "In the whole area of the United States, not including Alaska," he asserted, "there is not an important valley unoccupied by white men. The rapid spread of civilization since 1849 has placed the white man and the Indian in direct conflict throughout the whole area, and the 'Indian problem' is thus thrust upon us, and it *must* be solved, wisely or unwisely." "Many of the difficulties are inherent and cannot be avoided," he continued, "but an equal number are unnecessary and are caused by the lack of our knowledge relating to the Indians themselves. . . . a thorough investigation of North American ethnology would be of great value in our Indian Office."[44] Just as the Geological Survey was to provide knowledge of rivers, mountains, and alluvial valleys for a growing young country, so the BAE was to generate information about the Apache, Ute, and Arapaho peoples. It was to create a map of the Indian social and cultural landscape as extensive as the maps of the USGS. Tellingly, Powell served as director of the Survey and the BAE at the same time.

While the goal of the BAE was to create a map of Indian culture, however, the maps it made were not simply a collection of facts and figures. Instead, the BAE situated its facts in a theoretical framework. That framework was developmentalism, the dominant theoretical position in anthropology at the time, which argued that all human societies followed the same unilinear path of progress, moving from primitive to advanced stages of culture and social organization. Also known as social evolutionism, developmentalist theories were espoused by a number of prominent social thinkers in the latter half of the nineteenth century.[45] Foremost among these were Herbert Spencer, whose sociology held that human societies advanced from simple to complex and from military to industrial forms of organization; E. B. Tylor, who envisioned a unilinear evolutionary transformation of mental and cultural life; Karl Marx, who saw economic modes of production evolving from primitive communism through feudalism to capitalism; and Lewis Henry Morgan, whom I discuss below. Above all, developmentalists sought to classify human social facts by placing them in teleological order. Defining "science" as the "*discernment, discrimination, and classification of facts, and the discovery of the relations in sequence,*" Powell thus wrote in a memorial essay on Charles Darwin: "Facts have genetic relations." He explained, "If one thing is done something else will follow, and the highest function of scientific philosophy is to discover the order of succession of phenomena—how phenomena follow phenomena in endless procession, how every fact has had its antecedent fact, and every fact must have its consequent fact. This part of science is called *evolution*, and by this expression scientific men mean to be understood that phenomena go on in endless consequences."[46]

The scholarly implications of this theory are clearly intelligible in the displays of cultural artifacts that proponents of developmentalism created for the new institutions of natural history museums. Today, such museums feature exhibition cases that contain a variety of different artifacts from a single culture, grouped together to convey a coherent and unified portrait of the society. Zuñi knives, Zuñi pots, Zuñi clothes: objects are understood in relation to other objects through juxtaposition. They form an integrated symbolic system meant to be examined and evaluated on its own terms. Developmentalist museums were very different. They displayed items of a single type from a variety of cultures, arranging them in a line from the simple and crude to the complex and refined. This was the museological materialization of the comparative method, which constructs evolutionary social schemes by comparing a wide variety of divergent ethnographic and historical fields of data. A hypothetical exhibition case might begin with a knife from Neolithic France on its far left, continue with a recently made Zuñi knife placed to its right, and so on until a knife from eighteenth-century New England appeared at the edge of the case. This form of presentation was intended to illustrate the cultural transformation all human societies had undergone or ultimately would undergo in their development from what was deemed societal infancy to adulthood. An exhibit designed by Powell associate Otis T. Mason at the National Museum, for instance, was based on a checkerboard pattern, in which visitors could walk along a single axis and follow a given tool type across ethnographic regions and view its transformation from the simple to the complex. (When Franz Boas, the era's most prominent opponent of developmentalism, toured the exhibit in 1885, he signaled the sea change that was to come in both anthropological theory and jurisprudence by claiming that the display was unscientific. Such evolutionary classifications could not be made a priori, Boas argued; each culture "can be understood only by studying its productions as a whole," in a single, noncomparative museological unit.[47])

Significantly for the work of the BAE, and for Indian affairs generally, the most influential developmentalist of Powell's time was also a lawyer: Lewis Henry Morgan, often described as the father of American anthropology, and one of the most influential practitioners in the history of the discipline.[48] He was born in 1818 in Aurora, New York and studied at

Union College, whose Presbyterian president Eliphalet Nott taught his students that human progress was directed by natural social laws. Later, Morgan was admitted to the bar, and he made his career in Rochester, New York as a legal counsel to railroad companies. Yet, like many lawyers then and now, Morgan's real passion lay outside the law, in the study of Native American societies. He was particularly interested in the Iroquois, and he founded a social and academic club called the Grand Order of the Iroquois, which he consciously modeled on the political organization of the Iroquois League. After he amassed a small fortune, in part through railroad investment, Morgan devoted himself full time to his passion for Indians, bringing his legal training and worldview to bear upon his ethnology. This intellectual synergy was evident throughout Morgan's works on the Iroquois and their kinship systems (his *League of the Iroquois* [1851] and *Systems of Consanguinity and Affinity of the Human Family* [1871] remain classics in the field), but it received its fullest expression in his magnum opus, *Ancient Society* (1877).[49] In this breathtaking work, known also for its influence on Friedrich Engels (it is the intellectual foundation of *The Origin of the Family, Private Property, and the State* [1884]), Morgan outlined a system of evolutionary classification in which cultures began in "savagery," moved through "barbarism," and ultimately reached a stage of "civilization," passing through a variety of gradations in each period.[50] "The history of the human race," wrote Morgan, "is one in source, one in experience, and one in progress."[51]

In Morgan's scheme, each epoch in human evolution was marked by a particular set of characteristics, the most important of which was its conception of property and the rules governing its use and inheritance. According to Morgan, scholars could classify a society as belonging to a given stage in its development by considering how it viewed the relation between land and jurisprudence. In this legal-historical scheme, scholars could lay out the property laws of various societies along a scale of evolutionary change, just as museums of the period might lay out knives to illustrate the course of human cultural transformation.[52] Lower forms of society were those that lacked both a definite notion of private property and the legal codes giving that idea social sanction. Among savages, for instance, "ideas concerning [the] value [of property], its desirability and its inheritance were feeble." In this stage, lands were "owned by the tribes in common, while tenement houses were owned jointly by their occupants."[53] Among peoples in the lower stage of barbarism, the "variety and amount of property were greater than in savagery," thought Morgan, "but still not sufficient to develop a strong sentiment in relation to inheritance."[54] For those in barbarism's middle stages, the "territorial domain still belonged to the tribe in common; but a portion was now set apart . . . [and] divided among the several gentes, or communities of persons who resided in the same pueblo"—but, Morgan emphasized, "[t]hat any persons owned lands or houses in his own right, with power to sell and convey in fee-simple to whomsoever he pleased" was "not only unestablished but improbable."[55] More advanced, civilized societies, he argued, were those that already had developed or were in the process of forming some notion of fee simple absolute. These societies had cultivated "into full vitality that 'greed of gain' (*studium lucri*), which is now such a commanding force in the human mind," and created specific juridical instruments to capture that force and increase its strength.[56]

This was an anthropological system animated by juridical-racial principles. As I explained in my introduction, juridical racialism treats the concepts of race and law as mutually constitutive and contains within its account of legal and racial ontology a dialectical "mythology of modern law."[57] The historical cultural scheme Morgan developed in *Ancient Society* can be understood as juridical-racial in characterizing racial groups as belonging to distinct "ethnical periods" and in turn describing those periods as the material social embodiment of particular stages in the development of the law of property, while defining the law of property itself as the outgrowth of specific peoples, in Morgan's case Semites and Aryans.[58] Morgan's was not a vision of permanent juridical-racial difference. He did not argue that races manifest the capacity or incapacity for property-holding on the basis of their biology. Instead, as a social developmentalist, an advocate of evolutionary cultural principles, Morgan's juridical-racial system was a plastic one, in which racial groups were not permanently caught in lower forms of legal behavior, but rather, over time, tended to modify their lives on the basis of progressively changing ideals of title. Morgan's anthropological vision was a developmentalist juridical racialism, a juridical-racial system that was evolutionary in character and based on the fundamental legal concept of property.

When the future director of the BAE first encountered *Ancient Society*, he was deeply moved.[59] As Powell wrote to Morgan, he read the book "in one time and the first night I read until two o'clock," and he promised to "take it into the field with me and in my leisure hours study it carefully."[60] It ultimately became his theoretical touchstone, and he made the work required reading for BAE anthropologists.[61] One reason Powell was so enamored of Morgan's theoretical framework was that it was well suited to advance his optimistic dream of scientific social management. In particular, Morgan's developmentalism understood all peoples to be capable of legal-cultural transformation. An essentially Lamarckian rather than social Darwinist view, it claimed that human civilizations undergo jurisprudential change as a result of learning achieved through experience or the instruction of others.[62] The implications of this scheme were congruent with the positivist, Comtean worldview held by many intellectuals of the time. For if one could use the methods of developmentalist ethnology to chart the course of evolutionary social change, then one could create a map of human historical laws just as one could create a diagram of the laws of the physical world. And with this map, one could formulate legislation with a precise view as to its ultimate effects, thereby creating a more efficient and ordered society. For instance, if one knew just how Indian peoples were different from their civilized, white neighbors, in just what ways their legal and property regimes represented earlier stages of social evolution, then one would better know how to alter those societies through the wise and informed use of state power. With its vision of social plasticity, that is to say, Morgan's *Ancient Society* and its juridical-racial worldview were well suited to bind statecraft to sociology, to become part of the knowledge of the natural world Powell had always used to guide his actions, whether on his family farm in Wisconsin, in the Civil War, or with the USGS.

In this respect, it is important to emphasize that Morgan's juridical-racial framework also was well suited to advance Powell's own social authority. By asserting a particular narrative of cultural and legal transformation, the developmentalists of Powell's day were making a claim not only to knowledge per se but also to professional knowledge. Like the Brahmins involved in civil service reform or Sanitary Commission activists memorably described by George Fredrickson, developmentalists were asserting their own status as individuals and groups worthy of social deference in a world of proliferating knowledge elites. During the period in which Powell served as the director of the BAE, professional organizations and publications were being established in a variety of academic and quasi-academic fields.[63] The American Association for the Advancement of Science, reconstituted in 1873, published *Science*; the Anthropological Society of Washington, established in 1879, published the *American Anthropologist*; the American Bar Association was created in 1878. A primary function of this growing professional apparatus, this expanding network of institutions and journals, was to police the boundaries of legitimacy in emerging disciplines, helping to consolidate the authority of their members. Powell addressed and actively served in many of these societies (including the ABA, to which he gave a speech on primitive law), and much of his work with the USGS and the BAE can be understood as directed toward the task of professional legitimization to which these groups were also dedicated.[64] Powell was an intellectual institution builder, a man who sought to establish the centrality of his own organizations to government administration. And here too, Morgan's scheme served him well. Making claims to scientific knowledge of history (rather than to metaphysical, romantic, or moral ways of knowing), Morgan's social evolutionary framework could advance the goals of a professional class of knowledge workers. It could buttress the authority of an expanding, distinctively modern elite.

Indeed, Powell attempted to put Morgan's social evolutionary, juridical-racial framework into political and professional practice, using a version of his developmentalism to call for comprehensive federal action in Indian affairs—action that was to focus specifically on the transformation of native property and native law. An extended passage from Powell's writing reveals the ways in which his concern for Indian people, his specific legal-anthropological knowledge (here, about inheritance and property law), and his claims to scientific and social authority reinforced one another, even tending to blend into one. "The enlightened people who have overwhelmed and destroyed the savagery," wrote Major Powell in 1893, "have, as a body, from the first endeavored to save the savage people and to train them in the better ways of life." He continued:

> The conquering race, impelled by motives of humanity, has ever endeavored to raise the savage in culture. It has been a difficult task, because the things which we most desired to do for them they scorned with contempt. That for which they prayed, that for which they fought, could not be yielded. They wanted a wilderness for bounding game and blushing fruits; they wanted the primeval condition of savagery; they wanted beast-gods, scalp-dances, and Terpsichorean worship. The conquering race wanted the continent for higher and holier purposes,—for a transcendent state of culture, for homes and cities and temples in which to worship God. The price in money, the price in terror of savage neighbors, the price in bloodshed, which we have paid for the land may possi-

bly be large compared with its value to savagery, but it is small, very small indeed, in comparison with its value to enlightenment. . . . There is one thing, [though, that I believe] would be a boon to the tribes and ultimately afford great relief to the dominant race. A system of complete registration by clans and by families as they are known to civilized men should be made, and record kept of births and deaths, and the line of civilized inheritance plainly marked out for the people, in which they should be carefully instructed. This would prevent the lapsing of titles in severalty and encourage the sentiment of enlightened property-holding. . . . Slowly, by law and by instruction, teach them the value of our property laws. . . . If such a policy is maintained for two generations more, the problem will be solved; the remnant of the Indians will be saved and absorbed in modern enlightenment.[65]

While Powell's advocacy of assimilationist policies often was tempered by caution, by an admonition not to move too quickly to make a yeoman farmer from the Indian savage, such sentiments should not obscure his ultimate commitments. Writing to Senator Henry M. Teller of Colorado, for instance, Powell outlined three basic principles for government relations with native peoples: first, he wrote, the "removal of the Indians" from tribal lands was "the first step to be taken in their civilization" because these lands represented "everything most sacred to Indian society"; second, "ownership of lands in severalty should be looked forward to as the ultimate settlement of our Indian problems," as it would undermine "traditional modes of inheritance"; and third, Indians should be made to conform to the standards of "Anglo-Saxon civilization." "Here," writes one historian, "was a chilling condensation of the social evolutionist blueprint: separate Indians from their homes and their past, divide their land into individual parcels, make them citizens, and draw them into American society."[66] Powell's developmentalist juridical-racial vision may have differed in some aspects, largely temporal, from the more extreme assimilationists of his time, but its implications were fundamentally similar.

I discuss other assimilationist-era Indian reforms further below, but it is relevant at this point to note that a version of Powell's juridical-racial vision was put into practice with the Dawes Act, and that this policy was a disaster.[67] The goal of the Dawes Act, consistent with Powell's juridical-racial principles, was to abolish Indian tribal property and impose civilized notions of land upon savage peoples. Specifically, the Act authorized

Congress to divide tribal reserves into one-hundred-sixty-acre plots and allot them to individual owners, granting title in fee simple absolute after a twenty-five-year trust period (the remaining land was to be sold in a checkerboard pattern to white settlers, whose presence among the Indians was to serve as a further civilizing influence). Both Christian reformers and western land interests were optimistic about the Act's potential, calling it the "Indians' Magna Carta." With great enthusiasm, Theodore Roosevelt later called it a "mighty pulverizing engine to break up the tribal mass."[68] And, indeed, it was. By 1887, the final military campaigns against American Indians had already been fought and won, but with the Dawes Act the war against native peoples continued with the weapons of the rule of law. Over the next ten years, Indians lost 75 percent of their lands, over ninety million acres (40 percent of the land remaining was desert), and they began to suffer even more than before the scourges of poverty, despondency, and spiritual death. Not until the New Deal did Indian policy slowly begin to change for the better, and it was not until the 1970s that American Indians truly began to recover the sovereignty that had been battered by that mighty pulverizing engine of allotment in severalty. Like Powell's developmentalist anthropology of law, like the historical social sciences in general during the late-nineteenth century—like the prevailing American vision of order and legality—the Dawes Act claimed to be an instrument of enlightenment. And like so many manifestations of the Enlightenment itself, in the Indian country of Major Powell's America, a dream of reason became its precise and haunting opposite.

Federal Jurisdiction from Crow Dog *to* Kagama

Under the Dawes Act, the United States fundamentally restructured the property regime of scores of individual societies, and it did so without the consent of their people—an extraordinary imposition of state power. At the time, the Act was viewed as a legitimate, unproblematic exercise of Congressional authority under the terms of what became known as the plenary power doctrine of Indian affairs, a judicial interpretation of how much power the Constitution granted Congress in its dealings with Indian tribes. That doctrine asserted that Congressional authority over natives was absolute: not only did Congress hold power over indigenous peoples above and against individual states, but that power also was more or less unlimited. The original basis for the Indian plenary power doctrine lay in Chief Justice John Marshall's decisions in the *Cherokee Cases* of the early 1830s, but the doctrine took its distinct, modern form only between 1883 and 1886 in the course of *Crow Dog* and *Kagama*.[69] These decisions consolidated and expanded the plenary power doctrine first intimated by Chief Justice Marshall, paving the way for the Dawes Act and for a host of other laws intruding into native culture. Moreover, the intellectual themes of John Wesley Powell's personal and professional life sounded through those cases, recapitulating the dynamics of his thought at the level of legal decision-making.

Significantly, the two cases concerned not property, the centerpiece of Morgan's legal anthropology and of the Dawes Act, but crime. The assimilationist-era reform efforts to extend American law over native peoples entailed a special concern that the Indian law of murder was based on the concept of "blood revenge," in which a deceased person was avenged when one of their family members killed the offending party.[70] "The Indian has but little knowledge of law save the *lex talionis*," argued the winning attorney in *Elk v. Wilkins* (1884), echoing a common view; "[i]t is stretching the principle of universal citizenship and impartial suffrage to the verge of absurdity for the government to extend its hand to the subjects of an independent political community, who have made the tomahawk the arbiter of their wrongs, and in the twinkling of an eye invest them with all rights and privileges of American citizenship."[71] Indeed, as Indian reformers noted, the implications of the institution of blood revenge extended beyond the world of crime to that of land, for the security of title requires the same protective state that also meets out criminal punishment. Indian tribes were said entirely to lack such interlocking legal mechanisms. As in the case of the Philippines, examined in chapter 2, the principle underlying white concerns about Indian crime and criminal administration was that natives were, in the words of James Bradley Thayer, a "People without Law," that they existed in an early stage of legal development and could be brought into civilization, and into the circle of American civic belonging, only through a transformation of their legal system.[72]

This view was especially popular within the Bureau of Indian Affairs (BIA).[73] "It is much to be hoped that Congress will at its next session take this subject into careful consideration," wrote the Commissioner of Indian Affairs in 1866, "and provide a plain, comprehensive code, by which the superintendents and agents may dispense justice within their jurisdiction, and the infliction of appropriate penalties may be rendered certain, whether the offender be red or white. Retaliation is the law of the Indians; and if, in his early approaches to civilization, he is compelled to abandon that law, he looks for a substitute in the white man's law."[74] The annual reports of the commissioners contain many such calls, which came to visible fruition with the establishment in 1878 of Indian police forces, natives dressed in modern uniforms who enforced American laws and regulations in the absence of federal military force.[75] During the assimilationist era, a variety of such federal policies were set in motion to place Indians under the power of what one judge called the "educative and disciplinary instrumentalities" of U.S. courts.[76] Just as supporters of the Dawes Act hoped to abolish communal Indian land, constituting natives as individual property-holders, so others wished to abolish Indian criminal law, asserting national jurisdiction over Indian offenses and so binding native people to a liberal government that was to be the ultimate source of coercive power. They wished to infuse the Indian self with an Anglo-Saxon vision of law and so destroy the Indian as a social fact.[77]

It was in this volatile political context that a deadly fight broke out between two Indians on the Rosebud Sioux reservation in Dakota Territory one afternoon in 1881.[78] The two parties embodied opposite poles of Indian responses to the United States in the late-nineteenth century. One was named Kan-gi-shun-ca or Crow Dog. Crow Dog was one in a line of medicine men still active today, and he was firmly set against any accommodation to white settlement in North America. For some, Crow Dog was a troublemaker; for others, an uncompromising rebel. The other man was named Spotted Tail or Sin-ta-ge-le-Scka. Spotted Tail was the leader of the Brulé band of Sioux, and he was celebrated in Washington as a "progressive" Indian willing to negotiate with the federal government.[79] His supporters saw him as a statesman who could guide his people through a new and difficult political landscape; his enemies saw him as a quisling. For reasons unknown, though possibly related to Crow Dog and Spotted Tail's political differences, on the afternoon of August 5, Crow Dog jumped from behind the rear wheel of his wagon, pointed his rifle, and fired a single shot into Spotted Tail's side, killing him almost instantly. Traditionally, the trial of crimes committed by Indians against other Indians on reservations in the United States had been left to the authority of Indian tribes, a custom codified in § 2146 of the General Crimes Act of 1817.[80] The act extended federal authority over crimes committed on Indian lands, but it made an exception for crimes committed by one Indian against another. Accordingly, Spotted Tail's murder was settled under Sioux tribal law, with Crow Dog undergoing an act of ritual purification and compensating Spotted Tail's family with six-hundred dollars, eight horses, and one blanket. Tribal harmony was restored, and the matter was apparently at an end. The Bureau of Indian Affairs, however, viewed the matter differently. Seeing in Spotted Tail's murder a possible test case that could advance federal jurisdiction over Indian crimes, the agency initiated prosecution against Crow Dog in the spring of 1882 in Dakota territorial court. There, under federal law, Kan-gi-shun-ca was sentenced to hang.[81]

As with so much else in United States history, the words of Alexis de Tocqueville are relevant to Kan-gi-shun-ca's case. In *Democracy in America* (1835, 1840), Tocqueville offered an ironic account of federal law and policy regarding Native Americans. Noting that "the expulsion of the Indians often takes place at the present day in a regular and, as it were, a legal manner," Tocqueville described in detail the sufferings inflicted on native peoples through the coercion that took place under cover of legality. American policy for Tocqueville, in this respect, contrasted with the naked aggression and force used by Spanish conquerors. The Spanish, he wrote, had "pursued the Indians with bloodhounds, like wild beasts; they sacked the New World like a city taken by storm, with no discernment or compassion." Such force, he argued, while horrific, ultimately had an amalgamating consequence: "destruction must cease at last and frenzy has a limit: the remnant of the Indian population which had escaped the massacre mixed with its conquerors and adopted in the end their religion and their manners." The Americans, he argued, were different. "The conduct of the Americans of the United States towards the aborigines is characterized," Tocqueville wrote, "by a singular attachment to the formalities of law"—the consequence of which was not amalgamation but death. "It is impossible to destroy men," concluded Tocqueville, "with more respect for the laws of humanity."[82]

True to Tocqueville's vision, in the extension of U.S. jurisdiction over Indian crime, close attention was paid to whether this assertion of state power had constitutional and statutory legitimacy. After Crow Dog was sentenced to die, his counsel petitioned for a writ of habeas corpus, and the Supreme Court granted certiorari to consider the matter. The issue at bar was whether the Dakota court had subject matter jurisdiction over the case at all. Should the killing have been allowed to come under the consideration of federal legal institutions, or should it have ended with the exchange of six-hundred dollars, eight horses, and a blanket, under the purview of tribal authority? The answer to this question hinged on a more general question of statutory interpretation. The exception made in § 2146 of the General Crimes Act for crimes committed by one Indian against another included Crow Dog's murder of Spotted Tail, and so apparently invalidated the Dakota court's assertion of jurisdictional authority. In an 1868 treaty, however, the Sioux had agreed to submit to U.S. jurisdiction when specified crimes were committed on their land, including cases of murder committed by Indians against other Indians (Congress had codified this 1868 treaty, and the subsequent Treaty of 1876, as statutory law in 1877).[83] But while this treaty and statute appeared to uphold the Dakota court's jurisdiction, contradicting the force of the General Crimes Act, its language was ambiguous in a critical respect: it was not clear whether the treaty was intended to include the crime of murder committed by one Indian against another Indian of the same tribe. The question the Supreme Court faced was thus whether one could read into the 1868 treaty and 1877 statute the implied repeal of § 2146 of the General Crimes Act as it applied on Rosebud to Crow Dog's killing of Spotted Tail.

It may at first be surprising that the Court was unanimous in its opinion that Crow Dog should be set free. All nine justices ruled that the Dakota court had no jurisdiction over the case: the relevant section of the General Crimes Act had not been repealed through the ambiguous language of the Sioux treaty and statute. The Court granted Kan-gi-shun-ca his writ of habeas corpus, and he returned to the Rosebud reservation a symbol of the persistence of native legal autonomy in the face of American political dominance.[84] It is the vast difference, however, between what the Court's decision immediately did as a performative utterance and what the Court actually argued as a matter of law and stated in dicta that is essential for understanding the historical significance of the case, which directly belies the politically symbolic meaning often ascribed to Crow Dog's release. It is true that the Court invalidated the Dakota territorial court's assertion of power and, in this sense, the Court's decision did uphold the authority of Indian criminal law above and against the law of the United States. But the Court reached its decision not out of respect for native sovereignty. Quite the contrary, the Court asserted that the federal government probably did in fact have the authority to extend its criminal jurisdiction over cases such as Crow Dog's. The problem, asserted the Court, was simply that Congress had not extended its authority in explicit language, and that therefore jurisdiction still lay with the Sioux tribe. The Court invalidated the Dakota court's assertion of power because it refused to find the repeal of one Indian statute by another through mere implication. Just as *Marbury v. Madison* (1803) accrued authority for the Court through temporary abnegation of its power, so *Crow Dog* advanced national authority over Indians by denying one specific use of state force while suggesting that a still larger governmental capacity lay within constitutional reach.[85]

This assertion of broad national power through its specific abnegation was underwritten by juridical-racial principles of the kind Powell advanced. The opinion in *Crow Dog* was written by Justice Stanley Matthews, formerly a railroad attorney in Ohio, a devout Presbyterian known not only for his pragmatism but also for his legalistic cast of mind ("his decisions," wrote Senator John Sherman upon his death, "were mathematical demonstrations").[86] In approaching the issues in the case, Justice Matthews first turned to two provisions of the 1868 treaty that were alleged explicitly to override the General Crimes Act. He dismissed the first out of hand, and it does not warrant discussion here.[87] The second provision was article eight, which stated that Congress "shall, by appropriate legislation, secure to [the Sioux Indians] an orderly government; they shall be subject to the laws of the United States, and each individual shall be protected in his rights of property, person, and life." This provision, argued Matthews, could not override the General Crimes Act, because the tribal, group-based character of Indian life was incapable of upholding the individualist law of American civilization. He argued:

> The pledge to secure to these people, with whom the United States was contracting as a distinct political body, an orderly government, by appropriate legislation thereafter to be framed and enacted, necessarily implies, having regard to all the circumstances attending the transaction, that among the arts of civilized life, which it was the very purpose of all these arrangements to introduce and naturalize among them, was the highest and best of all, that of self-government, the regulation by themselves of their own domestic affairs, the maintenance of order and peace among their own members by the administration of their own laws and customs. They were nevertheless to be subject to the laws of the United States, not in the sense of citizens, but, as they had always been, as wards subject to a guardian; not as individuals, constituted members of the political community of the United States, with a voice in the selec-

tion of representatives and the framing of the laws, but as a dependent community who were in a state of pupilage, advancing from the condition of a savage tribe to that of a people who, through the discipline of labor and by education, it was hoped might become a self-supporting and self-governed society.[88]

For Justice Matthews, in other words, the 1868 treaty and 1877 statute could not be said explicitly to override the General Crimes Act, because its invocation of "orderly government" had to be read in the context of the widely acknowledged ethno-legal differences between Euro-Americans and native peoples, differences that were precisely of the kind that the Bureau of American Ethnology was devoted to collecting and classifying. A government of order could only be a government of imposed federal law.

Justice Matthews next turned to whether the 1868 treaty and 1877 statute could be said to override the General Crimes Act by implication. Justice Matthews argued that this could not be the case, because of the rule of *generalia specialibus non derogant*, which states that exceptions must be special and express and that general acts do not repeal specific provisions of previous statutes. Justice Matthews concluded the opinion with its most eloquent and forceful statement, which argued that even if the results of the case would seem to deny justice, the "nature and circumstances" of *Crow Dog* "strongly reinforce[d]" its more widely applicable hermeneutical position. Justice Matthews described those circumstances in explicitly juridical-racial terms:

It is a case of life and death. It is a case where, against an express exception in the law itself, that law, by argument and inference only, is sought to be extended over aliens and strangers; over the members of a community separated by race, by tradition, by the instincts of a free though savage life, from the authority and power which seeks to impose upon them the restraints of an external and unknown code, and to subject them to the responsibilities of civil conduct, according to rules and penalties of which they could have no previous warning; which judges them by a standard made for others and not for them, which takes no account of the conditions which should except them from its exactions, and makes no allowance for their inability to understand it. It tries them, not by their peers, nor by the customs of their people, nor the law of their land, but by superiors of a different race, according to the law of a social state of which they have an imperfect conception, and which is opposed to the traditions of their history, to the habits of their lives, to the strongest prejudices of their savage nature; one which measures the red man's revenge by the maxims of the white man's morality.[89]

In *Crow Dog*, juridical racialism of the kind used by Powell in his developmentalist approach to human variation thus bridged a gap between the ambiguous language of a contemporary statute and that of a past treaty, resolving the interpretive difficulty at issue by presenting itself as a set of social axioms that should be axioms of law. The Court's reference to the "traditions" of savagery, to an as-yet-unknown and thus ultimately knowable code, to social states of which people have an imperfect and so ultimately perfectible conception, and to differing standards of ethical measurement, instantiate a juridical-racial system homologous to that of developmentalist anthropological theory—a legal-racial vision forged in state-funded social scientific groups such as the BAE and employed at law to expand federal power over Indian criminal offenses and, ultimately, to extend the legitimacy of the state itself.

When the Court handed down its decision in *Crow Dog*, many in Congress and the Bureau of Indian Affairs were outraged.[90] "It is an infamy upon our civilization," stated Congressman Byron M. Cutcheon of Michigan, "a disgrace to this nation, that there should be anywhere within its boundaries a body of people who can, with absolute impunity, commit the crime of murder, there being no tribunal before which they can be brought for punishment. Under our present law there is no penalty that can be inflicted except according to the custom of the tribe, which is simply that [of] the 'blood avenger[.]'" The "law of the tribe," stated Cutcheon, is "no law at all."[91] But the decision, which stood not for the absolute right of native peoples to maintain their legal traditions but for the absolute need of Congress to be explicit in any statute that in part or in whole abolished Indian laws, was more clearly understood by Congress as a challenge to which it was invited to respond. Within a year, federal legislators passed the Major Crimes Act of 1885, which extended federal criminal jurisdiction over specified offenses, including all cases of murder, not just onto Rosebud but onto all reservations. As the Court's opinion in *Crow Dog* had advised, Congress extended its jurisdiction explicitly, in language clearly overriding pertinent parts of the General Crimes Act of 1817.[92] "Just so long as they are left without the developing and educating restraint and protection of civilized law, so long will they be lawless," stated Henry Pancoast of the Indian Rights Association in late 1883, in a form of analysis also popular within the BIA: "Side by side with the power of religion and the power of education to redeem the remnant of this people, there should stand the power of the law. To introduce this law is the task which those who work for the Indian should set before them."[93]

In its turn, the Major Crimes Act of 1885 invited its own judicial response, the case of *United States v. Kagama*, which established the Indian plenary power doctrine. The facts of the *Kagama* case are tawdry and brutal, incidents of a displaced people in a desperate time.[94] About one month after the passage of the Major Crimes Act, a Klamath Indian named Kagama, also known as Pactah Billy, killed another named Iyouse, also known as Ike, on the Hoopa reservation in northern California, in a dispute over land. The fight ultimately may have been caused by a poor geographic survey of the area, which placed two Klamath villages on an Indian reservation granted to the Hoopa, and so made the legal rights of the Klamath unclear. What exactly happened that afternoon in June 1885 is not certain, but in the course of a discussion of their respective property claims, Kagama stabbed Iyouse and cut his throat, while Kagama's son Mahawaha, also known as Ben, held back Iyouse's wife and prevented her from intervening. Kagama and his son were indicted for murder in federal district court in San Francisco. Their attorney demurred to their indictment, and after the federal circuit court for the district of California certified its division of opinion on the matter of jurisdiction, Kagama's case found its way on interlocutory appeal to the Supreme Court. There, just as Crow Dog's attorney had contested the federal government's assertion of power over his client's case, so Kagama's counsel argued that the part of the Major Crimes Act of 1885 granting territorial courts jurisdiction over a killing committed by one Indian against another on a reservation lay outside the constitutional authority of Congress.

In a unanimous ruling, the Court upheld Congressional authority to pass the Major Crimes Act of 1885 and so also upheld the jurisdiction of the territorial court. Whereas Crow Dog was released from federal authorities, Kagama would be subject to their power. Significantly, the opinion in *Kagama* was written by Justice Samuel Miller, a man who bore many similarities to Major Powell in his physical energy and professional development.[95] Born on April 5, 1816 in Richmond, Kentucky, Miller was the descendant of Pennsylvania Germans who had immigrated to the state in 1812. After a sporadic education, he studied medicine, earning a degree from Transylvania University in Lexington in 1838. Miller practiced medicine for approximately ten years in the backwoods of Barbourville, but he became bored and turned to law, which he taught himself. Moving to Iowa, he soon became a prominent and prosperous member of the state bar, specializing in property and commercial cases. One biographer describes him as "a large man, with a well-built frame, standing six feet tall and weighing over two hundred pounds. His features, too, were large and clear-cut; he had a massive head, a sharply chiseled face, and a pair of bright, penetrating eyes. One looked at him and sensed his massive power and indomitable will." "Not only was he rugged," continues the biographer, "but his zest for living made him love his family, work, and play. He liked to ride horse, dance a jig, sing a song."[96]

Miller's politics were representative of an important trend of the time. On one hand, he was a nationalist, a liberal Republican appointed to the bench by President Lincoln, a man who in a variety of decisions had advocated an extensive construction of national power. In the *Legal Tender Cases* (1870–71), for example, he upheld the authority of the greenback as a payment for national Civil War debt; in *Wabash v. Illinois* (1886), he lay the groundwork for modern regulatory agencies through his interpretation of the Commerce Clause.[97] In addition to being an advocate of federal power, however, Miller was also an Anglo-Saxon racist, regarding foreigners with deep mistrust. In an 1886 interview with the *New York World*, for instance, Miller was asked if he believed justices of the Court should wear silk robes (the journalist contended they might be incompatible with "the simplicity of our republican institutions"). Miller responded that such badges of hierarchy were, in fact, an unfortunate necessity in changing ethnic times. "[T]he Anglo-Saxon people are the only people on the face of the earth who have much respect for law in the abstract," Miller argued. "Other nations have it in a measure, but such is the respect of the Anglo-Saxon mind for abstract law that I believe that the future development of the world depends largely upon the predominance of the Anglo-Saxon element. . . . If we had predominant in this country at this present time the [Anglo-Saxon] . . . then I feel quite certain if the judges sat upon the bench in plain clothes they would exercise as much influence as they ought to."[98] Miller thus exhibited the odd union of a fiery commitment to liberal state-building and an intense ethnocentrism that, as in Powell's work as director of the BAE, was part of the folkways of many American Republicans in the late-nineteenth century.

I use the term "folkways" deliberately, because in deciding that Congress did, in fact, have power to pass the Major Crimes Act, Justice Miller did not rely on an expansive analysis of the constitutional text. He rejected the argument that the ability to regulate Indian tribes arose from Congressional commerce power, from its Article I, Section 8 authority to "regulate commerce with foreign Nations, and among the several States, and with the Indian tribes."[99] Instead, Justice Miller turned to the custom-based world of the common law and its juridical-racial implications. In particular, in his analysis, Justice Miller relied on the common-law doctrine of wardship, which defines the legal obligations of wards to guardians. Treated in Kent's *Commentaries* under the law of persons, wardship was considered a subtopic of laws concerning parents and children, and in this sense, it was an area of knowledge imbricated with ideas from developmentalist anthropology, which compared the growth of a society from savagery to civilization to the growth of an individual from childhood into adulthood.[100] The language of wardship first had been employed by Chief Justice Marshall to describe the relation of Indians to whites as one of semisovereignty, in which Indians and the federal government maintained mutual rights and obligations. In Justice Miller's hands, however, that language came to describe a condition of almost complete national authority, in which the autonomy of native tribes was subsumed by their greater dependence. In Kent's treatment of the law of persons, the dependent status of children required that parents care for them, and parents were said to be able to exercise such care only if they had the legal authority to do so; parental rights arose from parental duties. Similarly, in the Court's opinion, the dependent condition of Indians, and not any explicit constitutional grant of power, implied the existence of federal authority over them.[101] But in an implicit extension of the wardship doctrine, the Court also asserted that the extent of federal rights was commensurate with the extent of parental duties, and that because Indians were "remnants of a race once powerful, now weak and diminished in numbers"—because they were wards whose dependence was becoming absolute—the federal government's authority was becoming absolute as well. "From their very weakness and helplessness," asserted Justice Miller, who emphasized Indian dependence in the strongest terms, "there arises the duty of protection, and with it the power."[102]

That power included, naturally, the Major Crimes Act (passing it was entirely within the authority of Congress, stated Miller; after all, it had written the act in very explicit terms, consistent with the Court's demand in *Crow Dog*). And it included much else besides. By the early-twentieth century, in *Lone Wolf v. Hitchcock* (1903), the Court would hold that Congress had the authority unilaterally to abrogate specific provisions in federal-Indian treaties if it deemed such abrogation necessary.[103] This was the Indian plenary power doctrine, and here, the juridical exchange about Indian affairs initiated by *Crow Dog* reached its end. When Congress passed the Dawes Act two years later, its constitutionality was a foregone conclusion. The United States could lift its Indian children through the juridical-racial path of social progress, from the childlike state of property-less savagery to the adulthood of individualist, fee-simple civilization, in almost any way it saw fit. In this sense, the relation between the U.S. government and American Indians was similar to that which Kent had described in his examination of the rights of parents among groups in the upper stages of barbarism—and in this sense, a nineteenth-century ideal of reason can be said to have undergone a reversal on the level of legal doctrine as well. "[T]he ancients generally carried the power of the parent to a most atrocious extent over the person and liberty of the child," wrote Kent in his *Commentaries*. "The Persians, Egyptians, Greeks, Gauls, and Romans, allowed to fathers a very absolute dominion over their offspring, and the liberty and lives of the children were placed within their power. . . . [And] in many instances, this paternal power was exercised without the forms of justice" (Kent was thinking, in this regard, of infanticide).[104] So it also was in federal-Indian affairs during the assimilationist era. In the Supreme Court's mapping of federal authority, based upon its earlier discussion of federal jurisdiction in *Crow Dog*, the power of the national government over Indian property was vast indeed; and when viewed within the familial metaphor of wardship and the juridical-racial vision of Powell's anthropology, one might say that the stage was set for disinheritance.

Conclusion

There are at least two ways of describing the historical significance of the juridical racialism advanced by Powell and in *Crow Dog* and *Kagama*, and while they are not mutually exclusive, they are quite different. The first takes what might be called a multiculturalist perspective on the American past. From this perspective, the story of the developmentalist juridical racialism that links anthropology to Indian law is one of social annihilation. It is one in which ideas that had been developed in part by anthropologists were employed within the law to advance an ethnocentric vision of American identity and thereby to trammel cultural diversity—one in which the historical framework of juridical-racial evolution espoused by Powell transformed a varied cultural landscape into a more flat and even plane when it became manifest in both legislation and court decision-making. In this view, developmentalism was an instrument of legal-cultural homogenization, a means by which the number of social and normative worlds extant in North America gradually was reduced. To gesture toward the work of Robert Cover, developmentalism served a jurispathic rather than a jurisgenerative project, destroying the juridical universe of Indian tribes rather than fostering their growth.[105]

There is a second perspective on the history of developmentalist juridical racialism and Indian law, however, more compelling for legal history, based on materialist and state-centered concerns. This view brings into focus the intellectual mechanisms that underlay and justified the process by which assimilationist-era Indian policy served the interests of emerging and expanding economic forces in the late-nineteenth century by displacing Indians from their lands. Developmentalist models of juridical-racial evolution were employed by those advocating Indian land allotment, and developmentalist thought helped bind together the alliance of Christian social reformers and western land interests that was instrumental to the legislative and administrative shifts in federal Indian policy. More important, before Indian lands were redistributed by the state, the federal judiciary handed down a series of rulings legitimizing this large-scale property redistribution in the terms of liberal constitutional democracy. As I have suggested, juridical racialism played a role in this legitimization process. Juridical-racial ideas were used to adjudicate questions of criminal jurisdiction, territorializing Indians in legal doctrine before their territory itself became more fully subject to the law. And in another, deeper sense, apparent in *Crow Dog*, juridical-racial ideas were used to further the interests of dominant economic forces by helping the state assert its apparent autonomy from those very forces, strengthening the state's legitimacy and its power by offering an occasion for it to perfect the formalization of its procedures of coercion.

This materialist approach highlights the ways in which our national government and its jurisprudential principles, like American anthropology, came of age in the context of an Indian presence, defining itself against a legal-cultural other in the same way that ideas of political freedom arose from the presence of slavery in colonial Virginia. In this sense, it demonstrates that the history of Indian law truly is national history. Moreover, it points toward how the state facilitated national economic transformation while maintaining its own liberal ideological continuity. Earlier, I contrasted developmentalist museum presentations with the presentations common today, in which cultures are meant to be examined and evaluated on their own terms. These presentations are the legacy of Franz Boas, and in 1883, the year in which *Crow Dog* was decided, Boas set sail to Bafflinland for his first work among the Inuit. The ideas Boas began to develop on this trip were poised precisely against, as they would come to displace, those of the developmentalists who initially gave him their institutional and financial support. In the intellectual and legal revolution effected by Boas's conceptions of race, culture, and the law, the central terms of developmentalist anthropology and of the constitutional interpretation of the status of minorities would be inverted, while the instrument for putting American civic ideals into practice would be strengthened and their economic potential realized to an even further degree. In particular, Boas's work would play a central part in a case that, like *Kagama* and *Crow Dog*, concerned race and geography, invoked a language of childhood development, required an unprecedented extension of federal state force, and initiated a new phase of capitalism in America: *Brown v. Board of Education* (1954), the decision with which I conclude this study.[106] In other words, in the volatile exchange through which Boasian ideas replaced those of Morgan and his followers—an exchange in which a transformation in the idea of law would help to create a change within the law itself—the socioeconomic order of the United States would assume a quite different form; nevertheless, the national state that began to develop in the wake of Major John Wesley Powell's Civil War, and which grew still greater in the wake of World War II, would become an increasingly powerful figure on the political and economic landscape. It is this phenomenon that lies at the heart of the broad historical significance of the developmentalist constitutional theory of culture, and at the heart of juridical racialism during the assimilationist era of United States Indian affairs. To understand why in greater detail, it is necessary to turn attention away from North America, toward the Philippines.

2

Teutonic Constitutionalism and
the Spanish-American War

The closing years of the nineteenth century began a new era in American history, one of overseas empire, brought into being through the Spanish-American War. In a host of ways, this new era grew from the national experience with American Indians examined in chapter 1. As an economic matter, the war provided increased access to overseas markets and so furthered the process of economic growth begun with the redistribution of Indian lands in the West. As an ideological matter, U.S. contact with native peoples provided a basis upon which political leaders reconciled imperial policy with traditional republican ideals.[1] Significantly, this reconciliation operated at two related levels of socio-legal argument. First, the Supreme Court's encounter with Indian affairs beginning in the 1830s was said to establish a basis in legal doctrine for American power over its new "insular," or island, possessions.[2] Second, and more important for this study, the socio-legal link between American Indians and overseas imperialism existed within the rhetorical field of juridical racialism. For like Indians, the inhabitants of insular lands frequently were described as incapable of upholding American legal norms and so fit largely for subjugation. "[Y]ou, who say the Declaration [of Independence] applies to all men," proclaimed Senator Albert J. Beveridge to anti-imperialists in Congress, "how dare you deny its application to the American Indian? And if you deny it to the Indian at home, how dare you grant it to the Malay abroad? . . . [T]here are people in the world who do not understand any form of government . . . [and] must be governed."[3]

The closing years of the nineteenth century thus marked not only a new era in American history, but also a new period in the history of juridical racialism. That new era is the subject of this chapter, which examines the place of juridical racialism during and immediately after the

Spanish-American War. I am interested specifically in the role juridical racialism played in the *Insular Cases* (1901–4), which determined the constitutional status of Puerto Rico, Hawaii, and the Philippines in the wake of the Treaty of Paris (1898) and limited the extent to which residents of the insular possessions were members of the American nation.[4] At the jurisprudential foundation of the *Insular Cases*, I argue, lay a particular manifestation of juridical racialism associated with the Teutonic origins thesis of American government, a blend of legal history and legal anthropology central to academic life in the late nineteenth century.[5] Exponents of the Teutonic origins thesis claimed that the greatest American legal achievements found their spiritual origin in the legal thought of the free and strong warrior peoples Tacitus describes in his celebrated account of ancient Germany. They accordingly characterized Anglo-Saxons as a people with a special genius for law and state-building, viewed the state and legal order itself as Anglo-Saxon in character, and understood dark-skinned peoples as incapable of legality and congenitally criminal.

I begin my analysis by examining the life and work of Senator Henry Cabot Lodge, blue-blooded Bostonian, influential advocate of U.S. imperialism, and early student of the Teutonic origins thesis, a man whose personal and professional self-development rested on a juridical-racial vision of self and society. I then discuss how Lodge and his allies employed this vision in Congress in their promotion of American imperial policy overseas. Turning to the *Insular Cases*, I suggest how the juridical-racial view Lodge espoused also formed the jurisprudential basis of *Downes v. Bidwell* (1901), which I describe as advancing a "Teutonic constitutionalism."[6] An otherwise mundane case concerning the constitutionality of a tax levied on a shipment of oranges sent from Puerto Rico to New York, the case announced the doctrine of territorial incorporation, which granted Congress wide powers in governing the colonial possessions acquired through the Treaty of Paris and which represents the doctrinal analogue of the Indian plenary power doctrine for this period of American political history. In the conclusion, I follow the logic of Teutonic constitutionalism from Puerto Rico to the Philippines, considering how assertions of inherent Anglo-Saxon legality facilitated and justified behavior precisely unlawful in character. In this way, I argue, juridical racialism elided the human suffering wrought by imperial expansion during an age of progressive state development.

Henry Cabot Lodge and the Anglo-Saxon State

Even a brief history of the Spanish-American War must begin not with the lands under dispute but with the instability and corruption that marked Spanish political life at the end of the nineteenth century.[7] After being overthrown in 1868, the Spanish monarchy was reinstated by a coup d'état in 1874, beginning a notorious period known as the Restoration. Upon the death of King Alfonso XII in 1885, the country came under the regency of the child princess María Cristina of Austria and was governed by the rule of *caciquismo*, which one scholar describes as "a system of scheming and manipulation which enabled the political bosses . . . in alliance with the wealthy landowners, military leaders and government officials to rule the state for their own personal advantage."[8] Caught between a glorious past and a banal present, Spain fell under a "curious mood of self-deception," in which any symbol of its self-ascribed national greatness, no matter how small or dubious, assumed prominence in Spanish identity. Within this political universe, the colonies of Puerto Rico, the Philippines, and, most important, Cuba, played a special role as emblems of a yearning for national power and renown. They were said to be "living proof that God's blessing continued to shine on Spain's imperial status."[9] As such divine proofs often do, these symbols belied actual conditions of exploitation, relations of extractive colonial rule that in the late 1860s sparked a Cuban rebellion for independence. Beginning in the poor and underdeveloped province of Oriente, the revolt failed to spread across the island, and the fighting ended in 1878 with a truce brokered by Spanish General Arsenio Martínez Campos, who offered a variety of concessions to the rebels. These concessions were never fulfilled, and in the 1890s the independence movement resurfaced, this time under the leadership of José Martí, who in 1892 established the Cuban Revolutionary Party and in 1895 launched a new fight for *Cuba libre*.

This renewed rebellion drew brutal resistance from the Spanish military. With the failure of the Cuban peace, Spain replaced General Campos with General Valeriano Weyler y Nicolau, a highly professional soldier of German descent who had developed a "reputation for ruthlessness" in earlier campaigns in Cuba and Catalonia.[10] With 200,000 troops fighting approximately 20,000–30,000 Cuban rebels, General Weyler undertook a multipronged counterinsurgency campaign. One prominent tactic involved the construction of vast trenches, approximately six-hundred feet in width, filled with "trees, boulders, barbed wire and explosives" and guarded by "forts, towers and blockhouses," to surround Cuban towns and divide revolutionary forces from each other.[11] A second, more notorious action, for which Weyler is still remembered today, was the first widespread use of "reconcentration camps" as a pacification strategy. In his attempt to combat rebel forces, General Weyler "emptied the countryside of people, crops and livestock" and relocated Cuban civilians to detention centers. By recent scholarly estimates, at least 100,000 Cubans died as a result, though assessments at the time put the number at 400,000.[12] General Weyler's campaign aroused international outrage and earned him the nickname "butcher." Neither trenches nor reconcentration, however, fulfilled Spanish hopes, and the rebels were gaining ground despite Weyler's campaign. Though Spain attempted to concede a certain degree of home rule to Cuba in 1897, the die had already been cast. Spain was waging a total war against revolutionaries who made a reasonable claim that their opponents were committing systematic acts of lawlessness.

Americans were deeply moved by Cubans' struggle for independence, and many wished to further their cause. As descendants of a revolution, some sympathized with movements for national independence everywhere. Others feared the economic and political consequences of Cuban unrest and Spanish misrule. Still others, such as Josiah Strong, were animated by a Protestant hatred of Catholic monarchy. The United States, moreover, continued to be torn by sectional strife between North and South, and it hungered for a common cause that could provide a measure of reconciliation by helping to wash the "bloody shirt." Amid disparate calls for intervention, and after repeated attempts by Presidents Grover Cleveland and William McKinley to escape direct military confrontation, the United States threw itself into war against Spain in 1898 after the notorious explosion of the *Maine*. The war sought to free Cuba from Spanish domination, though the conflict had consequences far beyond its stated purpose. The United States quickly conquered Spain in Cuba, Puerto Rico, and the Philippines, and the fighting came to an end with the American acquisition of a variety of island colonies through the Treaty of Paris.[13] Congress soon began the task of reforming the Spanish legal system and replacing it with American law to establish social and economic order.

Senator Henry Cabot Lodge was one of the primary architects of American foreign policy, and he was one of the most vociferous voices calling for U.S. participation in the war against Spain.[14] Born in 1850,

Lodge was a Republican who began his political career in the Massachusetts state legislature in the early 1880s, moving to the federal House of Representatives in 1887 and the United States Senate in 1893. Lodge had a special interest in foreign affairs and was a longtime member of the Senate Committee on Foreign Relations. It was in his role as a member of Congress during the Republican McKinley administration that Lodge put his imperialist beliefs most effectively into practice. In his advocacy of American expansion, Lodge was a disciple, like his friend Theodore Roosevelt, then Assistant Secretary of the Navy, of the historian Alfred Thayer Mahan.[15] In *The Influence of Sea Power upon History* (1890), Mahan had argued that naval power was the central component of international political influence and that the United States should look outward and develop an overseas empire like those of great European states.[16] Lodge's imperial designs were bitterly opposed by Senators such as George Hoar of Massachusetts and Eugene Hale of Maine and by anti-imperialist Republicans. This diverse group of men shared the belief that overseas expansion was fundamentally at odds with the republican principles of the American nation, which itself had revolted against colonial domination; they forcefully argued that the development of an empire would undermine the very nature of American political identity.[17] Still, it was Lodge who ultimately won the ear of the President, almost single-handedly persuading the more cautious McKinley to declare war on Spain whatever concessions it might offer to Cuba or the United States.

Those who supported the Spanish-American War did so for a variety of reasons.[18] To understand what the conflict meant for Lodge as an exponent of juridical racialism, however, it is helpful to bear in mind a sense of historical periodization. The late-nineteenth century in the United States was an era of economic and state modernization similar to that undergone approximately thirty years earlier in Europe, and the war was a national event that materially advanced this historical movement. This modernizing trend included those phenomena that typified what scholars once called the Progressive Era: the consolidation of national unity, the concentration of domestic wealth, the construction of a professional state apparatus, and the creation of new markets for surplus capital—or, more strongly put, the militant assertion of an overarching American racial identity, the rise of trusts, the construction of expert reform organizations and civil service bureaucracies, and the quest for foreign markets overseas. Some of the legal aspects of this transformation have been described in detail by Martin Sklar.[19] Its cultural components have been examined by Alan Trachtenberg and characterized as "the incorporation of America."[20]

The Spanish-American War played a key role in these shifts. First, the war offered an occasion for national unity at home, healing sectional divisions across the Mason-Dixon line, providing a common cause around which a shared national racial identity might be constructed from a fragmented political self. Second, the war brought the United States onto the world stage, launching its career as a global power, by creating an overseas empire for a nation previously limited to its own continental territorial boundaries. Third, the war propelled industrial economic development and the concentration of domestic capital by expanding global markets. By opening Cuba, Puerto Rico, the Philippines, and various Pacific regions to commercial exploitation, and providing coaling stations for ships on their way to Asian ports, the war offered an outlet for surplus capital generated at home.[21] Finally, the war required the creation of a complex bureaucratic state apparatus to provide for the central administration of colonial peoples. In the wake of the Treaty of Paris, non-Western societies came under the direct military and civil authority of the United States government, which was forced to construct rational bureaucratic procedures and administrative agencies for maintaining an efficient peace. In these and other respects, the war not only was driven by the symbolic and emotional issues of national liberation, but also participated in and was guided by the creation of a distinctly modern form of social and economic life. It was a war that brought the United States into the twentieth century.

The modernizing or progressive nature of the war is significant for understanding Lodge, because the Senator from Massachusetts was hardly representative of the new nation America would become. Instead, he was a figure from the past, born into an old, distinguished line of Boston Brahmins, a class that had played an enormous role in national culture and politics in previous years but that was becoming increasingly marginal. Born under the roof of a "granite mansion, in the best part of residential Boston," Lodge was guaranteed by his very pedigree "[w]ealth, social position, intellectual stimulation, even a healthy body and reasonably good looks."[22] His father was a prominent Boston merchant with a stern and rigid cast of mind. His mother, Anna Cabot, who doted on him, sprang from an old and venerated New England family. Her grandfather, Federalist George Cabot, had been elected to the United States Senate and was a close associate of George Washington, Alexander Hamilton, and John Adams. The family lived within the highest ranks of Boston society, and its home was the site of visits by Charles Sumner, Henry Wadsworth Longfellow, Francis Parkman, William Prescott, John Lothrop Motley, Charles Bancroft, and Louis Agassiz. Lodge attended grade school with the sons of the Bigelows, Cabots, and Parkmans, and later studied at a "private Latin school" with the Chadwicks and the Lymans.[23] He came to know and love William Shakespeare, watching Edwin Booth in *Julius Caesar* and *Hamlet*; he grew patriotic for the Union during the Civil War without becoming unduly rash or abolitionist in his sentiments; he traveled to Europe with servant and tutor in tow; he enrolled in Harvard College.

Lodge's relation to his family history was deeply reverent, verging on ancestor worship.[24] After spending several years at Harvard as a self-described mediocre student, in 1871 Lodge launched a career as a scholar, critic, and essayist, writing about the past in which his ancestors had played such an important role. His first major work concerned George Cabot. "A sentiment of respect for the memory of my great-grandfather, and a desire to rescue his name if possible from complete oblivion, induced me to undertake [this] work," begins Lodge, in a book whose frontispiece bears the Cabot coat of arms and the inscription "SEMPER COR CAPVT CABOT." "Wise and patriotic in public affairs," he concludes, "respected by his friends, and beloved by his family, of high honor and unspotted integrity, Mr. Cabot left a memory which must ever be venerated by his descendants."[25] In addition to writing this ancestral hagiography, Lodge contributed to the *Nation* and the *Atlantic Monthly*, and he served as an assistant editor at the prestigious *North American Review*, publishing numerous articles on political topics that indicate his patriotic cast of mind: "Critical Notice of Henry Dexter's *As to Roger Williams and his Banishment from the Massachusetts Plantation*," "Critical Review of Von Holst's *Constitutional and Political History of the United States*," "Notice of George Shea's *Alexander Hamilton*" and "New England Federalism."[26] Lodge's other book-length works during this period sound a similar patriotic theme. In addition to his biography of George Cabot, within only a few years, he published *A Short History of the English Colonies in America*, an edited volume of *The Federalist*, various collections of essays on civic themes, and biographies of Alexander Hamilton, Daniel Webster, and George Washington; and, with Theodore Roosevelt, the equally representative work *Hero Tales From American History; or the Story of*

Some Americans Who Showed that They Knew How to Live and How to Die.[27]

Though successful in this literary career, beginning in the late 1870s, Lodge left his life in letters for a life in politics. Driven in part by a sense of aristocratic distaste with contemporary American social affairs, he continued to write while devoting himself increasingly to progressive political causes and moving to Washington to enter the highest levels of the federal government. Despite the contempt with which Lodge is often treated by academic liberals today, it is important to recognize that in the context of his own day he was a reformer. He advocated civil service professionalism, for example. "The system of patronage in offices," he explained, "we have always had, but it is none the less a system born of despotisms and aristocracies, and it is the merest cant to call it American."[28] Similarly, he supported the use of federal power to protect southern black voting rights, sponsoring the Federal Elections or "Force" Bill as a matter of both principle and politics. He also advocated the use of the Sherman Antitrust Act, partly from a cultured opposition to the society of the industrial new rich and to what he notably termed their "lawlessness."[29] In this respect, Lodge's political career, and his ultimate support of imperialist foreign policy, was a movement at once forward and back, an attempt to bring the past into the present. In the rapidly changing society of the Gilded Age, in an incorporating America, Lodge chose to forsake scholarship so as to rescue himself and his class from irrelevance, from being merely backward-looking men of breeding and history, merely writers and editors of the *North American Review*. While the United States was undergoing the structural changes shaping it into a modern nation, Lodge was attempting to modernize himself.

Significantly for the history of juridical racialism, in this process of self-modernization Lodge drew on the lessons he learned in the backward-looking scholarly career he set aside, especially from his study of legal history. After graduating Harvard, Lodge remained in Cambridge to receive a degree in law and in 1876 a Ph.D. in political science. This was one of the first doctorates awarded in the discipline in the United States, where the social sciences were just beginning to become professionalized, and Lodge received it less for the study of contemporary policy than for the study of what has been called historico-politics.[30] Lodge's teacher, in fact, was Henry Adams, the anti-modernist Boston Brahmin, an unruly scholar-statesman who was an early enthusiast of the German historical method that became the foundation of much American scholarship in the early twentieth century. When Lodge began his graduate studies, Adams had just returned from a European honeymoon during which he met with some of the most significant German historians of the day. These included Heinrich von Sybel, the chief student of Leopold von Ranke; Theodor Mommsen, a scholar of Roman legal history; and Heinrich Rudolph von Gneist, a historian of German law (in London, Adams also met with Sir Henry Maine, William Stubbs, who was researching the *Constitutional History of England* [1873–78], and other English scholars).[31] Upon his return, Adams led Lodge and two other graduate students in a doctoral seminar on "Medieval Institutions" (the term "institutions" was often used as a synonym for "law" during the period). Under Adams's direction, Lodge spent long hours reading German, Anglo-Saxon, and Latin legal texts, immersing himself in the arcane, retrospective historical subject toward which his teacher had steered him, Anglo-Saxon land law. Adams's pedagogical advice to Lodge and his colleagues was simple: be thorough in research and emulate German scientific standards.[32]

Lodge's work was published as "The Anglo-Saxon Land-Law" in *Essays in Anglo-Saxon Law,* a volume to which Adams contributed an essay titled "The Anglo-Saxon Courts of Law" and Lodge's fellow students offered accounts of "The Anglo-Saxon Family Law" and "The Anglo-Saxon Legal Procedure." The volume is exceptionally recondite, if not dusty and parched, as Lodge himself would allow years later, partly in an effort to distance himself from the life of the mind with which he contrasted his later political career.[33] "I doubt if I could have selected a drier subject," Lodge recalled ruefully; "I certainly could not have found drier reading than the latest and most authoritative German writers of that day . . . [Rudolf] Sohm, [Georg Ludwig] Von Maurer, and the rest, at whose books I toiled faithfully for some weary months." The process of writing a dissertation, he explained, "was not inspiriting, it was in fact inexpressibly dreary, and I passed a depressing winter so far as my own labors were concerned. I seemed to be going nowhere and to be achieving nothing."[34] Still, despite such objections, Lodge's dissertation was deemed important enough to merit extended analysis by Frederick Pollock (he was deeply critical of Lodge's work, though he thought it showed "much ingenuity"), and it certainly revealed Lodge's mastery of the German methods of social science in which Adams had taken care to school his students.[35]

Anglo-Saxon land law was a relatively underdeveloped subject in Lodge's day, and the basic purpose of his project therefore was theoretically modest. He hoped simply to classify the various forms of landholding among ancient Anglo-Saxons and trace their changes over time. Yet behind this basic empirical work lay a larger purpose, one appropriate to Lodge as a seasoned practitioner of family history. This was to bolster respect for the English common law and thereby strengthen the ideological foundations of the American political order. Encouraging reverence for American politics through a dry study of ancient German landholding may seem like a dubious proposition from the perspective of today, but it is important to bear in mind that the common law at the time was thought to have developed directly from the law of the Anglo-Saxons before the Norman invasion, and that its spirit in turn was said to find its highest expression in the political institutions of the United States. In this regard, Lodge's work took part in a larger debate among late-nineteenth-century legal scholars between those who revered the Romanized Normans and their way of life and those who favored the Teutons. While Lodge was partly descended from Huguenots and so appreciated the Norman position, he generally sided with the Teutonists. "Free from the injurious influences of the Roman and Celtic peoples," Lodge wrote in his dissertation, "the laws and institutions of the ancient German tribes flourished and waxed strong on the soil of England. . . . Strong enough to resist the power of the church in infancy, stronger still to resist the shock of Norman invasion, crushed then, but not destroyed, by foreign influences, the great principles of Anglo-Saxon law, ever changing and assimilating, have survived in the noblest work of the race,—the English common law."[36]

The idea that the greatest English and American political institutions derived from ancient Germany was culturally central to the late-nineteenth century, forming the basis of a historical and anthropological set of ideas known as the Teutonic origins thesis of American government.[37] Advanced by an array of writers, and associated with John Burgess at Columbia and Herbert Baxter Adams at Johns Hopkins, the Teutonic thesis asserted that Americans were to play a unique role in world history because they were the spiritual and institutional descendants of the warrior peoples described in the writings of Tacitus, tribes of free, strong, and hardy men and women who shunned gold, avoided pompous ostentation, and were steadfast in battle.[38] In particular, like the Teutons of the *Germania*, the English and Anglo-American people were understood to be specially endowed with a racial genius for law. They were thought to possess the basic self-discipline necessary for political liberty and an innate capacity for state-building and the maintenance of legality. Currently discredited as a scholarly idea, the Teutonic origins thesis held an important place in the social sciences in the years that Henry Adams taught "Medieval Institutions" and Henry Cabot Lodge poured over his Latin texts. Though scholars have emphasized the ways in which the thesis offered a scholarly narrative about racial development, with the important exception of Richard Cosgrove they have not stressed enough the ways in which the Teutonic thesis formed a scholarly narrative not only about racial development but also about legal history, based firmly on the work of legal historians and anthropologists.[39] This professional class, from Sir Edward Coke to Maine to Paul Vinogradoff to Maitland, the intellectual forebears of contemporary legal academics, played a critical role in generating the academic belief that Anglo-Americans were a people especially capable of law and government.[40]

I use the terms legal history and anthropology somewhat interchangeably in describing the academic origins of the Teutonic thesis, and the conflation is deliberate. In the late-nineteenth century, amid the increasing professionalization of the social sciences, the boundaries between the disciplines were not as clear as they would later become.[41] This was true of anthropology, which frequently produced works with historical ambitions, and also of history, which often referred to the anthropology of aboriginal peoples in its narrative and analysis. The central conceptual link between these two areas of knowledge was a unifying idea, that of progressive social evolution.[42] The link, that is, was the study of the laws that guided societies in their growth toward more complex and rule-bound forms of self-government—and in the case of the Teutonic thesis, in particular, the evolution of the open-air councils, folk-moots, and early parliamentary capacities into the ordered state. The titles of two books of the preceding era signal the points at which the two disciplines overlapped: Henry Maine's *Ancient Law* (1861) and Louis Henry Morgan's *Ancient Society* (1877), the first a classic work of legal history that relied heavily on anthropological data and analysis, the second a classic work of anthropology whose main focus was the law (and whose author, as I discussed in chapter 1, was a New York corporations lawyer).[43] Similarly, Albert Kocourek and John Henry Wigmore's important edited series *Evolution of Law*, published in the 1910s, drew most of its scholarly material from late-nineteenth-century legal historians such as Maine and anthropologists and ethnological jurisprudes such as John Wesley Powell and Joseph Kohler.[44]

One also might turn in this light to the words of Lodge's teacher Henry Adams, contributing to the collection of *Essays in Anglo-Saxon Law*. An admirer of the Romanized Normans, Adams nevertheless advanced historical ideas essentially congruent with those of the Teutonic theory to which Lodge more explicitly subscribed. Describing ancient Germanic society and the place of the modern legal historian in uncovering its meaning for his own age, Adams mustered more than his usual eloquence. "The long and patient labors of German scholars," he writes in "The Anglo-Saxon Courts of Law," "seem to have now established beyond dispute the fundamental historical principle, that the entire Germanic family, in its earliest known stage of development, placed the administration of law, as it placed the political administration, in the hands of popular assemblies composed of the free, able-bodied members of the commonwealth." Adams continues:

> This great principle is, perhaps, from a political point of view, the most important which historical investigation has of late years established. It gives to the history of Germanic, and especially of English, institutions a roundness and philosophic continuity, which add greatly to their interest, and even to their practical value. The student of history who now attempts to trace, through two thousand years of vicissitudes and dangers, the slender thread of political and legal thought, no longer loses it from sight in the confusion of feudalism . . . but follows it safely and firmly back until it leads him out upon the wide plains of northern Germany, and attaches itself at last to the primitive popular assembly, parliament, law-court, and army in one; which embraced every free man, rich or poor, and in theory at least allowed equal rights to all. Beyond this point it seems unnecessary to go. The State and Law may well have originated here.[45]

In the eyes of many, including Lodge the young doctoral candidate, America originated here as well. From those wide plains of northern Germany, moreover, the United States drew its special destiny, to bring to those peoples of the world sitting in the darkness of legal incapacity the law of a nation whose racial genius was jurisprudential—whose innate, Teutonic juridical abilities lay in the construction and administration of modern bureaucratic governance.[46]

Teutonic juridical racialism bears some similarity to developmentalist juridical racialism in its evolutionary focus, but there are two important differences between these rhetorical systems. First, as explained in chapter 1, the primary point of mythological negative transcendence in developmentalist juridical racialism concerns the law of property. Indians are characterized as a race incapable of holding title to land, and the concept of fee simple absolute is described as peculiarly Euro-American. In contrast, the specific point of negative transcendence in Teutonic juridical-racial rhetoric is the state. In Teutonic juridical racialism, Anglo-Saxon peoples are characterized, above all, by their capacity for state-building. They are described as a people with special talents for governance, and the state itself is seen as Anglo-Saxon in character. At the same time, dark-skinned others are described as incapable of living within an ordered society and essentially criminal. The second difference between developmentalist and Teutonic juridical rhetoric lies in their conceptions of racial plasticity. In developmentalist juridical racialism, races are marked by their particular legal qualities, yet racial character is subject to change, sometimes indeed to rapid transformation (thus, American Indians in the late-nineteenth century were seen as capable of assimilating into the larger white American legal community). In Teutonic juridical racialism, racial-legal character is intractable. Racial groups are understood to have juridical qualities anchored in the very depths of their individual and collective souls. While not explicitly genetic, Teutonic juridical racialism suggests that race and its legal manifestations are innate and cannot change over the course of a lifetime or even over the course of a century. In contrast to developmentalist systems, Teutonic juridical racialism advances a vision of permanent racial-legal hierarchy.

In this respect, Teutonic juridical-racial rhetoric is evident not only in those works of anthropological legal history that advanced the notion that Anglo-Saxon peoples were uniquely endowed with law—a positive assertion—but also in those works advancing the negative corollary that darker races were incapable of legal order, that they were slavish children in earlier stages of evolutionary development. Teutonic constitutionalists made such claims particularly in their accounts of the Malay people of the Philippines, who, they argued, were governed by opinion and caprice rather than by law and were racially incapable of the order required by the rule of a state (a view ultimately derived from Johann Friedrich Blumenbach's "On the Natural Variety of Mankind").[47] Thus, Kocourek and Wigmore write in their *Evolution of Law*, "The greatest productive value of an inquiry into the juridical life of remote ages and of arrested developments lies in providing an indispensable standard by which the processes of human reason, so far as they enter the sphere of legal evolution, are guided and corrected."[48] More dramatically, Daniel Brinton, president of the American Association for the Advancement of Science and a primary opponent of Franz Boas's theories of race and culture, in 1895 called on anthropology to become the handmaiden of government by proclaiming, "there is in some stocks and some smaller ethnic groups a peculiar mental temperament, which has become hereditary and general, of a nature to disqualify them for the atmosphere of modern enlightenment . . . an inborn morbid tendency, constitutionally recreant to the codes of civilization, and therefore technically criminal."[49] For Brinton, in a very practical sense, peoples without law were peoples outside America, forever alien and apart.

This was Lodge's intellectual milieu, and he brought varying shades of these ideas with him into the Senate, in his formulation of American imperialist policy, in his discussion of the character and capability of the dark-skinned peoples the United States came to dominate, and in his analysis of the appropriate administrative measures to be taken by colonial rulers in insular governance. In his work in Congress, even beyond foreign policy, Lodge consistently spoke in the language of Teutonic juridical racialism, his political concerns deeply driven by its worldview. In an 1896 speech on immigration restriction, for instance, Lodge argued that race "is something deeper and more fundamental than anything which concerns the intellect." "When we speak of a race," he proclaimed, "[w]e mean the moral and intellectual characters, which in their association make the soul of a race, and which represent the product of all its past, the inheritance of all its ancestors, and the motives of all its conduct. The men of each race possess an indestructible stock of ideas, traditions, sentiments, modes of thought, an unconscious inheritance from their ancestors, upon which argument has no effect."[50] The greatest race of all was, of course, the Anglo-Saxon, "descended from the Germanic tribes whom Caesar fought and Tacitus described."[51] Storming in waves across the channel into England, over centuries these tribes "were welded together and had made a new speech and a new race, with strong and well-defined qualities, both mental and moral."[52] Lodge wished to restrict immigration because it would degrade this Anglo-Saxon purity and erode the racial "motives" of which the U.S. system of government was but a single expression. "Mr. President," announced Lodge, "more precious even than forms of government are the mental and moral qualities which make what we call our race. While those stand unimpaired all is safe. When those decline all is imperiled."[53]

Lodge's discussion of Philippine policy followed a similar line of argument. When addressing the question of whether the United States should annex the Philippine Islands and rule their inhabitants as a colonial power, for instance, he turned to the fundamental racial motives animating Philippine society and to a juridical consideration of the nature of race itself. "The capacity of a people . . . for free and representative government is not in the least a matter of guesswork," argued Lodge in 1900, two years after the Treaty of Paris had ended Spanish-American hostilities: "The forms of government to which nations or races naturally tend may easily be discovered from history." Echoing Adams's discussion in *Essays in Anglo-Saxon Law*, Lodge continued, "You can follow the story of political freedom and representative government among the English-speaking people back across the centuries until you reach the Teutonic tribes emerging from the forests of Germany and bringing with them forms of local self-government which are repeated to-day in the pure democracies of the New England town meeting." This historical perspective revealed not simply the permissibility but the need for American colonial power. "The tendencies and instincts of the Teutonic race which, running from the Arctic Circle to the Alps, swept down upon the Roman Empire, were clear at the outset," Lodge stated with blunt facticity. "Yet the individual freedom and the highly developed forms of free government in which these tendencies and instinct have culminated in certain countries and under the most favorable conditions have been the slow growth of nearly fifteen hundred years." "You can not change race tendencies in a moment," Lodge warned. "[The] theory, that you could make a Hottentot into a European if you only took possession of him in infancy and gave him a European education among suitable surroundings, has been abandoned alike by science and history as grotesquely false. . . . We know what sort of government the Malay makes when he is left to himself."[54]

Other imperialists echoed Lodge's juridical-racial views. For instance, his colleague Albert J. Beveridge, whom Theodore Roosevelt described as having "views on public matters [that] are almost exactly yours and mine," proclaimed that Filipinos "are not yet capable of self-government. How could they be? They are not a self-governing race. . . . What alchemy will change the oriental quality of their blood, in a year, and set the self-governing currents of the American pouring through their Malay veins?"[55] The Anglo-Saxon people, on the other hand, "is the most self-governing but also the most administrative of any race in history," he argued; "Our race is, distinctly, the exploring, the colonizing, the administrating force of the world." American imperialist policy, for Beveridge, thus arose "not from necessity, but from irresistible impulse, from instinct, from racial and unwritten laws inherited from our forefathers." "[W]herever our race has gone," he announced, "it has governed."[56] Indeed, even more so than Lodge, Beveridge viewed the U.S. Constitution as but one of many expressions of the deeper Anglo-Saxon racial character. In arguing that the Constitution granted Congress extremely broad powers in colonial administration, for instance, Beveridge asserted that the seemingly limiting provisions of the Bill of Rights should be read in light of what he called Anglo-Saxon "institutions," the fundamental juridical-racial character of Americans as a race. "Institutional law is older, deeper, and as vital as constitutional law," argued Beveridge. He proclaimed:

> Our Constitution is one of the concrete manifestations of our institutions; our statutes are another; decisions of our courts are another; our habits, methods and customs as a people and a race are still another. . . .
> It is our institutional law which, flowing like our blood through the written Constitution, gives that instrument vitality and power of development.
>
> Our institutions were not established by the Constitution. Institutional law existed before the Constitution. . . . Partisanship shrieks "imperialism," and asks where we find words to prevent the development of a czar [in the Philippines]. . . . I find it in the speech of the people; in the maxims of liberty; in our blood; in our history; in the tendencies of our race.[57]

In espousing such arguments, Beveridge and Lodge considered themselves to be the forces of progress. Far from representing reactionary or antedated thinking, their opinions were legitimated by one of the most modern groups of the early-twentieth century, anthropological social scientists. For Lodge, it was the academic teachings of this new class, ensconced though it might have been in the seemingly removed sphere of the university, that enabled both his own personal modernization and the economic and political modernization of the United States—the latter of which was based on a break with the civic tradition that Senators Hoar and Hale so admired: the notion that if America ever acquired an over-seas colonial empire, it would forfeit its very identity.

Progressive Anglo-Saxon Interpretation in the Insular Cases

The United States, of course, did acquire that empire, and when it did, American jurists faced a series of pressing constitutional questions, the answers to which recapitulated Lodge's own personal drama of modern-ization at the level of legal doctrine. With the conclusion of the Treaty of Paris on December 10, 1898, and the exchange of formally ratified agree-ments between Spain and the United States on April 11, 1899, the Amer-ican national government found itself in a new geopolitical position. By the terms of the treaty, Spain had agreed to "relinquish" its sovereignty over Cuba, thus remaining accountable for prewar debts to the island while at the same time enabling the United States to establish a military protectorate in Havana; it ceded outright the islands of Puerto Rico and Guam; and for the sum of twenty million dollars it "sold" the islands of the Philippines. The American government took somewhat different ap-proaches to each of its new acquisitions. Despite the desire of many im-perialists, the United States did not annex Cuba directly but instead granted it semisovereignty, ruling it first through military force and, fol-lowing the transfer of power to a new government under President Tomás Estrada Palma, through a form of economic colonialism. To Puerto Rico, the United States extended a liminal status still operative today. And in the Philippines, the source of the greatest geopolitical difficulty after 1898, the United States established itself as the ultimate sovereign power, incurring the resentment of many Filipinos, who began a protracted struggle against their American guardians. Despite the different strategies the nation developed for each of its new territories, in all cases it insti-tuted social engineering policies and wide-ranging reforms designed to dismantle the Spanish legal system with which the territories had been governed and replace it with American law.[58]

Until the Spanish-American War, the history of United States expan-sion had been a continuous one. In 1787, the nation grew to include the Northwest Territory. The Louisiana Purchase of 1803 extended its boundaries across the Mississippi. Texas became a part of the nation in 1845, and Mexico ceded its lands in the West and Southwest in 1848 and 1853. Washington and Oregon joined the nation in 1853 and 1859, respectively; Alaska was purchased in 1866. Throughout this history, the United States was guided by a "pattern of territorial development" already outlined in the Northwest Ordinance, which defined three basic stages in the acquisition of a territory.[59] The first entailed federal plenary control lasting from one to eight years, in which Congress appointed a governor, judiciary, and other governmental officers and assumed a strong hand in decision-making for the region. The second period extended to territorial residents the right to elect their own legislature and form a constitution (the governor of the territory, however, was still appointed by Congress, with the ability to overturn the efforts of the legislative body). The final stage was statehood, the creation of an independent government within the federal system. This pattern of territorial transformation, in which a territory was acquired, briefly ruled under federal plenary control, and then granted statehood, was definitively broken in 1898. Whereas the territories of the western United States had always been understood as destined for eventual membership in the Union, such was not the case with Guam, Puerto Rico, and, especially, the Philippines. None of these insular possessions was considered a possible candidate for statehood in the foreseeable future. With the Treaty of Paris, the United States thus broke a pattern of republican territorial acquisition and entered into a truly imperial phase of national political development.

Among the many reasons the insular possessions were not deemed eligible for statehood, one played a central role: a sense of Anglo-Saxon racial superiority. Shared by imperialists and anti-imperialists alike, the belief in the racial inferiority of residents of the insular territories, especially Filipinos, passed as common wisdom. There were exceptions to this general rule, but popular knowledge tended to associate the new territories with the basest forms of savagery, especially with the headhunting of the Ilongots, Igorots, and Ifugaos.[60] Significantly, juridical racialism provided the rhetoric within which this perception of racial inferiority was articulated in popular discussion. Filipinos, for instance, were described as unable to live within an ordered state, their traditional society serving as an emblem of the negation of modern law. "Every Igorot *barrio* has its judicial body of old men, who dispose of all cases from petty theft to murder," wrote one commentator:

> Most penalties take the form of a fine payable in cattle, or other property. Trial by ordeal is commonly practiced. The *podung*, or bloody test, consists in boring holes in the scalps of the suspect and his accuser. The

verdict goes to the one who bleeds the least. When one of a number of persons is believed to be a criminal, each of them is given a mouthful of dry rice to chew. After mastication this is spat out upon the hands of the judges and he whose mass exhibits the least saliva is deemed convicted, in accordance with their proverb, which says, "A guilty man has a dry mouth."[61]

In accordance with the views of legal scholars of the day, such popular writers asserted that the natives of the Philippines were in the very early stages of the development of criminal law and the construction of an absolute legal sovereign, with its attendant willingness to submit to state command.[62]

Such descriptions also appeared in official government anthropology and were included by the secretary of the interior in the annual reports of the Philippine Commission of the War Department. As the United States began to govern the Philippines, it commissioned a series of studies to gather data that might be of use in insular administration, undertaking a general ethnographic survey of the islands, first with the Bureau of Non-Christian Tribes.[63] The Philippine Commission was headed by William Howard Taft, a man who himself later would serve on the Supreme Court and who met with the high praise of Theodore Roosevelt and Justice Henry Billings Brown, author of the opinion of the Court in *Downes*.[64] Among the products of the Commission's survey were Albert E. Jenks's "Bontoc Igorot," William Allan Reed's "The Negritos of Zambales," Emerson Christie's study of native languages, Otto Scheerer's "The Nabaloi Dialect of Benguet," E. Y. Miller's "The Bataks of Palawan," and a translation of thirty-three manuscripts by N. M. Saleeby on the "History and Laws of the Moros."[65] Like the studies of the Indians supported by the Bureau of American Ethnology, to which anthropologists of the Philippines explicitly looked for guidance, these studies aided colonial administrators.[66] In the process of strengthening American sovereignty, they also supported the expansion of American commercial interests, providing knowledge not only for tribal governance but also valuable information to manufacturers regarding the possibility of commercial exports, information also to be placed on display in a "Commercial Museum."[67] While many of these studies were strictly factual, revealing great scholarly care, some included descriptions of native peoples, especially those living in small-scale tribes, that rested on the same vision of racial hierarchy that animated popular accounts of the region.[68] "It is universally conceded," stated the Commission, for example, "that the Negritos of to-day are the disappearing remnants of a people which once populated the entire archipelago. They are, physically, weaklings of low stature, with black skin, closely-curling hair, flat noses, thick lips, and large, clumsy feet. In the matter of intelligence they stand at or near the bottom of the human series, and they are believed to be incapable of any considerable degree of civilization or advancement."[69]

It was in this context of juridical-racial discourse, state power, and economic modernization that the Supreme Court heard the series of disputes that together would be known as the *Insular Cases*, especially the case of *Downes v. Bidwell*. *Downes* began in 1900 as a case brought against the customs collector of New York by Samuel Downes, who was conducting an import business under the firm of S. B. Downes & Company. Downes was forced to pay the collector $659.35 in tariff duties on a shipment of oranges, which he transported to New York from the port of San Juan. The tariffs were authorized by the establishing or organic law of Puerto Rico, known as the Foraker Act.[70] The act provided Puerto Rico with a civil government, the governor of the island to be appointed by the president of the United States, and a legislature to be elected by Puerto Ricans. In addition, the act allowed the levying of a duty on commercial goods from Puerto Rico of up to 15 percent of that charged on goods arriving into the United States from "foreign" countries (a duty from which goods arriving from within the United States were exempt). In objecting to the tariff, Downes claimed that, after the Foraker Act, Puerto Rico had, in fact, become part of the United States and that imposing the duty thus was an illegitimate exercise of the collector's power. He paid the duty under protest and thereafter brought suit to recover his exacted funds, hiring the firm of Coudert Brothers, with Frederic R. Coudert, Jr. and Paul Fuller leading the case.[71]

The specific legal questions of the dispute in *Downes* revolved around the Uniformity Clause of Article I, section 8 of the U. S. Constitution, which requires that "all Duties, Imposts and Excises shall be uniform throughout the United States."[72] While the case included a variety of legal and factual complexities, the basic issue the Court faced was relatively straightforward: Was Puerto Rico part of the "United States" or not? If the Court held that the Foraker Act made Puerto Rico part of the United States by establishing a civil government on the island, then Downes's oranges were exempt from the collector's tariff, because the imposition of duties on goods arriving from Puerto Rico would violate the Uniformity

Clause. It would be an unconstitutional use of federal power to place duties on imports arriving from one part of the United States to another, as if the federal government were to place special duties on goods arriving from California to New York. On the other hand, if Puerto Rico were a foreign country despite the Foraker Act, then duties placed on goods arriving from Puerto Rico fell under the legitimate power of Congress, and the New York customs agent could have his way. In this reading, the Foraker Act could be understood as both establishing a civil government on the island of Puerto Rico under American control and at the same time imposing duties on the region as a territory that was not part of the United States itself.

At one level, then, *Downes* was a case about money. As often in such cases, however, the issues at stake were more far-reaching; as in much American constitutional history, for instance in *Heart of Atlanta Motel* (1964) and *Katzenbach v. McClung* (1964), issues of civic belonging were adjudicated in the context of commercial disputes. As Justice Brown noted in the opinion of the Court, the primary query was whether the revenue clauses of the Constitution "extend of their own force to our newly acquired territories," that is, whether Congress could rule the regions America acquired in 1898 without regard to the revenue provisions of fundamental U.S. law except in those particular instances in which it explicitly intended to be bound by that law and registered that intention when it established insular civil governments.[73] This was a significant issue, for its answer bore upon an even larger matter: whether any, all, some, or none of the protections afforded by the Constitution extended to the new American territories, particularly to those that might never become states. If it were found that the Uniformity Clause did not apply as a matter of legal course to Congressional legislation concerning Puerto Rico, then what of trial by jury (no moot point, as we will see)? Could Congress create a system of justice for Puerto Rico, the Philippines, or Guam that failed to provide for this symbolically central right of the Anglo-American legal order? In fact, the issues in *Downes* were weightier still, for behind all these questions lay the most fundamental query of all: To what extent were the people of the insular territories members of the American nation, a community bound together by a shared commitment to live under liberal constitutional principles? Would these dark-skinned people automatically be entitled to the basic protections of the founding political document of the United States, or would they live, potentially forever, under the plenary power of Congress? Would they have

a legal status not typically associated with American republican principles, not citizens, but subjects?

The justices of the Supreme Court were not the first legal thinkers to
consider these questions. The decisions in the *Insular Cases* were pre-
ceded by a series of articles in the *Harvard Law Review*, widely believed
to have influenced the Court. There, Christopher Columbus Langdell and
James Bradley Thayer argued that the Constitution applied only to the
states, and that Congress had the authority to establish separate revenue
systems for each of its new territories as it saw fit.[74] Simeon E. Baldwin
and Carman Randolph, on the other hand, asserted that the revenue
clauses, and the Constitution as a whole, were applicable wherever the
United States exercised its power, and Abbott Lawrence Lowell expressed
a view that straddled these positions.[75] Despite their disagreements, however, all these legal scholars assumed the ethnic superiority of Anglo-Saxons as legal actors and the racial inferiority of insular residents, especially
Filipinos, describing them as a race incapable of living within an ordered
state. Langdell wrote that the guarantees of the Bill of Rights were "so peculiarly and so exclusively English" that they were inapplicable to "ancient" and "alien races." While favoring the extension of constitutional
guarantees, Baldwin admitted that "[o]ur Constitution was made by a
civilized and educated people" and conceded the point that "[t]o give the
half-civilized Moros of the Philippines, or the ignorant and lawless brig-
ands that infest Puerto Rico, or even the ordinary Filipino of Manila, the
benefit of such immunities from the sharp and sudden justice—or injustice—which they have been hitherto accustomed to expect, would, of
course, be a serious obstacle to the maintenance there of an efficient government." Lowell argued that the full extent of the Constitution should
apply only "among a people whose social and political evolution has been
consonant with our own," that the "Anglo-Saxon race was prepared for
[self-government] by centuries of discipline under the supremacy of law,"
and that the peoples of "infant states," especially Filipinos, lacked the
"self-restraint" necessary for complete political freedom.[76]

In adjudicating *Downes*, the intensely divided Court broke between
two general camps that might be called the judicial traditionalists and the
judicial modernists.[77] The outspoken traditionalist was John Marshall
Harlan of Kentucky, the great dissenter of the Court. The traditionalists
asserted, in the words of the day, that the Constitution "follows the flag,"
that all provisions of the Constitution extend by their own force, or *ex
propio vigore*, into areas over which the United States exercises civil con-

trol. For Harlan, the decision to acquire territories that included alien races could be made in any way Congress chose, but once those territories were acquired, the Constitution applied to them completely. No such distinctions could be made between territories and states. "The idea that this country may acquire territories anywhere upon the earth, by conquest or treaty," he wrote, "and hold them as mere colonies or provinces—the people inhabiting them to enjoy only such rights as Congress chooses to accord to them—is wholly inconsistent with the spirit and genius as well as with the words, of the Constitution."[78] After all, he asked, how could Congress not be bound by the Constitution in the administration of its new possessions, when it was the Constitution that created and granted those administrative powers, and in fact created Congress itself? The threat feared most by the traditionalists was that the United States would become an agent of tyranny. If the full force of the Constitution did not apply, they argued, Congress could maintain territories such as Puerto Rico and the Philippines entirely according to its own will—as Chief Justice Fuller wrote, "like a disembodied shade, in an intermediate state of ambiguous existence for an indefinite period."[79]

American imperialists should tread cautiously, traditionalists warned, because the fundamental law of the United States, the Constitution, would be interpreted strictly regardless of changing geopolitical circumstances. "Whether a particular race will or will not assimilate with our people," wrote Justice Harlan, "and whether they can or cannot with safety to our institutions be brought within the operation of the Constitution, is a matter to be thought of when it is proposed to acquire their territory by treaty. A mistake in the acquisition of territory, although such acquisition seemed at the time to be necessary, cannot be made the ground for violating the Constitution or refusing to give full effect to its provisions."[80] Traditionalists also relied on a line of precedent suggesting that the term "United States" in the Constitution denotes both states and territories, rather than merely formal members of the Union. This position was suggested by Chief Justice John Marshall in *Loughborough v. Blake* (1820), a case concerning a direct tax levied by Congress on the District of Columbia, where the Court upheld Congressional authority, in dicta defining the "United States" broadly. "The power then to lay and collect duties, imposts, and excises," wrote Chief Justice Marshall, "may be exercised, and must be exercised throughout the United States. Does this term designate the whole, or any particular portion of the American empire?" "Certainly," he responded, "this question can admit of but one answer. It is the name given to our great republic, which is composed of both States and territories."[81] For traditionalists, Chief Justice Marshall's assertion of the wide scope of the term "United States" in the Constitution served as a general restraint on American power overseas.

The judicial modernists, for their part, viewed the prospect that Congress might maintain its insular possessions "like a disembodied shade" as precisely the desired outcome, and the course most supported by the Constitution and American legal ideals. The modernists included Justice Edward White, the author of the majority opinion in *Downes*, as well as the author of an influential concurrence in the case, Justice Brown, a man whose autobiography begins, "I was born of a New England Puritan family in which there has been no admixture of alien blood for two hundred and fifty years."[82] Brown was born in 1836 in South Lee, Massachusetts, a small manufacturing village where his father operated saw and flour mills, and the family later moved to Stockbridge and, in 1849, to Ellington, Connecticut. He enrolled in Yale College in 1852, at the age of sixteen, and graduated in 1856, the same year as his eventual colleague on the Supreme Court, Justice David Brewer. Following legal studies at Yale and Harvard, Brown moved to Detroit and served as U.S. deputy marshal and assistant U.S. attorney for the Eastern District of Michigan. He later entered private practice and developed a specialty in shipping. Brown was a staunchly Republican unionist and in 1875 he was appointed to become a federal district judge by President Ulysses S. Grant. A nationally respected expert in the difficult field of admiralty law, and a successful professor at the University of Michigan, he was appointed to the U.S. Supreme Court by President Benjamin Harrison in 1890. He was known to be an agreeable justice, well-liked by his colleagues and judicious in temperament. Assuming office upon the death of Justice Samuel Miller, a proponent of both liberal state-building and racial bigotry discussed in chapter 1, Justice Brown abided by his predecessor's jurisprudential persuasion.

As they looked forward into the coming century, Justice Brown and his fellow modernists were concerned that too strict an adherence to the Constitution and too limited a reading of Congressional powers would hinder the United States in its ability to act within new geopolitical circumstances. For modernists, the issue in the *Insular Cases* involved the future expansion and progressive development of the United States. "Patriotic and intelligent men may differ widely as to the desireableness of this or that acquisition," asserted Justice Brown, "but this is solely a political question. We can only consider this aspect of the case so far as to say that no construction of the Constitution should be adopted which would prevent Congress from considering each case upon its merits." "A false step at this time," he continued, "might be fatal to the development of what Chief Justice Marshall called the American empire. Choice in some cases, the natural gravitation of small bodies towards large ones in others, the result of a successful war in still others, may bring about conditions which would render the annexation of distant possessions desirable."[83] "Take a case of discovery," wrote Justice White in his concurring opinion in *Downes*, offering an example of the potential consequences of the views advanced by Justice Harlan: "Citizens of the United States discover an unknown island, peopled with an uncivilized race, yet rich in soil, and valuable to the United States for commercial and strategic reasons. Clearly, by the law of nations, the right to ratify such acquisition and thus to acquire the territory would pertain to the government of the United States. Can it be denied that such right could not be practically exercised if the result would be . . . the immediate bestowal of citizenship on those absolutely unfit to receive it?"[84]

The judicial modernists, then, were caught in a contradiction. They agreed with Lodge that the United States was about to enter a new world in which its power would flow in part from the acquisition of territories inhabited by peoples without law. On the other hand, they had to respond to the judicial traditionalists who, like Lodge's enemies in the Senate, had raised the fear that departing from strict constitutional construction could lead to tyranny and so undermine national self-definition. Significantly, both Justice Brown and Justice White's solutions to this conundrum strongly relied on Teutonic juridical racialism, forging a rhetorical amalgam one might call Teutonic constitutionalism. Indeed, Justice Brown argued explicitly that the residents of the insular territories were not entitled to the guarantees of the Constitution because they were a racially alien people incapable of maintaining Anglo-Saxon notions of law. According to Justice Brown, there might be an extremely limited number of universally applicable personal rights, to which the people of Puerto Rico or the Philippines might be entitled. Most of the guarantees of the Constitution, however, were simply "remedial rights which are peculiar to our own system of jurisprudence."[85] The greatest portion of American constitutional law, that is, applied only to a very limited group of people. When Congress legislated for dark-skinned others, it could not be bound by a document written for white Englishmen over one hundred years ago: the document applied only to a superior civilization that had reached a higher stage of social development. When the United States acquires new possessions "inhabited by alien races," Justice Brown wrote, "differing from us in religion, customs, laws, methods of taxation, and modes of thought, the administration of government and justice, according to Anglo-Saxon principles, may for a time be impossible."[86] This was the negative corollary of the Teutonic origins thesis of American government.

Justice Brown disposed of Justice Harlan's concern that such a view could lead to tyranny in a similar manner, invoking the positive principles of the Teutonic origins thesis. Specifically, like Lodge Justice Brown believed that "more precious even than forms of government are the mental and moral qualities which make what we call our race."[87] He further argued, as had Lodge and Beveridge, that the Constitution was merely an expression of the Anglo-Saxon racial genius for law, which needed no document to prove or bind itself—that beneath the Constitution lay the more fundamental racial principles of what Beveridge called "institutional law," the juridical-racial spirit passed down to Anglo-Saxon peoples from Tacitus's Germanic tribes. In their administration of islands overseas, in Justice Brown's view, the American people would necessarily be restrained by the innate ideals they carried in their blood, ideals that were foundational to and in fact superseded the Constitution. "Grave apprehensions of danger are felt by many eminent men," wrote Justice Brown in *Downes*, "a fear lest an unrestrained possession of power on the part of Congress may lead to unjust and oppressive legislation, in which the natural rights of territories, or their inhabitants, may be engulfed in a centralized despotism. These fears, however, find no justification." "There are certain principles of natural justice inherent in the Anglo-Saxon character," he explained, "which need no expressions in constitutions or statutes to give them effect or to secure dependencies against legislation manifestly hostile to their real interests." This is to say that Justice Brown disposed of the concerns of the traditionalists, those who relied on a strict reading of the Constitution for their vision of national identity, by asserting that any action undertaken by an Anglo-Saxon American government overseas was ipso facto within the bounds of a transcendent, racially based legal order.[88]

Although Justice White's opinion differed in some respects from Justice Brown's, and was more sophisticated in its reasoning, it too found its basis in Teutonic juridical-racial principles—and, in fact, Justice White sought to grant Congress even greater control over its insular affairs than did his colleague.[89] Making a distinction between incorporated, unincorporated, and foreign territories, Justice White argued along lines advanced by Abbott Lawrence Lowell in the *Harvard Law Review*, proclaiming that the Constitution applied only to those territories Congress explicitly had "incorporated" into the Union. This became known as the "doctrine of territorial incorporation," a judicial principle first fully articulated and endorsed by the Court in *Dorr v. United States* (1904).[90] The *Dorr* case involved the great Anglo-Saxon right of trial by jury in criminal cases, and posed the question of whether that right extended to the Philippine archipelago. The Court held that because the Philippines, like Puerto Rico, had not been explicitly incorporated into the American constitutional order, trial by jury was not guaranteed. It held, in other words, that a right symbolically central to Anglo-Saxon claims of racial superiority did not apply to Filipinos, who under the terms of juridical racialism were incapable of legal behavior. For Justice White, as well as for Justice Brown and Henry Cabot Lodge, it was a seemingly antedated racial worldview that allowed the constitutional contradictions of twentieth-century imperial expansion to be overcome. If the Spanish-American War and the desire for territories overseas created a gap between state ambition and fundamental principles, between modernizing, progressive will and traditional constitutional standards, that gap was bridged at the level of jurisprudence by the social scientific notion of Teutonic legality. It was bridged by a Teutonic constitutionalism, a method of juridical-racial legal decision-making that was as modern as the world it helped to bring about.

Death, Law, and the Philippines

After ratifying the Treaty of Paris, the United States began to face a long, protracted struggle with the native inhabitants of the Philippines, who previously had been engaged in a movement for national independence against Spain.[91] As Spain had done, the United States chose to resist this independence movement, suffering the consequences of that choice in precisely the ways anti-imperialists had predicted. That is, the United States switched places with Spain and became an imperial power exerting violence, even tyranny, against forces of national political liberation.[92] Ideology, like dreams in Freudian psychoanalysis, often function through a process of reversal, positing the very negation of the social world it conceals, an inversion evident in the rhetoric of Anglo-Saxon legal genius and Filipino legal incapacity and the course of American military action on the ground. For all the references to the Anglo-Saxon genius for law made during the Spanish-American and Philippine-American wars—whether in the formation of imperialist policy, in the adjudication of claims arising from imperial expansion, or in the writings of men in the armed forces[93]—in fact, American soldiers in the Philippines shed many of the restraints of that ethnic genius and engaged with "surprising . . . alacrity" in what historian Stuart Miller calls a "penchant for lawlessness."[94] This was especially the case on the island of Samar, the "most vicious, and certainly the most controversial, campaign of the Philippine War," the site of Ferdinand Magellan's landing in 1521 and of Douglas MacArthur's in 1944.[95] Over the course of 1902, Americans at home were treated to repeated news reports of the terrible cruelty inflicted on Filipinos by the American military: rape, the burning of villages, the indiscriminate murder of civilians, the killing of the wounded, the use of the water cure as a form of torture. These were *crimes* of war, and indeed the Philippine conflict came to a conclusion through what most agreed was an illegal act, in which high-ranking American military officers dressed in enemy uniform and infiltrated enemy headquarters, capturing the commander of the Philippine forces, General Emilio Aguinaldo.[96] In the Philippines, Americans often seemed very much like their own worst image of the Malay savage: a people without law.[97]

Ironically, or perhaps naturally, juridical racialism proved capable of justifying such behavior and the apparent rift it opened between the rhetoric of Teutonic constitutionalism and the reality of an imperial war fought against a nationalist rebellion. The charges of critics such as Moorfield Storey, for instance, were forcefully met by Teutonic constitutionalists such as Yale University's distinguished professor Theodore S. Woolsey, whose assistance was sought by the Roosevelt administration. Son of the illustrious Theodore Dwight Woolsey, for whom the university named Woolsey Hall (one can still walk through the hall today and gaze upon moving plaques commemorating men who died in the Philippine Insurrection, including on the island of Samar), Woolsey was a central academic defender of the Philippine-American War and an expert in international law. In regard to the capture of General Aguinaldo, Woolsey counseled the administration that the United States was not at war with "a civilized power," and that because Aguinaldo "was not a signatory of the

Hague Convention . . . there was no obligation on the part of the United States Army to refrain from using the enemy's uniforms for the enemy's deception." On the other hand, Woolsey stated, it was the duty of Filipinos to adhere to the Hague Convention as their enemy was a civilized power and a signatory of that agreement. The strategy used by Americans in capturing Aguinaldo, in other words, would be illegal "only with a lawful belligerent."[98]

Henry Cabot Lodge also did his part to justify such illegalities, becoming chair of a controversial Senate committee investigating U.S. war crimes.[99] Lodge stacked the hearings with witnesses friendly to the administration, but repeated reports of brutality from American soldiers who had seen it firsthand served to undermine the very position they were brought to support. The notorious General Arthur MacArthur began his testimony with what he called his "ethnological premises," a close variant of the Teutonic origins thesis. "Many thousands of years ago," he proclaimed, "our Aryan ancestors raised cattle, made a language, multiplied in numbers, and overflowed. By due process of expansion to the west they occupied Europe, developed arts and sciences, and created a great civilization, which, separating into innumerable currents, inundated and fertilized the globe with blood and ideas, the primary bases of human progress, incidentally crossing the Atlantic and thereby reclaiming, populating, and civilizing a hemisphere." "The broad actuating laws which underlie all these wonderful phenomena," continued MacArthur,

> are still operating with relentless vigor and have recently forced one of the currents of this magnificent Aryan people across the Pacific—that is to say, back almost to the cradle of its race—thus initiating a [new] stage of progressive social evolution. . . . [T]he human race, from time immemorial, has been propagating its higher ideals by a succession of intellectual waves, one of which is now passing, through our mediumship, beyond the Pacific, and carrying therewith everything that is implied by the beautiful flag which is a symbol of our nationality.

"We are now living," gloried MacArthur, "in a heroic age of human history."[100] The grim statistics of the war, and the thousands of Filipino dead, suggested very much the opposite.

Soon after General MacArthur gave his testimony, Albert Beveridge, instructed by Lodge, closed the Senate investigation over a storm of protest, but not before Lodge's witnesses thus revealed in retrospect one of the central functions of Teutonic juridical racialism in an age of modernization: the rhetorical elision of violence and the concealment of death. While national administrative capacities expanded under a broad reading of Congressional power, necessitated by a war that set the stage for further national economic growth, juridical racialism hid the human price of the bold new American era.[101]

3

The Biological Politics
of Japanese Exclusion

More than any other modern state, America traditionally has welcomed immigration, which forms its economic life-blood and provides the basis for the expansive conception of civic identity for which the country is known and admired today. The primary period under discussion in this chapter, the 1920s, however, witnessed a substantial departure from this tradition in relation to a group about which white Americans already had felt ambivalent or actively hostile for two generations, namely immigrants from Asia—and, especially in the early-twentieth century, from Japan. As with the story of juridical racialism as it concerned both American Indians in the 1880s and the insular territories in the 1900s, the ideological source of the restrictive stance toward Asian immigration in the 1920s was a form of juridical racialism that blended modern racial thought, specifically of a biological variety, and national economic interest. Its statutory result was the Immigration Act of 1924, also known as the Japanese Exclusion Act, which placed strict national quotas on immigration from southern and eastern Europe and, by prohibiting immigration by groups ineligible for naturalized citizenship under federal law, including, as I will explain, the Japanese, imposed an absolute bar on immigration from Asia.[1] This chapter examines the juridical-racial features of the movement for Asian and Japanese exclusion that led to the Immigration Act, exploring the homological conceptual relation between a now-discredited form of social scientific thought, that of racial eugenics, judicial approaches to state and national economic regulation, and the construction of increasingly restrictive American civic boundaries within an expansive conception of national power. In addition, this chapter highlights the relation of the socio-legal worldview underlying Asian exclusion to a particular elite understanding of masculinity.

I begin by examining the racial and legal ideas that shaped the life of Madison Grant, lawyer, zoologist, and prominent advocate of immigration restriction, whose views about race and American civic life the Immigration Act enshrined. In portraying Grant's potent mix of masculine self-fashioning and biological politics, I also reveal how Grant's vision of a strictly consolidated, independent, and inviolable self, the self of the legal field of contract, found its political counterpart in the ideal of a strictly consolidated, Anglo-Saxon nation state.[2] In the course of my analysis, I examine Grant's upbringing, education, and work as an advocate for both environmental protection and the notorious Nordic doctrine; in addition, to illuminate his thought and motivations, I consider Grant's close relationship with his brother Deforest, a Northeast industrialist; and I discuss how Grant's theories of race, law, and citizenship were advanced by Representative Albert Johnson of Washington, who cosponsored the Immigration Act in Congress. Next, I turn to two decisions by the U.S. Supreme Court concerning Asian immigration. The first, *Chae Chan Ping v. United States* (1889), advanced Congressional plenary power over immigration as an incident of national sovereignty.[3] The second, *Takao Ozawa v. United States* (1922), formed the basis for the Japanese exclusion provision of the Immigration Act of 1924 by establishing that Japanese were not "white persons" and so ineligible for naturalized citizenship under Title XXX of Revised U.S. Statutes § 2169.[4] In examining *Chae Chan Ping* and *Ozawa*, I consider the men who wrote each opinion of the Court, Justice Stephen J. Field and Justice George Sutherland; the economic interests the decisions affected, including those of domestic American labor and of Japanese immigrants in the western United States who sought to own title to real property; the individual agreements and international treaties the decisions helped abrogate; and, finally, the indirect interplay of issues of race and contract in the Court's decision-making.

Madison Grant, the Nordic Myth, and Japanese Unconscionability

For the first hundred years of its existence, with the notable exception of the Alien Act of 1798, the U.S. federal government was largely uninvolved in immigration issues, leaving what minimal regulation of aliens existed to the states.[5] This was the era of the "open door," when American immigration policy enabled a plentiful supply of workers to settle a growing country. But the national approach to immigration began to change in the last quarter of the nineteenth century, in large part due to pressure from western states, whose residents feared economic competition from Asians.[6] In the face of sometimes violent labor agitation on the Pacific Coast, Congress began to assert increasing control over immigration, and it passed a variety of statutes aimed at restricting the influx of immigrants, especially from China. By 1882, the nation had prohibited entry of all Chinese laborers, a policy extended to nearly the entirety of Asia in 1917, when Congress established the "Asiatic barred zone." But Japan was something of an anomaly in this policy transformation. The Meiji government was quickly becoming a power to be reckoned with on the world stage, and any explicit affront to the Japanese people was considered diplomatically inadvisable. Japan thus was excluded from the barred zone, and restriction of Japanese immigration was instead achieved through a treaty known as the Gentlemen's Agreement (1908). Under the terms of what might be called this contract between two states, Japan promised not to issue travel documents to émigré laborers and, in exchange, its nationals who had settled in the United States were to receive a series of benefits. The American government, for example, was to pressure the San Francisco School Board to rescind its policy of racial segregation, and it was to permit the wives of Japanese men already residing in the United States to join their husbands (the absence of women migrants was a source of particular social devastation among the Chinese).[7] This arrangement allowed the United States to tighten its borders, and at the same time allowed Japan not to lose face.

But the Gentlemen's Agreement was not to last—and Madison Grant was to play an important intellectual role in its dissolution. Grant was born in 1865 in New York City into an old and distinguished family.[8] His first American ancestor, William Grant, arrived in New Jersey from Scotland in 1745. His father, Dr. Gabriel Grant, was a well-known Union Army surgeon during the Civil War; an authority on epidemics, he served as a brigade and later division surgeon to General William French, and he received the Congressional Medal of Honor for personal gallantry in action. Grant was very much a New Yorker—according to his obituary in the *Times*, every member of his family since the colonial era had been born within fifty miles of City Hall—and his life and work were intricately connected with the metropolis and its history.[9] He received his preparatory education in New York private academies, and like many

New Yorkers of his class, his family supplemented his schooling with extensive travel in Europe, especially Germany. Grant graduated from Yale College in 1887 (he was particularly influenced there by the teachings of sociologist William Graham Sumner, known today as a proponent of social Darwinism), and he received a Bachelor of Laws degree in 1890 from Columbia Law School, which at the time was located on East 49th and Madison.[10] It had been ten years since John Burgess had left the institution to establish his separate program in political science, in which students studied constitutional questions while students at the law school concentrated on bread-and-butter legal and municipal issues; it was the year of the retirement of celebrated law school president Theodore Dwight, who taught Grant contracts during his first year by lecturing through Blackstone and Parsons; and it was just before the school instituted its revised curriculum under reformist president Seth Low.[11]

Grant possessed independent means, and after his admission to the New York bar in 1891, he was able to devote a good deal of energy to nonlegal pursuits, particularly his lifelong interest in zoology.[12] Many legal scholars and historians know Grant as an advocate of immigration restriction, but among biologists he is remembered as an authority on North American mammals. The author of numerous books and articles on native wildlife, including *The Rocky Mountain Goat* (1905) and "The Vanishing Moose" (1894), he spent much of his time and resources traveling through the West studying and categorizing the diversity of American species.[13] Grant's name, in fact, will live forever in Linnaen classification: a unique variety of Alaskan caribou he discovered was named in his honor, the *Rangifer tarandus granti* (a taxidermic diorama of "Grant's Caribou" is still on display at the American Museum of Natural History in New York). Significantly, zoology contained a particular cultural meaning for Grant, one rooted in the class and gender terms in which he experienced his life. Over six feet tall, of "very upright carriage," and a confirmed bachelor, Grant was an active participant in an upper-class world, often associated with Theodore Roosevelt, in which the masculine self was groomed for leadership, and its strict borders defined, through a series of difficult encounters with nature.[14] Both Grant and Roosevelt, in fact, were members of the Boone & Crockett Club, a social society of big game hunters that required applicants to have bagged at least three large animals before admission. This was a world for gentlemen, and as Grant reveals in his frontier memoir *Hank* (1931)—published under the pseudonym "The Major"—in that masculine province, zoology and hunting were part of a linked set of pursuits designed to create a sense of sovereign mastery over the self (the first line of the story "The Debtor," reads: "Hank sat quietly contemplating the camp fire and then suddenly inquired, 'Major, you ain't a lawyer, are you?'"; the last line of the book: "'Yes,' said the Captain, 'women are queer'"). The natural world offered an escape from an effeminate modernity and trained men in the rugged, frontier individualism deemed necessary for political and economic stewardship.[15]

A sense of stewardship indeed was a leitmotiv of Grant's life. A powerful yet erroneous current runs through the historical literature that paints Grant as simply a wealthy New York socialite. This portrait neglects that Grant was a lawyer by training, groomed by the study of Blackstone, with a firm commitment to the responsibilities of his familial station and a wide network of connections to political and economic affairs in New York and beyond. Grant's connection to the male civic sphere of public responsibility was secured especially by his relationship with his brother Deforest, with whom he was extremely close (the two shared connecting apartments on Park Avenue for over a decade).[16] Deforest Grant was born in 1869, received his preparatory education at Dresden Polytechnic School in Germany, and in 1891 graduated from Yale. Until 1893, he served as superintendent of the Harlem line of the New York Central Railroad and, soon after, founded a series of highly successful firms that manufactured architectural terra cotta, including the Atlantic Terra Cotta Company, the Federal Terra Cotta Company, and the Federal Seaboard Terra Cotta Company. Terra cotta is a hard, semifired ceramic clay of great importance to the architectural history of early-twentieth-century New York, where it was used as fronting for skyscrapers. Deforest prospered (in 1928, he had nine hundred workers under contract), and one can still view the terra cotta from his firms across Manhattan, including on the Biltmore Hotel, the Woolworth Building, and throughout the subway system.[17] In 1916, he married Emilia Brinton—daughter of the Civil War surgeon and anti-Boasian anthropologist Daniel Brinton, discussed in chapter 2—and together they maintained homes in Washington, Maine, New York, and Tucson, and a plantation in southern Georgia.[18] Deforest also became a prominent political conservative, immersing himself in the study of political economy and serving as a member of the National Industrial Conference Board, notorious for its hostility to labor and the ostensible research wing of the National Association of Manufacturers.[19]

Deforest helped launch Grant in the public career for which he was to become known to history, particularly what one might call his environmental and biologically oriented social reform. Soon after he left Yale, Deforest became president of the Good Government Club A, an important chapter of a group of reform-minded political associations. Under his leadership, the club became a significant force in the campaign to elect millionaire businessman William Strong mayor of New York in 1895. Strong was a Republican whose platform advocated professionalizing the civil service, especially the police department, improving city sanitation, and opposing the power of Tammany Hall. "The tenor of his campaign," according to one historian, "was that his success as a business man guaranteed a comparable success as a political leader."[20] Strong served a momentous three-year term, during which he presided over the legal consolidation of greater New York, instituted a variety of sanitation measures (including the creation of public baths), and appointed Roosevelt president of the New York City Police Commission. Deforest took a particularly active role in campaigning for the mayor, but Madison participated in the election effort as well, gaining entry into circles of metropolitan political power—an opening he used to advance the biological interests most dear to him. Grant had long discussed with members of the Boone & Crockett Club the need to establish a zoological park, an institution that would preserve and bring to urban youth the natural world, in which the masculine self was challenged and from which it drew its vitality. With Roosevelt a prominent member of the new administration, Grant seized the moment, and through his efforts, we now have the New York Zoological Society and the Bronx Zoo, of which Grant served as president for thirty years. Grant later would extend such public-spirited work for the environment as president of the Bronx Parkway Commission and as founder of the American Bison Society and the Save the Redwoods League (one of the tallest trees in the world, located in northern California, is named after Grant and his associates).[21]

These aspects of Grant's background—his political approach to masculinity and the self, his proximity to American industry through his brother Deforest, and the centrality of biology to his civic stewardship and social perceptions—established the foundation for his later work in immigration reform, thereby securing his importance in the history of juridical racialism. Grant surely would be a widely celebrated figure among American liberals today had demographic and economic changes, especially in the fields of agriculture and transportation, not driven southern and eastern Europeans from their countries of origin en masse to seek refuge in America. Most of the thirteen million immigrants who arrived in the United States between 1900 and 1914 passed through Ellis Island, and nowhere were the changes they wrought more strongly felt than in Madison Grant's New York. Over the course of his lifetime, Grant saw his home transform into the disorienting, heterogeneous polyglot that so troubled Henry James, and he witnessed firsthand how immigrants seemed to bring crime, disease, and strange, often radical ideas into the world of his fathers.[22] He was particularly troubled by the growing presence of eastern European Jews—and then there was his beloved West, threatened by immigration not so much from Europe but, worse, from Asia. Grant responded to the problems he saw around him by jumping into public action, becoming a central part of the immigration reform movement during the 1920s. As an organizer and administrator, he served as vice president of the Immigration Restriction League, a Boston-based group of wealthy and established activists, who fought to alter the view that the United States should act as a "refuge of the oppressed."[23] And as an author and intellectual, he wrote the series of anti-immigrant works for which he is best known, particularly *The Passing of the Great Race* (1916) and *Conquest of a Continent* (1933).[24]

In their discussion of the perils of the open door, these works drew heavily on the arguments and key terms of modern anthropology and racial science. By the early-twentieth century, the discipline of anthropology had branched into two divergent fields, both of which sought to define the meaning and definition of race and, by implication, to control the meaning and limits of American identity.[25] Those in the first field, including biological determinists such as Harry Laughlin of the Carnegie Institution in Washington and Henry Fairfield Osborn, director of the American Museum of Natural History (and cofounder of the Save the Redwoods League), were influenced by Charles Darwin, the rediscovery of Mendelian genetics after 1900, and the scientific spirit of Francis Galton. These scholars looked to biological determinants in their analysis of human behavior and social structure, and they argued that racial categories were based on inborn, unchanging characteristics with little or no relation to environment. Often, though not exclusively, associated with the modern eugenics movement, these men viewed the United States as an Anglo-Saxon nation. The second group, the culturalists, emphasized the importance of culture for human behavior and also rejected the unilinear scale of societal development and value that had long been central to developmentalist anthropological thought. The culturalist position was developed especially by and frequently associated with Franz Boas, who dedicated his life to discrediting the eugenicists' biological classification of race and their ascription of unchanging, inborn mental characteristics to human groups. By the early part of the twentieth century, Boasian anthropology and the concept of culture it advanced had achieved a firm foothold in the American academy, particularly at Columbia, where Boas trained a generation of scholars in the methods associated with the terms "culture historicism" and "cultural relativism." The work of these scholars found its political expression in arguments for America as a melting-pot of races and ethnicities, as well as in the advocacy of various forms of pluralism, from that of Horace Kallen to that of Randolph S. Bourne.[26]

Grant was allied firmly with the first of these two branches of modern racial science, and indeed, the struggle between Boasian culturalists and hereditarian eugenicists often played out as a conflict between Boas and Grant himself. Take, for instance, Grant's reaction to Boas's "Changes in Bodily Form of Descendants of Immigrants."[27] In this detailed investigation, Boas surveyed thousands of immigrants and their children and found that their cephalic index, which measures skull size and shape, had changed significantly in the course of a single generation after settlement in the United States. Boas concluded that what traditionally had been considered an inborn racial trait was in fact the immediate product of environment, and that other such apparently hereditary characteristics might also change depending on social circumstances. Grant thought Boas's study perilously tendentious and made his views clear in both private and public pronouncements. Writing to an acquaintance who had expressed sympathy with a melting-pot vision of national identity, for instance, he characteristically warned that "[c]urrent literature is being swamped by a mass of misleading articles emanating from a group of Jews, financed by those who are trying to encourage immigration on the theory that America is the refuge for the oppressed. This campaign is especially led by Boas, who has spread abroad a lot of nonsense to the general effect that the races of men are products of their immediate environment rather than of heredity." The president of the Bronx Zoo and the cofounder of the Save the Redwoods League knew otherwise. "To any zoologist," Grant continued, "[Boas's] thesis that skull shapes can change in one generation by the transplantation of its owner from Polish ghetto or Italian slum to the East side of New York is the height of absurdity. 'The elixir of American institutions' . . . [and] 'public education' will do much, but we have yet to find that it modifies physical structure." Grant's warning was stern, a call to resist the ideology of slaves that masked as science: "I trust you will not unwittingly lend yourself to the promulgation of unscientific theories of the superficiality of race which are brought forward in the interests of helot peoples."[28]

For his part, Boas thought Grant's views extremely "dangerous," and he took him to task in scalding reviews in the *New Republic* and elsewhere.[29] In particular, Boas sought to discredit Grant's "Nordic doctrine," a set of racialist beliefs drawn from contemporary ethno-history on which Grant based his approach to immigration policy—and which ultimately came to be enshrined in the 1924 Immigration Act.[30] Like other adherents of this virulent ideology of Anglo-Saxon supremacy, Grant divided Europeans into three distinct racial groups: Alpines, Mediterraneans, and Nordics. According to Grant, each of these peoples was endowed with particular physical and mental characteristics that were passed down through generations by heredity and that were essentially immutable. The largely Slavic Alpines, for instance, had wide heads and were "always and everywhere a race of peasants . . . [a people] submissive to authority both political and religious."[31] Similarly, the Greek and Italian Mediterraneans possessed a set of bodily and spiritual traits peculiar to them (none of them especially positive). The focus of Grant's personal and political interest was the third group, the Nordic race, which he believed represented the highest human type, or "the white man par excellence"—and which defined the best in the American national character.[32] Physically, Nordics were tall, blond, doliocephalic (or long-skulled), sometimes though not necessarily light-eyed, with the men tending toward a high degree of body hair. Mentally, they were dedicated to organization, administration, business, and law—in this, they were like Henry Cabot Lodge's Teutons—had great capacity for self-government, and above all, were energetic individualists. The hearty folk Grant so admired on the western frontier, they embodied the pluck, strength, and decisiveness that Roosevelt sought to emulate in politics and foreign policy. Moreover, they were a people whose borders of the self had been consolidated and defined through persistent battles with the environment, the kind of masculine encounters Grant sought in his zoological adventures and as part of the Boone & Crockett Club.

For the past five thousand years, Grant argued, Nordics had been involved in two world-historical racial struggles, an appreciation of which suggested the urgent need for immigration reform in the United States.

First, Nordics had fought against Alpines and Mediterraneans for control of Europe, a battle they ultimately won, enabling the social and economic development of the continent. Second, and more fundamentally for Grant—and of greatest implication for America—Nordics had long provided Europe's last defense against the human threat from Asia, specifically against the repeated invasions in which Asiatic hordes had swept across the Balkans and to the north and east, leaving hazardous genetic and cultural offshoots in their wake. From Ghengis Khan to Attila the Hun, these invaders had always encountered stiff resistance from Alpines and Mediterraneans, but they had been stopped finally only by the manly forces of Nordics or Nordicized cross-breeds. According to Grant, though Asia had been prevented from military conquest of Europe, its danger lingered in two genetic legacies. The first was to be found in Alpine people, whom Grant thought largely the heirs of soldiers who had spread across the Balkans from Asia Minor. The second was represented by eastern European Jews, whom Grant believed constituted a cross between the descendants of Tartar invaders, converted Kahzars, and orientalized Alpines. For Grant, nowhere was the continuing world-historical battle against the ancient Asiatic threat so dire as in the United States. For there, Nordics faced the Asian peril not only from Jews arriving from Poland and Russia and from Alpines arriving from the Balkans (those displaced by the population explosion and the transformation of European agriculture), but also in its purest form, direct immigration from Asia—a danger located this time not "on the [traditional] east" but "on the *west*."[33] Grant thought an Asiatic presence in the United States would destroy the very essence of his country, and he called on citizens to halt Asian immigration through force of law, just as Nordics earlier had stopped the advance of Asian tribes into Europe through force of arms.

In Grant's writing, Asiatics were not simply a group of lesser beings with whom it was demeaning to associate; instead, they posed a specific socio-legal threat. Like many intellectuals of his day, Grant believed that Asians were constitutionally incapable of recognizing the authority relationships grounding Western democracy, and that they would undermine American political institutions if their numbers were allowed to increase. Over the course of evolutionary history, Grant argued, Asians and Jews had learned to survive under extremely difficult social conditions. In the Darwinian struggle for survival, they had become able to endure conditions of extreme poverty, thriving in worlds in which others would wither. He saw them as "like rats," able to flourish off the filth of society.[34] The danger such ratlike people posed to the Nordic element in the United States, especially to Nordic laborers, was that they would outcompete them in the workplace and then simply outbreed them. By virtue of their biology, Asians threatened to undersell, or undercontract, Nordic workers, driving down their earnings and leading to their demise as a people, the "replacement of [the white] race."[35] Like the juridical-racial description of American Indians as incapable of holding real property, and that of Filipinos as essentially criminal and incapable of the self-regulation necessary to citizenship in a democratic state, Grant's account condemned Asians by way of a claim that they were incapable of a particular form of legal behavior. In Grant's ethno-historical model, Asians had an incapacity for contract, for all forms of legitimate exchange agreements; to employ the language of contemporary contract doctrine, Asians existed in a natural state of unconscionability.[36] Much of Grant's writing about Asiatics thus expressed what might be called a "contractual juridical racialism," a normative language for understanding the proper boundaries of American civic life in which race and contract were mutually constitutive terms. That juridical-racial worldview, it is worth emphasizing, also was an explicitly masculine one, Grant's world of honest Nordic contract, positing a self independent of intersubjective social relations, an individual with a sense of sovereign self-mastery and rigorous self-control.

This bond between race, contract, and manhood—and, more broadly, ethnicity and economics—also animated the political work of Grant's closest ally on Capitol Hill, the legislator who cosponsored the immigration statute both men saw as a personal triumph.[37] Albert Johnson was born in Springfield, Illinois in 1869 to a family descended from fugitive Scots Highlanders who had revolted against the British with Prince Charles Edward Stuart in 1745. He began his career as a newspaper man, serving briefly in the 1890s as managing editor of the *New Haven Register* and in 1897 accepting a position with the *News* of Tacoma, Washington, where his sharp editorial commentaries quickly helped establish him as a prominent figure in state and city politics. He later moved to Seattle, and in 1912, his fame as an editor carried him to Congress. In his political life, Representative Johnson was driven by two linked ambitions that implicated the fields of race and political economy. The first was to crush labor radicalism and its challenge to the inviolability of individual property and national economic growth; he particularly opposed the increasingly visible Industrial Workers of the World (IWW). The second was to curtail immigration, particularly from Japan. Despite the Gentlemen's Agreement, many voters in the western United States remained worried about the Asian presence. Like Grant, many were concerned that culturally unassimilable Asiatics were unfairly competing with white workers, driving down their wages. Others were disturbed by the influx of "picture brides," women who were married through the mail to men they had never met. These women entered the United States under the terms of the Gentlemen's Agreement, and many Americans were frustrated by their participation in farm labor, which seemed to make them precisely the type of workers the Meiji government promised to restrict.[38] Battling hard for his constituents, and unwavering in his commitment to racial exclusion, Johnson threw himself into immigration politics from the very start of his Congressional career, eventually becoming chair of the powerful House Immigration Committee.

Johnson's chairmanship of the Committee was characterized not only by his unyielding promotion of restrictive immigration reform, but also by his use of scientific data to advance his views. Known as the "one who must be shown," Johnson called numerous expert witnesses before Congress to testify to the mental and physical qualities of the various groups of immigrants who sought refuge on U.S. shores.[39] The majority of scholars who testified for the Committee sympathized with the anti-culturalist arguments of the eugenicists. Harry Laughlin, for example, cofounder with Grant of the American Eugenics Society, who considered immigration to be an insidious form of foreign "conquest," was appointed the Committee's "expert eugenics agent," and presented numerous studies purporting to show that certain nationalities were associated with inborn mental and physical characteristics that would be detrimental to the health of the nation and its workforce. The most famous of these, "An Analysis of the Metal and Dross in America's Modern Melting-Pot," can be viewed as the intellectual opposite of Boas's "Changes in Bodily Form of Descendants of Immigrants," a scientific rallying point for those, like Grant, who advanced a hereditarian analysis of racial classification and group character and who sought to discharge their duties of civic stewardship through public advocacy (Grant himself served as an informal advisor to Rep. Johnson, traveling to Washington to discuss policy matters).[40] Those who questioned such views, as did the ecumenical advocate for Japanese-American friendship Sidney Gulick, were given harsh treatment at the hands of the Committee, their culturalist, pluralist writings ignored.[41] Perhaps nowhere in the history of American lawmaking were the arguments of modern eugenics given such an open reception and allowed to exercise such deep influence over the formation of national policy.

The ultimate result was the Immigration Act of 1924, also known as the Johnson-Reed Act, which remained law until 1952.[42] Under the terms of the act, the extent of immigration from Europe was dictated by a complex set of quotas that severely curtailed the number of Alpines, Mediterraneans, and orientalized Semites who could enter the United States each year. Even more, Japanese immigrants were excluded altogether under the act's section 13(c), which flatly barred entry of all aliens "ineligible for citizenship" under federal naturalization law, a group that included the Japanese—the subject of the following section of my analysis. The act was harsh by any measure, as indeed was its intention. As one historian sympathetic with Representative Johnson asserted, throughout his campaign for reform, the chair of the Immigration Committee had simply refused to let his statute be "emasculated."[43] Given the personal and intellectual history of Madison Grant, the term was ironically appropriate, illuminating the juridical-racial dynamics the great change in immigration policy of the 1920s set in motion. For one, Johnson's law undermined one of the basic contracts of gendered human experience, that of marriage, effectively denying it to Japanese men residing in the United States. Moreover, the act abrogated the contract that had been fundamental to Japanese-American relations for years, the Gentlemen's Agreement. And that abrogation, which led to heated anti-American demonstrations throughout Japan, represented a curious ideological reversal. Consolidating the boundaries of the nation in the interest of white contracting labor, Congress implied that the nation was not bound by the contracts it itself had made. In this respect, one might say, when the Nordic mastery Grant desired to cultivate in the masculine self, and which he saw as an essential aspect of American identity, was expressed at the level of national policy, it showed a janus visage. It showed that in the matter of race, contract would find its stark and absolute limit; that in the central concept of market relations, there would exist a community fully outside the circle of exchange and beyond the limits of obligation.

Asian Immigration and Federal Power before the Supreme Court

The juridical-racial themes central to Grant's analysis of the perils of Asian immigration also were central to the story of Asian immigration before the Supreme Court, especially in *Chae Chan Ping* and *Ozawa*. The direct relation in the immigration reform movement between racial theories of human variation and issues of political economy, however, took a refracted form in the arena of judicial doctrine. Specifically, where questions of political economy and the force of domestic labor unrest helped propel Grant's hereditarian, anti-culturalist views onto center stage in the legislative arena, a constitutional jurisprudence with economic concerns at its heart ironically prevented those same views from being determinative on the judiciary in adjudicating matters of Asian citizenship under federal naturalization law. At the same time, the modernizing concerns that lay behind that jurisprudence, a body of legal thought commonly known as economic substantive due process, contained (at least in the judicial work of one of its primary exponents, Justice George Sutherland) expansive implications for federal power that effected the same racial consolidation of civic life envisioned in hereditarian racial arguments and the immigration reform movement they supported—and, in turn, effected the same ironic cultural reversal set in motion by the Immigration Act of the contractual ideals said to form the basis of American national identity. In this dynamic socio-legal process, the Court furthered the principles of contractual juridical racialism in its *Ozawa* decision, making the exclusion of Japanese immigrants possible within the Immigration Act of 1924, at the same time that it rejected the influence in its decision-making process of the racial science Grant advocated.

The tangled relation between racial civic exclusion, questions of political economy, and the expansion of national power traces to the construction of the "legal scaffolding" of the "new Americanism" embodied in the anti-Chinese immigration statutes of the 1870s and 1880s.[44] Fatefully, the Framers of the Constitution had kept silent on immigration issues; the document indeed makes no mention of immigration at all. Filling this gap, the Supreme Court until the late nineteenth century held that Congressional power to regulate immigration derived from its Article I, Section 8 authority to regulate commerce with foreign nations.[45] Congressional immigration authority, that is, was considered attendant to its commercial authority. Only in 1875 did the Court hold that authority to regulate immigration lay within the exclusive control of Congress, rather than with the states as well,[46] and only in 1889 did the Court place Congressional power over immigration on the exceptionally broad foundation on which it rests today and on the basis of which Congress passed the Immigration Act of 1924. That doctrinal shift took place in one of the series of disputes known as the Chinese Exclusion Cases, and the specific case from which its companions garnered their collective name, *The Chinese Exclusion Case*, or *Chae Chan Ping v. United States*. As I will explain, *Chae Chan Ping* removed Congressional immigration authority from its Article I, Section 8 grounding—an interpretation in which federal authority was subject to internal limitations imposed by the Constitution itself—and placed it on an extraconstitutional basis that brooked almost no restriction.

The Court's opinion in the case was written by Justice Stephen Field, whose own life was animated by the connection between economic and state modernization that shaped the contours of the case.[47] Field was born in 1816, in Haddam, Connecticut, into an old line of New England Puritans. When he was a child, his family moved to Massachusetts, and there the bright young student came to know Theodore Sedgwick, Jr., a Jacksonian political economist whose ideas would influence him throughout his life. Sedgwick's work asserted the absolute inviolability of private property and called on the executive to use his national authority as president to protect individual ownership against legislative tyranny. Field attended Williams College, and later read law in the New York office of his brother, David Dudley Field, known today for his advocacy of legal codification. After his apprenticeship, Field moved to California, acquired a small fortune by speculating in real estate, and soon became one of the state's best-known attorneys. This fame won him a place on the state supreme court in 1857, and his distinguished and controversial career there brought an appointment to the U.S. Supreme Court in 1863 by President Lincoln. On the bench, Justice Field fought to put his Sedgwickian commitment to private property into practice, and in doing so, he laid the basis for the jurisprudence of economic substantive due process. This school of legal thought takes as its central concern the judicial protection of certain natural rights that cannot be relinquished to the sovereign, asserting that the Constitution put these rights into effect, even if it does not mention them explicitly, by virtue of its status as the American fundamental law. Foremost among these natural rights, according to men such as Justice Field, was that of liberty of contract. Contractual freedom, that is, was understood by substantive due process theorists as a bedrock element of American national identity, a point powerfully made in Justice Field's celebrated dissent in the *Slaughter-House Cases* (1873). There,

Justice Field asserted that the Fourteenth Amendment consolidated the country around a vision of an independent, contracting self that could not be encroached by state legislative power.[48]

Significantly, it was precisely the inviolability of contract that was at issue, and that was breached, by Justice Field's opinion for the Court in *Chae Chan Ping*. As noted, in the last quarter of the nineteenth century, influenced in part by agitation in the West, Congress began to pass a series of statutes designed to restrict entry of Chinese into the United States. In 1882, it passed the Chinese Exclusion Act, which barred entry of all Chinese laborers, and in 1884, it amended the act with the requirement that Chinese residents traveling abroad obtain a certificate of reentry if they wished to return.[49] *Chae Chan Ping* was one of many legal challenges brought against these laws, and it was the most important. Chae Chan Ping was a Chinese citizen who had lived in San Francisco for twelve years, beginning in 1875. In 1887, he returned to China for a visit, first obtaining from the customs authority in San Francisco a certificate guaranteeing him the right to return. He boarded the steamship *Gaelic* on June 2, 1887, his certificate metaphorically in hand, arrived safely in China, and remained there for about one year. Then, on September 7, 1888, he boarded the steamship *Belgic* in Hong Kong for the return journey he had planned. On October 1, however, while he was steaming toward California in the middle of the Pacific Ocean, Congress passed the Scott Act. Named after exclusionist Representative William Scott of Pennsylvania, the act barred the reentry of Chinese citizens who had traveled abroad, even if they had obtained a reentry guarantee. The act, that is, rendered Chae Chan Ping's reentry certificate null and void. When he arrived in San Francisco harbor on October 8, he thus was denied admission by customs authorities and detained aboard his ship. He was not alone. As many as 20,000 other returning Chinese immigrants found themselves similarly stranded.

As his attorneys argued, in many respects the affair was a simple case of a breached contract, in which the obligations imposed by the certificate Chae Chan Ping received from customs authorities had not been fulfilled, and for which he could demand specific performance. Writing for a unanimous Court, however, Justice Field ruled otherwise. While Justice Field agreed that Chae Chan Ping had an interest in his certificate that typically could not be brooked by the legislature, he stated that the abrogation of such immigration agreements fell largely outside the reach of constitutional restrictions, and he based his reasoning on a reconceptualizaton of the source of federal immigration power. That power, stated Justice Field, was not granted specifically by the Constitution; rather, it was derived from a source that encompassed the Constitution itself: national sovereignty. Simply by virtue of being a nation, Justice Field argued, the U.S. government had the absolute power to determine who could and could not cross its borders. Moreover, according to Justice Field, that power would allow Congress legitimately to render any of its previous actions concerning immigrants' lives null and void, because immigration authority emanated directly from the sovereign will itself. "The power of exclusion of foreigners being an incident of sovereignty," Justice Field explained:

> the right to its exercise at any time when, in the judgment of the government, the interests of the country require it, cannot be granted away or restrained on behalf of any one. . . . Whatever license . . . Chinese laborers may have obtained, previous to the act of October 1, 1888, to return to the United States after their departure, is held at the will of the government, revocable at any time, at its pleasure.[50]

It was this doctrinal position, which construed the free movement of immigrants as subject to the pleasure of the legislature, that provided Congress with its authority to pass the Japanese Exclusion Act in 1924. Justice Field, a man who believed above all in the sanctity of contract, thus ironically provided the broad intellectual platform on which contracts with Asian immigrants could be broken almost at will, an ideological paradox homologous to the inverted juridical-racial logic of the Immigration Act itself.

This ideological inversion of the relation between race and contract also figured in the dispute that provided the immediate judicial basis for the Japanese Exclusion Act, *Takao Ozawa v. United States*. Like Justice Field, the author of *Ozawa* believed that contract was a defining element of national identity, and like *Chae Chan Ping*, the *Ozawa* decision supported the abrogation of individual contracts with Asians. *Ozawa* holds a special place in the history of U.S. immigration law, for while the Immigration Act of 1924 was intended to exclude Japanese from immigrating to the United States, the act itself did not specifically mention the Japanese by name. Instead, Congress provided in section 13(c) of the act that aliens would be barred from entry if they were otherwise "ineligible for citizenship."[51] Whom did this designation include? The answer to that question lay in another federal law, Title XXX of Revised Statutes § 2169, which defined who was entitled to become a naturalized American. First enacted in 1790, § 2169 originally limited the grant of citizenship to "free white persons," and after the Civil War, also came to include persons of "African nativity [or] descent."[52] Under section 13(c) of the Immigration Act, then, only "free white persons" and those of African birth or descent were able to enter the United States as immigrants, because only they had the ability to become naturalized citizens under § 2169. Although it seemed sufficiently clear who was of African nativity or descent, § 2169 did not enumerate what constituted a "white person." It left this critical term undefined. The Japanese exclusion provisions of the Immigration Act of 1924 thus were based on a statute with a potential definitional uncertainty: Were the Japanese white? Before *Ozawa*, federal and state courts, for their part, were divided. By 1910, 420 Japanese had become naturalized Americans on the judgment that they were white persons under federal law.[53] In *Ozawa*, the Supreme Court made a final determination of the matter.

Significantly, for Japanese both in and outside the United States, the question of whether they should be considered to be white under federal naturalization law had implications not only in the realm of immigration but also in that of real property.[54] In the late-nineteenth and early-twentieth centuries, Japanese were immigrating to the western United States, primarily to California, in increasing numbers, giving rise to the fears that led to the Gentlemen's Agreement and, later, the Immigration Act of 1924. There were about 111,000 Japanese in California by 1920, out of a total state population of about three-and-a-half million.[55] These first-generation immigrants, or *Issei*, generally came to till the land, sometimes as contract laborers, and over time they began to purchase farms and establish agricultural communities of their own. In 1905, Japanese owned, cash-leased, shared-leased, or contracted about 62,000 acres in California; by 1913, that amount had increased to 282,000; and by 1920, to 458,000.[56] Beginning in the early-twentieth century, a number of western states, fearing racial-economic competition, passed a series of anti-alien land laws forbidding aliens "ineligible for citizenship" from holding title to real property.[57] The California Alien Land Law of 1920, for instance, made it illegal for aliens ineligible for citizenship—a group defined not by state but by federal law, namely § 2169 of Title XXX—to purchase or lease agricultural land, to hold stocks in agricultural land companies, and to transfer or sell agricultural landholdings to each other, and it "disqualified them from being appointed as guardians of minors who had interest in such land."[58] Western legislatures reasoned that they could enact such obviously discriminatory legislation and evade successful constitutional challenge under the Fourteenth Amendment because their statutes would rely on a classification made by Congress under its plenary power over naturalization, granted by the Constitution in Article I, Section 8.[59]

But though both national immigration policy and western anti-alien land laws ultimately relied on the judiciary to determine who was "white," at least when anti-Asian administrative actions or state laws were challenged, as they often were, the federal naturalization statute itself provided no firm guidance as to how to interpret its terms, and judicial determination of what constituted a white person was fraught with difficulty. For instance, skin color clearly was an inadequate test, for the skin of many Europeans who were generally considered to be white was darker than that of many Asians, and at the same time, the celebrated Ainu people of Japan were as white as many Europeans. The possession of a stated level of "civilization" proved an equally elusive criterion; and while some argued that the term "white" in the federal naturalization statute had simply meant "not an African slave," few thought this to be a credible position.[60] There was, however, an entire professional field that seemed devoted to making such classifications between groups: anthropology. In the fifty-two federal and state court decisions that considered the question of who was white, attorneys and judges thus regularly cited anthropological science to support their judgments.[61] For the most part, anthropology was used to further arguments in favor of interpreting § 2169 restrictively, that is, to undercut the claims of aliens asserting their right to become naturalized citizens under federal law. In such cases, attorneys frequently cited Johann Friedrich Blumenbach's 1775 classification of man into five groups—the American race, or "red" people; the Ethiopian race, or "black" people; the Mongolian race, or "yellow" people; the Malayan race, or "brown" people; and "Caucasians," or "white" people—as well as to the array of anthropological work that built upon Blumenbach's typology.[62] At the same time, anthropological knowledge also was used to argue for a less restrictive interpretation of federal law; the case of *United States v. Cartozian* (1925), for example, included a lengthy deposition from Franz Boas, who testified that the Armenian immigrants at issue in the case should be classified as "white" and so eligible for citizenship.[63]

Consistent with this use of social science, attorneys marshaled the evidence of anthropologists and ethno-historians in the briefs they submitted to the Court in *Ozawa*. The facts of the case are noteworthy for what they reveal about its plaintiff. Born on June 15, 1875 in Kanagawa Prefecture, Takao Ozawa immigrated to San Francisco as a teenager in 1894. There, he graduated from Berkeley High School and studied for three years at the University of California. In the words of one scholar, Ozawa was "a paragon of an assimilated Japanese immigrant."[64] He worked for an American company; could speak, read, and write fluent English; had married an American-educated Japanese woman; belonged to an English-speaking American church; sent his two children to American schools; spoke only English to them so that they would not learn Japanese; and had made active attempts to sever his ties to the Japanese government, for instance by avoiding registering for military service. Eager to become an American citizen, Ozawa had filed a petition for naturalization in 1914 in Hawaii, where he had settled about eight years before. After the petition was denied, Ozawa filed an appeal to the territorial supreme court, which also was denied. He then filed yet another appeal, this time to the Ninth Circuit in San Francisco. At this point, the case drew the attention of the Pacific Coast Japanese Association Deliberative Council. The Japanese analogue of the NAACP in the 1940s and 1950s, the Council recently had begun looking for a test case to challenge the foundation of the anti-alien land laws. Ozawa's case seemed just right: the plaintiff embodied the ideals of the American melting-pot, and on purely political grounds it might be difficult for a court to deny his claim. Sensing an opportunity, the Council took Ozawa's cause as their own, retaining his original lawyer as part of the litigation and also appointing as principal counsel former U.S. Attorney General George Wickersham. Under Wickersham's leadership, Ozawa's case made its way on interlocutory appeal to the Supreme Court in May 1917.[65]

Although much of Ozawa's case concerned procedural and other technical legal matters, a significant portion of his substantive claims centered on issues addressed by anthropologists and other students of human variation and classification. Attorneys on each side of the litigation marshaled social scientific evidence to support their claims that Ozawa should or should not be allowed to become a naturalized citizen as a "white person."[66] Notably, whereas the government tended to rely on racial science with essentialist implications, Ozawa and his attorneys cited social science that challenged rigid classifications of racial difference and suggested, in a broadly Boasian vein, the importance of culture in human experience. The brief for Ozawa, for instance, not only prominently suggested that "the dominant strains [of Japanese] are, 'white persons,' speaking an Aryan tongue and having Caucasian root stocks," but also asserted that "[e]ven Blumenbach, who is the father of modern anthropology, says that 'Innumerable varieties of mankind run into one another by insensible degrees.'"[67] Ozawa himself submitted a sincere though clumsy brief that made much the same point, citing scholarship that indicated the fluidity of racial identity.[68] "For there is not an absolutely white person, nor absolutely yellow person existing on this earth," Ozawa wrote. "*[I]t is an undeniable fact that the cast of countenance depends as much, probably more, on the social than on anthropological traits*. . . . [A]ny theory [of rigid racial classification] proposed by any ethnologist is not stable."[69] Arguing that the framers of the 1790 law had not intended to create a rigid racial test—and, in any case, that they had not been aware of Blumenbach's five-part scheme—Ozawa asserted that § 2169 demanded simply that individuals applying for naturalization be culturally fit for citizenship in a republican polity, and that the critical term of the statute was not the word "white" but rather "free." Under this standard, Ozawa asserted, Japanese were more than capable of assimilation into mainstream America, as indeed he had shown through his own life, and should be allowed to gain citizenship under federal law.

The government's anthropological arguments were less sanguine about the possibilities of such assimilation, though they relied on anthropological evidence even more than did Ozawa. Sections of the amicus curiae brief filed by the California attorney general, for instance, read almost like an anthropology textbook, containing numerous references to a wide variety of social scientific work, from Blumenbach to Tylor to William Z. Ripley, all tending to undercut the melting-pot ideal. The attorney general's brief also relied heavily on expert testimony given before Congress by one of the primary anti-Boasian academic anthropologists of the day, Czech-American scientist Aleš Hrdlička.[70] Known as the founder of modern physical anthropology, Hrdlička fought Boas on a number of intellectual fronts. As a physicalist, for one, he tended to minimize the importance of culture in human experience, and thus while not himself an advocate of eugenics, he gave strong institutional support as secretary of the Committee on Anthropology for the National Research Council to the work of eugenicists such as Madison Grant. Moreover, Hrdlička was deeply opposed to Boas's left political activism. When Boas criticized

President Woodrow Wilson in the *Nation*, for instance, also accusing un-named anthropologists of acting as government spies during World War I—among other transgressions, a breach of the ideal of independent pro-fessionalism—Hrdlička helped pass a motion of censure against Boas within the American Anthropological Association. And when summoned before the Committee on the Territories in anticipation of the *Ozawa* lit-igation, Hrdlička gave lengthy testimony to the effect that Japanese were not white and could never be so classified:

> [Chairman]. Are the Japanese people a legitimate part of the yellow race? [Hrdlička]. The Japanese people are an inherent part of the yellow-brown race. [Chairman]. Would it be at all possible to regard the Japan-ese race as a white race, or a Japanese as a white person? [Hrdlička]. [All] reliable scientific men . . . without exception, class the Japanese as yellow-brown or Mongoloid people.[71]

The muscular scientific certainty of such statements, by Hrdlička and oth-ers, became a central feature of the arguments used to defend against Ozawa's suit.

And so, how did the Court deal with this mass of anthropological ev-idence that both sides of the case suggested was foundational to their claims? It ignored all of it; it chose, that is, not to rely on social science or a scientific standard in determining who was and was not a white per-son.[72] *Ozawa* was the first opinion written by Justice George Sutherland, who had only recently joined the Court, and it forcefully implicated two commitments that lay at the center of his judicial work: furthering the ju-risprudence of economic substantive due process and strengthening fed-eral power over foreign affairs—areas of law that each required the strict definition of boundaries, one of the self, the other of the nation state.[73] An immigrant from England who came of age on the Utah frontier, Jus-tice Sutherland believed that at the center of American citizenship lay the ability of individuals to enter freely into contracts, a belief he famously expressed in *Adkins v. Children's Hospital* (1923), in which the Court struck down minimum wage laws for women on the grounds that they vi-olated contractual liberty.[74] Through *Adkins* and similar decisions, Jus-tice Sutherland came to be known as a fierce opponent of New Deal eco-nomic reforms, and among the Four Horsemen who battled with Roo-sevelt until 1937, he was the acknowledged intellectual leader, the inheritor of the mantle of Justice Field. In his work on the bench, Justice

Sutherland sought to locate and reinforce bedrock principles that would keep the legislature from redistributive tyranny and the Court from interpretive contingency—a goal in which social science and sociological jurisprudence had almost no place.[75] Natural law limits were universal in character, unaffected by the ever-changing knowledge of professional thinkers. In this sense, Justice Sutherland was the precise opposite of Louis D. Brandeis, whom he first encountered in an exchange of letters concerning the treatment of IWW leader Joe Hill by the Utah authorities (Brandeis requested that Justice Sutherland use his influence to inquire into the case; Justice Sutherland flatly refused).[76]

Justice Sutherland undoubtedly felt his general aversion to using social science with particular force in adjudicating an international affairs matter like that posed by *Ozawa*. For in addition to having foregrounded economic substantive due process in constitutional interpretation, Justice Sutherland also is the jurist on the Court who most developed American foreign affairs power. Like John Wesley Powell ("the Major"), Justice Sutherland firmly believed in the inviolable integrity of the Union; he urged, for instance, that in everyday speech Americans should say not that "the United States *are* a Nation" but rather that "the United States *is* a Nation."[77] In his decision-making, he sought to further that national coherence by granting the federal government extensive powers over international affairs, a leadership manifest in his opinion in *Curtiss-Wright Export Corp.* (1936), which granted the president plenary, extraconstitutional authority in foreign relations.[78] In this respect, Justice Sutherland saw himself, as others also saw him, as a forward-thinking person whose jurisprudence strove to allow the government to respond to distinctively contemporary needs. He was much like Justice Field on this score, an innovator of national power; and indeed, like Justice Field, he also believed that certain powers, such as foreign relations, were granted to the national government merely as an incident of its sovereignty. In a series of lectures delivered at Columbia University in the wake of World War I, he clarified the motivation behind this jurisprudential conviction by warning that it was "time we realized not in phrases merely but in fact, that the Constitution is not a petrifaction, nor the charter of a petrifaction. This is a progressive Nation in a progressive world. . . . if the activities of the government are too strictly limited, a drag upon, instead of an aid to this forward progress will result."[79] For Justice Sutherland, as for Justice Miller in *Kagama* and Justice Brown in the *Insular Cases*, the nation as much as the self required the power of absolute self-mastery.

In a case such as *Ozawa*, then, Justice Sutherland would have thought it the height of folly to suggest that the scope of American international policy might depend on the writings of university ethnologists. And, indeed, nothing in the archival record suggests that Justice Sutherland thought *Ozawa* a difficult case. "The application of the naturalization statute has, from time to time, presented some very close questions," he wrote the director of the Carnegie Endowment for International Peace, "and will continue to do so, but that it does not include Japanese and Chinese seemed to the Court very clear."[80] For Justice Sutherland, the Japanese were not white and so not eligible for citizenship under § 2169, because they generally were not considered "Caucasians"—a term that was not, as some scholars have argued, a scientific one, but rather a figure of popular speech.[81] In using the term Caucasian as it was *"popularly known,"* Justice Sutherland flatly rejected the significance of the ethnological data in determining the outcome of Ozawa's dispute, no matter how it spoke to the question of race and citizenship at hand.[82] "We have been furnished with elaborate briefs in which the meaning of the words 'white person' is discussed with ability and at length, both from the standpoint of judicial decision and from that of the science of ethnology," he wrote with understated but firm disapproval. "It does not seem to us necessary, however, to follow counsel in their extensive researches in these fields."[83] One journalistic commentary on the decision, saved by Justice Sutherland in his personal papers, accordingly lauds *Ozawa* for the non-scientific bent of its reasoning. "The decision by the United States Supreme Court that Japanese cannot become citizens of the United States because they are not white is likely to amaze the average casual reader of newspapers," wrote its bemused author. "Every schoolboy knows that the Japanese is not Caucasian. . . . This decision . . . may be considered a happy augury of the quality of the service [Justice Sutherland] will perform. Those familiar with his career long have understood his belief that common sense and law are neither irreconcilable nor incompatible."[84]

In denying Ozawa's claim, Justice Sutherland's opinion for the Court in *Ozawa*, like Justice Field's opinion in *Chae Chan Ping*, contained its own series of ironies and reversals. First, and most immediately, while in *Ozawa* Justice Sutherland rejected the use of anthropological evidence in § 2169 disputes, his opinion formed the basis of legislation that itself was undergirded by racial social science: the Immigration Act of 1924. For in determining that Japanese were ineligible for citizenship under federal naturalization law, the Court also made possible the drafting of a statute that flatly excluded the Japanese from American shores (though without explicitly naming them). The *Ozawa* decision, that is, allowed the hereditarian anthropology of which the Court declined to take cognizance to be given legislative effect, allowed it to succeed in one legal arena because it was ignored in another. In this, the common civic contractual perspective Justice Sutherland shared with Grant, Johnson, and other immigration reformers may have produced different immediate outcomes as it was used in divergent legal institutions, legislative and judicial, but it finally drove toward the same exclusionary civic effect. Second, by determining that Japanese were not white under § 2169, *Ozawa* also forged the basis on which the Court later upheld western anti-alien land laws. Not long after *Ozawa*, those laws were deemed constitutional in opinions for the Court written by Justice Pierce Butler, another of the Four Horsemen who, like Justice Sutherland, passionately believed in the centrality of contract to human dignity. If Congress had made the determination that only "white persons" were eligible for citizenship, reasoned Justice Butler, then state land laws surely could not be challenged under the Fourteenth Amendment, for those laws simply relied on a classification already made by the federal government (the lower federal court in the case of *Terrace v. Thompson* [1923] had asserted that the Congressional bar to Asian naturalization was based on the perception that "[t]he yellow or brown racial color is the hallmark of the Oriental despotisms").[85] *Ozawa* thus ultimately undermined Japanese ability to participate in an institution Justice Sutherland held so dear, the ownership of real property, just as Justice Field circumscribed the sanctity of contract within more encompassing racial concerns.

Finally, *Ozawa* enacted a cultural reversal at the level of the human heart. The subject of that reversal was marriage, a contractual institution that creates bonds of obligation between two people in opposition to a traditionally masculine valuation of unbridled individual freedom. For in the wake of the Immigration Act of 1924, a series of cases arose that not only challenged the constitutionality of the law, but also glaringly revealed the price it exacted on foreign women who had married American citizens abroad and now wished to join their husbands in the United States. One of them was Chang Chan.[86] Sometime before 1924, Chan had married a Chinese-born American citizen, but while she was on the high seas aboard the ship *President Lincoln*, steaming toward the United States, Congress passed the Immigration Act. Although the act generally defined the spouses of American citizens as eligible for entry as nonquota immigrants, it was unclear on the face of the law whether that eligibility applied only to whites or also to those generally ineligible for naturalized citizenship under federal law. With the notorious Justice James C. McReynolds—lifelong bachelor, extreme conservative, and outspoken misogynist—as its spokesman, the Court decided in favor of Chan's exclusion.[87] Justice McReynolds upheld the law by approvingly citing earlier immigration decisions by Justice Sutherland, in which the Justice renowned for his thoughtfulness and care argued that the Court would simply turn a deaf ear to those who charged that immigration legislation was "cruel and inhuman in its results." "[T]he courts," Justice Sutherland had written, "have no choice but to follow [such statutes], without regard to the consequences."[88] Here was one more cruel irony in the strange cultural career of Asian immigration and American contract—and yet, as we will see in chapter 4, within three decades, the very principles of political economy and economic development that decisions such as *Chae Chan Ping*, *Ozawa*, and *Chang Chan* furthered also would lead to the ultimate rejection of the juridical-racial principles they supported, thereby beginning a new, still ongoing chapter in the history of American civic life.

4

Culture, Personality, and
Racial Liberalism

Contractual juridical racialism rested not only on a political vision of Anglo-Saxon racial supremacy, but also on theories of economic liberty ascendant at a particular stage in American capitalism. The Supreme Court's economic substantive due process jurisprudence and Madison Grant's anti-environmentalist model of racial-legal character were mutually supporting positions shaping the racial boundaries of American civic life. Yet neither view would sustain its cultural and legal dominance and, indeed, they would fall together at midcentury. Economically, the jurisprudence of contractual liberty that Justice Sutherland expressed so forcefully against the views of Louis D. Brandeis in cases such as *Adkins v. Children's Hospital* (1923) would not survive the 1930s.[1] By the time the United States entered the postwar period under discussion in this chapter, the *Lochner* era had long given way under the pressures of social and governmental need. American capitalism after the New Deal would be characterized instead by nationally regulated markets, corporate economic dominance, and high-growth consumer society. At the same time, racial beliefs like those Grant advanced in *The Passing of the Great Race*, from his particular claims that Jews and Asians were ratlike people who thrived off the filth of society to his generally hereditarian perspective on social difference, would buckle beneath the assault, among others, of American state mobilization against Nazism. While there still are meaningful bars to full civic membership for minority groups in the United States today, an explicitly geneticist approach to social differences has been almost entirely displaced in public discourse; in its stead, Americans across the political spectrum adhere to an essentially Boasian view of the centrality of culture to human variation.

In this chapter, I explore the significance for juridical racialism of this dual transformation and its emergence within the Afro-American struggle for civil rights. I focus my attention on the Supreme Court opinion in *Brown v. Board of Education* (1954), which held that racial segregation in public schools per se violates the Fourteenth Amendment guarantee of equal protection of the laws, overturning the separate-but-equal doctrine enunciated in *Plessy v. Ferguson* (1896).[2] My interest in *Brown* centers specifically on its eleventh footnote, in which the Court controversially cited a body of social scientific research concerning Afro-American self-esteem, most notably Kenneth B. Clark's "doll studies," that were based on views about law, self, and society advanced by Boasian scholars in the culture-and-personality school of anthropology.[3] The citation of this scholarship illustrates the psychological inflection with which the culture concept transformed modern approaches to citizenship—one recapitulated, I argue, in the argumentative structure of the *Brown* decision as a whole. Note eleven also prominently cited the most important midcentury study of race relations in the United States, *An American Dilemma: The Negro Problem and Modern Democracy* (1944), and before turning to *Brown* I examine the life and work of its author, economist Gunnar Myrdal, who also played a significant role in forging the liberal intellectual consensus that would implement the social ideals *Brown* expressed.[4] Like the Court's opinion in *Brown*, I argue, *An American Dilemma* traced the psychological and socio-legal pathologies of American life to an ontological state of legal self-contradiction, and it sought to remedy those pathologies not only through the linked establishment of jurisprudential and psycho-social equilibrium, but also through the symbolic integration of the self and the machinery of federal government, the self and the national state. This approach to civic life, I argue, which brought the tradition of juridical racialism to an end through its final expression, was an essential ideological component of postwar economic modernization.

The Court's citation of social science in *Brown* has been the subject of vigorous scholarly debate. Speaking broadly, this debate concerns the extent to which footnote eleven was "necessary" for the logic of the opinion and thus the extent to which the Court can be said to have fundamentally "relied" on social science in its argument.[5] Scholars tend to address this question in one of two ways. Some claim the Court relied heavily on social science and that its opinion is an important manifestation of the jurisprudential victory of legal realism after the New Deal. Ironically, such scholars tend to be among the decision's staunchest critics, and they frequently couple their characterization of the logical centrality of note eleven with a dismissive appraisal of the quality of the work cited there.[6] Other scholars, however, claim that the social science cited in *Brown* was incidental to the opinion and should be passed over as jurisprudentially insignificant. These scholars tend to support *Brown* both as a legal decision and as an exercise in consensus-building political rhetoric, and they wish to shield it from delegitimating attack.[7] I approach this issue somewhat differently. As noted in the introduction to this book, I believe the history of anthropology can shed light on the history of American law not simply to the extent that the judiciary has relied factually on anthropology in its rulings, but also because the social and civic vision of anthropology appears in broad, iterated patterns in legal doctrine concerning American citizenship. From this perspective, footnote eleven is significant for how the studies cited there, in particular those of Clark and Myrdal, mirrored the conceptual structure of the decision as a whole—for how Boasian social science is present in *Brown* not simply through specific citation but also, more important, as a patterned way of thinking about the self and its relation to its socio-legal environment.

Gunnar Myrdal and the Legally Fractured Self

Gunnar Myrdal was born in 1898 in the Swedish province of Dalarna, an impoverished and isolated part of the country in which his ancestors had lived for more than three hundred years. He was christened Karl Gunnar Pettersson, but his family changed their surname to Myrdahl in 1914 (the name, meaning "swamp-valley," was something of an embarrassment to Gunnar, who dropped the "h" four years later). His father, Carl Adolf, was an ambitious building contractor, and the family moved often. Even after settling in Stockholm in 1905, young Gunnar was shuttled from one house to another as the family patriarch bought, renovated, and then sold their homes for profit. The Pettersson marriage was not a happy one. A "heavy drinker and womanizer," Carl Adolf drove his wife to discontent and bitterness, and the two often fought.[8] Although Gunnar considered his philandering father a humiliation, he inherited from him the "driving ambition, restless energy, [and] contentious style" that he in turn directed toward escaping his provincial roots and unhappy home.[9] Enrolling in gymnasium in 1914, he threw himself into his studies, quickly proving a precocious student. It was there, amid the heady world of the Stockholm bourgeoisie, that Myrdal first encountered the rationalism and cosmopolitanism of the Enlightenment that would inform his mature thought. It was also there that he began to cultivate what would become equally characteristic elitist political views, coming to advocate the creation of a political party of intellectuals to institute national social reforms. In 1918, Myrdal registered as a law student at Stockholm University and soon after, while on a cycling trip to Sörmland, he stopped to rest at a farm and met Alva Reimer. A radical and powerfully intelligent young woman, Alva longed to flee the "Strindbergesque family inferno" in which she was raised and, like Gunnar, saw educational attainment as her means to escape.[10] The two fell deeply in love, and later were married in a small ceremony, to which neither invited their parents. As Gunnar pursued his legal studies, Alva directed her attention to psychology.

Myrdal began his law career in 1923 as a judicial clerk in Stockholm municipal court, and later became a magistrate and public prosecutor. But finding the actual practice of law dispiriting, he quickly decided to abandon the profession. With Alva's encouragement, he began to read economics and soon took up full-time study under the leading neoclassical scholar Karl Gustav Cassel. In 1927, he received his doctorate for a dissertation on price theory, in which he debunked models of static equilibrium, a theoretical project he would pursue throughout his life, and with Cassel's support he was appointed docent in political economy at Stockholm University. As a young faculty member, Myrdal published two works that would lead him into the center of the rising Social Democratic party. The first was *Monetary Equilibrium* (1939), which proposed the critical distinction in economics between ex ante and ex post expectations, especially between intended and realized investment.[11] The second was a major article titled "The Dilemma of Social Policy" (1932), in which Myrdal expressed his eagerness to use technocratic social engineering to solve the economic crisis menacing his country in the early 1930s.[12] Anticipating the later writings of John Maynard Keynes, he advocated for a mixed economy driven by deficit spending and stabilized by the strong fiscal hand of the central government. His were "prophylactic reforms" intended to rescue capitalism from impending catastrophe—the reforms of the modern liberal welfare state. After publishing a best-selling book on the declining Swedish birthrate, in which he and Alva called for the sterilization of those who were not fit for productive work in the modern economy and the use of redistributive policies to encourage population growth among those who were, Myrdal became a prominent advisor to the social democrats.[13] He soon would give himself over entirely to public life, becoming a leading member of parliament, a trustee of the Bank of Sweden, and a prominent figure throughout national affairs. His overarching goal in this public work, it might be said, was to modernize his nation just as he had earlier modernized himself.

Myrdal was granted the opportunity to extend this modernizing vision to the United States when, in August 1937, he received a letter with a surprising offer from the president of the New York-based Carnegie Corporation, Frederick Keppel. From its inception, the Corporation had directed part of its philanthropy to southern black colleges, a legacy of its founder's admiration of Booker T. Washington. In 1935, however, Newton D. Baker, a Carnegie trustee, suggested the organization alter its traditional giving policy. Mayor of Cleveland from 1912 to 1916 and a longtime board member of a variety of charities, Baker was struck by the great changes occurring in the lives of black Americans after World War I. Sensing the need for new approaches to racial questions, he proposed that the Corporation organize an in-depth study of blacks in northern cities. Keppel was intrigued, and under his directorship, Baker's promising idea soon blossomed into a broad initiative to undertake a comprehensive study of the "Negro problem" generally. When the Corporation began to search for someone to direct the ambitious project, it quickly decided that, for political reasons, it would seek a prominent foreign scholar from a country without a history of colonialism. Myrdal's name was put forward by Beardsley Ruml, former dean of social sciences at the University of Chicago, who had come to know the young economist in 1929, when he brought Gunnar and Alva to the United States for a year-long academic visit as fellows of the Rockefeller Foundation. Although Myrdal at first rejected Keppel's offer (he is said to have exclaimed, "These Americans are crazy!"), he reinitiated negotiations in October after Ruml urged him to accept, promising the Corporation would provide its full financial support.[14] Some accounts have it that Gunnar and Alva ultimately decided to leave their rich, full lives in Sweden after seeing a film depicting doctors rescuing yellow fever victims in Africa. In 1938, Myrdal delivered the prestigious Godkin Lectures at Harvard, and afterward met Keppel at the New York Century Club, where he sealed the bargain.[15]

Myrdal arrived in the United States that October and quickly established himself in lavish offices in midtown Manhattan. High above New York, he threw himself into his work, organizing his project, one historian writes, like a Swedish royal commission.[16] Although Myrdal was to be the author of the final report, he directed over thirty researchers and collaborators who gathered information and wrote memoranda on a wide range of topics concerning the social and economic status of blacks in America. Representative titles of the memoranda included "Conceptions and Ideologies of the Negro Problem," "Mental Disease Among American Negroes," "The Hybrid and the Problem of Miscegenation," "The Health of the Negro," "The Fertility of the Negro," "The Political Status of the Negro," "Negro Churches and Associations in the Lower South," "The Negro Press," "Negro Labor and Its Problems," and "The Negro in the American Economic System."[17] Though Myrdal did not think highly of most of the reports, they provided stark evidence of the grave disparities between whites and blacks in the United States and of the "social waste" of untapped black economic development.[18] Four years later, he began to write, working famously long hours at Dartmouth and Princeton, with the final product of his labors appearing in late 1944. It was the shadow of war's end, with questions about postwar planning beginning to loom in public discussion, and Myrdal's work seemed to symbolize in its sheer size the political direction of the period. Running almost 1,500 pages, it was a truly prodigious effort, driven by a faith that academic knowledge could fashion enlightened solutions to social problems. Bold, comprehensive, practical, it embodied all Myrdal believed as an intellectual and social engineer. Years later, speaking with one of his daughters, the aging economist would remember the afternoon he held the manuscript of *An American Dilemma* in his hands at the Princeton train station as the greatest moment in his life.[19]

The significance of *An American Dilemma* for the history of juridical racialism lies in three primary features of its analysis: its Boasian intellectual foundations; its reflection of the psychological concerns of the culture-and-personality school that grew from Boas's work; and its characterization of American national culture as based in a particular popular understanding of law. Each is worth examining in turn.

Myrdal's debt to Boas appears most immediately in his thoroughgoing environmentalism. In the debate as to whether nature or nurture is the primary determinant of individual and group identity, particularly group racial identity, Myrdal fell firmly on the side of nurture, and he believed that human beings, beneath their apparent differences, share a basic similarity of cognitive process. Myrdal traced the roots of this environmentalism directly to Boas himself, whom he praised for helping inaugurate *"the most important of all social trends in the field of interracial relations,"* the battle against racial hereditarians, a group notably exemplified by "the high priest of racialism in America," Madison Grant.[20] "The last two or three decades," Myrdal wrote, assessing the environmentalist approach in social science Boas championed, "have seen a veritable revolution in scientific thought on the racial characteristics of the Negro. . . . [A] handful of social and biological scientists . . . have gradually forced informed people to give up some of the more blatant of our biological errors."[21] In this light, Myrdal sought the advice of Boas himself when originally formulating his study and made prominent and repeated reference to Boas's *The Mind of Primitive Man* (1911) and "Changes in Bodily Form of Descendents of Immigrants" (1910) in his final text. He also forged strong academic and personal connections with Boasian scholars throughout his work.[22] Two Boas students, for instance, wrote research memoranda for *An American Dilemma*, publishing their reports as monographs that garnered substantial acclaim in their own right: Otto Klineberg's *Characteristics of the American Negro* (1944) and Melville Herskovits's *Myth of the Negro Past* (1941).[23] Moreover, Myrdal organized *An American Dilemma* around a principle drawn from Boas student Ruth Benedict, that "'to understand race conflict we need fundamentally to understand *conflict* and not *race*.'" For Myrdal the environmentalist, the study of race relations in the United States was to rest upon the investigation not of racial differences, but of popular attitudes toward race itself, for it is *"they only . . . which enter directly into the causal mechanism of interracial relations."*[24]

In addition to an environmentalism whose roots traced to Boas, *An American Dilemma* reflected the particular assumptions and preoccupations about the individual subject that were advanced by the culture-and-personality school of anthropology. The scholars of the culture-and-personality school, most prominently Benedict and fellow Boas student Margaret Mead, were environmentalists in the field of human variation who directed scientific attention to the relation between culture and the individual personality.[25] Their work grew directly from the academic tradition Boas had established with his particular approach to the study of individual societies. Boasian ethnographers worked to create total pictures of the societies they investigated by assiduously collecting their separate, individual elements. These scholars logically were led to ask how these individual pieces cohered into a synthetic whole, a process known as "cultural integration." The scholars of the culture-and-personality school, influenced by Gestalt theory, argued that the most important mechanism driving this integrative process was the individual personality. The human subject, in their view, naturally seeks to form symbolic arrangements from its environment and to create "patterns of culture," in Benedict's influential phrase, by fashioning its experience into a meaningful design and then communicating that configuration to others. Significantly for the juridical-racial structure of *An American Dilemma*, a central principle of this argument was that the self is an active mirror, forming a psychologically causal microcosm of the society in which it exists—including that part of its environment formed by law and the legal system.[26]

This approach to the nature of subjectivity represented a crucial, constitutive link between modern theories of culture and the social and political project of postwar liberalism.[27] For the theory of the self advanced by Boasian anthropologists and their followers rested the vitality of a society on the internal lives and personalities of the individuals whose health the society in turn reinforced. As a matter of social engineering, then, postwar liberals like Myrdal, whose environmentalism traced to Boas, were committed to intellectual and policy programs that would advance psycho-social equilibrium, advocating the integration of the self into society at the level of social theory, political policy, and therapeutic practice. This particular integrative commitment, in turn, was to serve as the foundation of the other integrative programs central to postwar liberal policy, namely integration in the realms of economics, state administration, and race relations. In economics, liberals looked to the mixed economy of the welfare state as an instrument of modernization; in administration, they sought the consolidation of state bureaucratic capacities within a federal government guided by experts trained in social scientific analysis; and in race relations, they advocated the legal reforms of the Civil Rights Movement and the spread of a cosmopolitan ideal of tolerance. All these reforms depended upon one another. Economic modernization required the expansion and rationalization of national state power, which in turn was necessary for the program of civil rights that alone could release the South from economic stagnation—and this cycle of progress, at bottom, relied on and furthered the psychological adjustment and integration of self and society whose understanding derived from the issues of cultural integration raised by Boasian ethnography.

This psychological account of culture also formed the basis of Myrdal's analysis of popular perceptions of race. From his arrival in the United States in 1938, Myrdal was deeply concerned with conflicts within the self, in particular with white psychological pathology. About a month after Myrdal settled in Manhattan, he traveled for two months through the South on what he later called an "exploratory journey," stopping in various towns and cities to speak with local residents and officials.[28] Aside from the raw fact of social and economic underdevelopment, what struck him most during this voyage was the way racial injustice distorted the American personality, especially that of whites. According to Myrdal, the southern caste system produced in white Americans a set of pathological symptoms he termed "escape psychology," a state of consciousness in which the self, pervaded by dishonesty, never fully knows itself as itself—in which the self is split at its core in an ontological state of injurious self-contradiction.[29] For Myrdal, this split was nowhere more evident than in white attitudes toward interracial sex, which he observed in numerous encounters with Southerners in which the towering Swede would "suddenly turn to a gracious [white] host in a fine home and ask: 'Why don't you want your daughter to marry a Negro?'" (the typical reaction was as one might expect).[30] These encounters convinced Myrdal that the "attitude of refusing to consider amalgamation—felt and expressed in the entire country—constitutes the center in the complex of attitudes which can be described as the 'common denominator' in the problem."[31] They also gave him what he called "the central viewpoint" of *An American Dilemma*, that the "Negro problem is a problem in the heart of the [white] American. It is there that the decisive struggle goes on."[32] Myrdal's views on race relations, that is, not only were cultural, focused on popular beliefs and attitudes toward race, but also, more important, they were psychological. His analysis of the "Negro problem" found its Archimedean point of leverage in the sexual manifestations of the fractured white self.

How did this fracture in the white personality arise? The answer reaches further into the heart of Myrdal's analysis and to its legal-cultural dimension. According to Myrdal, American civic life is bound together by a hegemonic body of liberal political ideals he termed the "American Creed." In the United States, Myrdal believed, there exists "a basic homogeneity" of belief, a common "social *ethos*" of Enlightenment principles shared by citizens "of all national origins, classes, regions, creeds, and colors."[33] The idea that American society had been liberal at its core throughout its history was widely shared at midcentury.[34] But Myrdal both viewed this liberal homogeneity as a positive political force and, ironically, saw it as the basis of a uniquely American cycle of economic degeneration and psychological pathology.[35] In particular, he argued, the American Creed, which "centered in the belief in equality and in the rights to liberty," was sincerely held by all Americans at the same time that it was fundamentally at odds with the way many of those Americans treated blacks.[36] The American Creed, in other words, conflicted with American reality, and there existed an identity fracture at the heart of civic life. Being a rationalist, Myrdal believed that whites generally wished to view themselves as rational people as well, and he therefore argued that the deep rupture in their Creed produced in white Americans a form of cognitive moral dissonance.[37] This dissonance not only created the complex body of white American psycho-sexual pathology, but also directed whites unconsciously to maintain anti-environmentalist ideologies of racial hierarchy to justify their treatment of Afro-Americans. "The influences from the American Creed," Myrdal wrote, "had, and still have, a double-direction":

> On the one hand, the equalitarian Creed operates directly to suppress the dogma of the Negro's racial inferiority and to make people's thoughts more and more "independent of race, creed or color," as the American slogan runs. On the other hand, it indirectly calls forth the same dogma to justify a blatant exception to the Creed. The race dogma is nearly the only way out for a people so moralistically equalitarian, if it is not prepared to live up to its faith. . . . *The need for race prejudice is, from this point of view, a need for defense on the part of the Americans against their own national Creed, against their own most cherished ideals.* And race prejudice is, in this sense, a function of equalitarianism."[38]

And here began a "vicious circle."[39] For Myrdal, the white self was the causal mechanism of American race conflict, making meaning from the split within the Creed and forming, one might say, an ideational and psychological pattern from its culture. These beliefs and attitudes, in turn, deeply injured black Americans by constricting their social and economic opportunities, thereby deepening black underdevelopment and feeding white prejudice by providing ex post confirmation that their ex ante evaluation of Negro inferiority was correct.

Significantly for the history of juridical racialism, in this vicious circle of psychological pathology and economic stagnation, law held a "crucial" place.[40] The theory of the self as a psychologically causal microcosm of its social whole, which the culture-and-personality school brought into American social science, included but did not place fundamental emphasis upon the recognition that the social whole was constituted in part by law. For Myrdal, that social world was jurisprudential at its core, for the American Creed was explicitly legal in character, centering around a body of ideals concerning liberty and equality derived most powerfully from the political tenets of the Enlightenment and developed within the fertile soil of English common law.[41] From the Enlightenment, Myrdal believed—by the term, he meant an amalgam of "French eighteenth century humanitarianism and equalitarianism . . . [and] English seventeenth century liberalism"—the United States derived a "national consciousness and political structure" that emphasized human dignity and sought to put the difficult process of democratic decision-making into practice.[42] The Enlightenment had given the United States its basic principles of democratic association. These democratic ideals, he further believed, had entered American thought with relative ease because a long history of legal developments in England reaching back to 1215 had prepared the way for the reception of legal order and due process. "[I]t is no exaggeration," Myrdal wrote, "to state that the philosophical ideas of human equality and the inalienable rights to life, liberty, and property, hastily sowed on American ground in a period of revolution when they were opportune . . . would not have struck root as they did if the soil had not already been cultivated by English law."[43] For Myrdal, the American self was both historically and essentially formed around juridical concepts; the fundamental social ethos that defined American life and whose fracture revealed itself in the pathological white personality was an ethos of legality.

In the previous chapters of this study, I have discussed the work of thinkers who believed that law was the defining element of a people. Those thinkers understood law as having a peculiar racial quality, some viewing it as racial in its very essence; the suggestion that civil and political rights might be applicable to all peoples, even to all those born in the United States, was to them highly suspect. In chapter 1, for instance, I examined how an idea of law congruent with developmentalist anthropology suggested that Indians were perhaps incapable of holding title to real property, and that property itself was not simply a specifically Anglo-Saxon concept but a uniquely Anglo-Saxon legal capacity. Similarly, in chapter 2, I discussed how an idea of law derived in part from the Teutonic origins thesis of American government suggested that Filipinos were criminal by nature, unworthy of the protections guaranteed by the U.S. Constitution. And in chapter 3, I indicated how a hereditarian discourse about Japanese immigrants suggested they were incapable of contracting according to Anglo-Saxon norms, and that contract itself was a white legal category. Although many significant aspects of his character and political vision were similar to those of men like Madison Grant, Myrdal's juridical racialism turned such formulations on their head. As a universalist body of legal ideals, the American Creed applied to everyone; all citizens were capable of holding the full range of legal rights it embraced. Myrdal's view of civic belonging in the United States, that is, nationalized the idea of law itself, breaking the strict association of law with racial essence that inhered in earlier forms of juridical racialism and replacing it with a strong association between law and national citizenship that transcended race. In this Boasian juridical-racial account, based implicitly upon the concept of culture and its environmentalist explanation of human variation, race and law remained mutually constitutive concepts only in the context of failure, only when the rationalist principles of human unity and universal legal capacity were prevented from being fulfilled by the force of psychological pathology. For Myrdal, that is, the idea of law was constitutive of the idea of race, and vice versa, only when both law and race existed in a state of symbiotic, mutually reinforcing fracture.

This was a juridical-racial understanding characteristic of the postwar era and, characteristically, it placed law not only at the center of the civic disease of caste and race conflict, but also at the heart of its solution. For in Myrdal's account, undergirding the split between American Creed and American reality lay an even deeper legal division, one that gave "a unique twist to each of the specific problems" examined throughout the Carnegie study. This was a fracture in Americans' "respect for law and order," a contradictory opinion of law itself.[44] On the one hand, Myrdal believed, Americans had great respect for law and order in the abstract. They had a deep regard for the "inalienable rights to life, liberty, and property" that animated the core of their Creed, and they inscribed these ideals into legislation. "The indebtedness of American civilization to the culture of the mother country is nowhere else as great," Myrdal wrote, "as in respect to the democratic concept of law and order, which it inherited almost without noticing it." On the other hand, he wrote, Americans had "a relatively low degree of respect for law and order" in the particular.[45] The liberal individualism of American civic consciousness, he believed, also gave Americans a faith in their own ability to interpret natural law principles. He saw in the United States, that is, a certain "anarchistic tendency" one might call legal antinomianism, in which each person became a law unto themselves.[46] This was not an uncommon view at the time.[47] Myrdal was influenced on this point, for instance, by the work of James Truslow Adams and Roscoe Pound (according to Pound, who with Felix Frankfurter and others had undertaken a comprehensive study of criminal justice in Cleveland, legal theories of "natural law" created a "popular impatience of restraint").[48] Still, the idea was articulated with a special inflection in Myrdal's work because of his concern for the relation between culture and personality. According to Myrdal, the psychological division of the white mind and the social split of legal self-contradiction could be unified only if "the common American citizen" acquired a greater degree of "personal identification with the state and its legal machinery."[49] A more rational world could come into being, that is, only once the self was made to identify with the sovereign (and that state, naturally, would be guided by policy experts trained in modern social science).

It is not necessary to accept every feature of Myrdal's juridical-racial analysis to recognize its power. One strength of *An American Dilemma* lies in its capaciousness; it contains an investigation of psychological pathology, a description of American political culture, a theory of the vicious circle of degeneration, an idea of law. It is hardly surprising that, soon after its publication, critics came to see the work for the grand accomplishment that it was, or that over the next two decades it became one of the central works around which the national liberal consensus on racial issues revolved.[50] The agenda for racial progress advocated by that consensus was a deeply admirable vision, and it remains so today: a battle against racial prejudice and hereditarian fallacy; a concern for the transformation of white attitudes and conscience; a promise that the social sciences could be used to great effect in the formation of political policy; and a concern for assimilation and cultural pluralism rather than racial nationalism. But during a time when modern liberal politics generally are being reevaluated, historians can also acknowledge the difficult questions its agenda raised at its inception and, notably, in the life and work of its most prominent exponents. For in addition to a project Ralph Ellison incisively characterized as a "blueprint for a more effective exploitation of the South's natural, industrial and human resources," Myrdal's study of race relations advanced a more basic juridical-racial integrative goal: to make the self united, to bring the self into itself, to resolve white psychological pathology in a kind of Hegelian *aufhebung* by integrating the self into the power of the federal government.[51] This program was, to use Michel Foucault's assessment of liberal political thought, at once individualizing and totalizing, its global, universalist ambitions intimately linked to its concern for personal and subjective matters.[52] It was a difficult balance, to be sure, but it was a high-wire act through which an unhappy boy from Dalarna, using a culturalist vision of law and race, would seek to bring the political rationalism he wished to infuse across the United States, in fact across the entire developing world, into the very center of the human heart.[53]

Enhancing Self-Esteem in Brown v. Board of Education

Like *An American Dilemma*, the Supreme Court decision in *Brown v. Board of Education* furthered both racial integration and national economic modernization through an understanding of the relation between self and society parallel to that of the culture-and-personality school of anthropology, recapitulating its conceptual structure at the level of constitutional doctrine. As with Myrdal's own program of racial social engineering, the roots of the intellectual homology between *Brown* and the culture-and-personality school trace to the development of the liberal welfare state: to the transformation of the Court's approach to issues of economic liberty in the 1930s and, specifically, its rejection of the jurisprudence of economic substantive due process and the restrictive reading of federal power under the Commerce Clause that defined the *Lochner* era. This rejection not only established the doctrinal foundation for the economic reforms of the New Deal and the rise of modern federal administration, but also planted the seed of the Court's future analysis of equal protection and race discrimination in *Brown*. This equal protection analysis, in turn, implicitly rested on a view of the relation between legal culture and individual subjectivity similar to Myrdal's psychological approach to the American dilemma—and, as in Myrdal's work and the liberal consensus it helped forge, the Court's equal protection analysis lay the basis for modern economic development through the extension of Afro-American civil rights by nationalizing the concept of law in American civic culture.

The story of *Brown* as a postwar legal decision about race begins during the Depression with a set of legal decisions about economics. As discussed in chapter 3, during the early twentieth century, the Court was guided by a body of jurisprudence that emphasized the liberty of contract as a basic right protected by the Fifth and Fourteenth Amendment guarantees of due process of law. As a practical matter, that doctrine, advanced most forcefully by Justice George Sutherland, threatened to undermine at both the state and national levels President Franklin Delano Roosevelt's program of economic regulation.[54] In the wake of President Roosevelt's threat to pack the Court, its approach to economic liberties shifted dramatically in the case of *West Coast Hotel v. Parrish* (1937), which rejected the position Justice Sutherland had taken in *Adkins v. Children's Hospital* (1923).[55] In upholding the constitutionality of a Washington State minimum wage law for women, the Court indicated that it no longer would review such legislation as a probable violation of due process rights, but rather would grant state governments wide power to regulate economic affairs (the shift was emphatically expressed in relation to federal legislation in *NLRB v. Jones and Laughlin Steel Corp.* [1937]). This rejection of economic substantive due process jurisprudence was accompanied by a shift in the Court's interpretation of the scope of Congressional power under the Commerce Clause. Articulated first in *NLRB* and, later, in cases such as *United States v. Darby* (1941) and *Wickard v. Filburn* (1942), the Court's grant of wide regulatory power to the national government formed with the rejection of economic substantive due process a tandem principle underlying the modern liberal regulatory and welfare state.[56]

With the same hand that it shifted its approach to economic affairs, the Court also planted the seed of its postwar analysis of race discrimination. Following quickly after *West Coast Hotel*, the case of *U.S. v. Carolene Products* (1938) concerned the interstate shipment of packages of Milnut, a creamlike product made from a blend of skim milk and coconut oil.[57] Under the Filled Milk Act, Congress had deemed such milk blends injurious to public health and banned their shipment across state lines. The question in *Carolene Products* was whether Congress possessed the authority to issue the ban. Though the question would have been answered in the negative before 1937, the act was now clearly constitutional, and in so deciding, the Court relied on the post-*Lochner* principle that social and economic legislation was to be upheld unless "it is of such a character as to preclude the assumption that it rests upon some rational basis"—a lenient standard of review that gave broad power to legislators.[58] Fatefully, in discussing governmental authority for the Filled Milk

Act, some members of the Court also considered a basic issue left open by the Court's recent decisions on economic affairs, namely under what circumstances it would be appropriate for a Court now generally deferential to lawmakers to overturn state and federal legislation as unconstitutional. A plurality of the Court addressed the issue in what has become the most celebrated footnote in American public law, footnote four.[59] There, Justice Harlan Fiske Stone, joined by Justices Charles Evans Hughes, Owen Roberts, and Louis D. Brandeis, enumerated instances in which the rational basis standard of review would be inadequate and the Court might examine with a higher degree of suspicion legislation enacted by democratic majorities. One such instance, wrote Justice Stone, might arise when laws affected "discrete and insular minorities," marginal, well-defined minority groups generally unprotected by the democratic political process.

The position that the Court should examine with particular care laws affecting discrete and insular minorities, first expressed in footnote four of *Carolene Products*, would lead the Court later to articulate the principle that laws classifying individuals on the basis of race should be examined under the high constitutional standard known as "strict scrutiny." The origin in New Deal jurisprudence of this central tenet of the Court's modern analysis of race discrimination, the constitutional spirit that also animates *Brown*, reveals one important link between the status of *Brown* as a case concerning racial injustice and the economic and nationalizing agenda of the Roosevelt administration, the liberal projects of racial integration and economic modernization. In addition, it was Justice Stone's conception of the Court's heightened, active role when examining legislation classifying individuals by race that ultimately led the Court to embrace a vision of self and society analogous to that expressed by Myrdal in *An American Dilemma* and implicitly to absorb a psychological approach to the culture concept into modern constitutional law. The transformation of the Court's due process and Commerce Clause jurisprudence, that is, formed the historical ground on which modernizing economic regulation, racial equalitarianism, and the postwar psychological turn in American social policy came together. This connection was present in *An American Dilemma* through its analysis of a socio-legal contradiction: that between the American Creed and white treatment of blacks, which generated white psychological pathology and black economic underdevelopment, both of which were to be resolved, in part, through a greater identification of the self with the apparatus of the modern state. In *Brown*, the Court's modernizing approach to the self also occurred within the context of a socio-legal contradiction, that present in state laws that classified individuals according to race but also were facially symmetrical between whites and blacks, laws that despite their facial demand for equality were held by definition to violate principles of equal protection.

To understand why, it is necessary to turn back to the decision that *Brown* commonly is said to have overruled, the 1896 case of *Plessy v. Ferguson*.[60] With the retreat from Reconstruction in the 1870s, the personal freedom of blacks in the South increasingly was restricted by state and local governments. Among the most symbolically significant of these new limitations was the establishment of separate facilities for blacks and whites in public transportation. Predictably, it was in racially diverse New Orleans that a group of Creoles and blacks organized to test the constitutionality of one such law, which required "equal but separate" cars on railroads traveling intrastate. Their case involved Homer Plessy, an "octoroon" who boarded the East Louisiana Railroad, sat in a car set aside for whites, and was arrested when he refused to leave. Plessy brought suit, asserting that the law violated the Fourteenth Amendment guarantee of equal protection. The challenge raised a special problem within constitutional jurisprudence. While the Court earlier had made clear that statutes would violate the Fourteenth Amendment if they directly discriminated against a particular race by imposing a burden on it, for instance barring blacks from jury service, it now faced laws that required physical segregation by race but were facially symmetrical, merely separating the races without explicitly imposing a burden on either (as they would have if, for instance, they had excluded blacks from trains altogether). Did such facially symmetrical statutes nevertheless violate the constitutional principle of equal protection? The Court answered, famously, in the negative, establishing what came to be known as the separate-but-equal doctrine. Nothing in the Louisiana law itself, the Court asserted, demanded racial inequality, nor on its face did the law "stamp . . . the colored race with a badge of inferiority," as Plessy had claimed. Instead, the law treated whites and blacks equally. If blacks felt the Jim Crow law to be injurious, the Court asserted, it was not "by reason of anything found in the act" itself, but simply because "the colored race chooses to put that construction upon it," a purely subjective reaction that hardly could be taken into account in constitutional decision-making.[61]

Today, as a result of *Brown*, the constitutional principle perched atop this implicitly psychological assertion is viewed as the essence of legal self-contradiction. "[T]he very term separate-but-equal," writes one prominent constitutional scholar, "is internally inconsistent."[62] The Court's move toward this view began in the 1930s, when the National Association for the Advancement of Colored People began a campaign to undermine Jim Crow by challenging the application of the separate-but-equal doctrine to public education. Seeking to make Jim Crow if not unlawful then at least too expensive, these "equalization suits" sought to force states with Jim Crow education to live up to the educational equality that the separate-but-equal doctrine demanded in theory by equalizing the material resources between white and black schools. These suits gradually whittled away at the principle of *Plessy* by making it increasingly difficult for defendants to prove as a factual matter that racially segregated schools had truly equal facilities and by removing any means by which lawmakers could escape the requirement of actually providing for black education in the same geographic region in which they provided education for whites (for instance, by paying the tuition for black students to attend graduate school outside a given state). The suits also eventually opened the door for the direct attack on the separate-but-equal doctrine in *Brown*, supported by the Court's citation of environmentalist social science in footnote eleven and its implicit reliance on a model of self and society parallel to that of the culture-and-personality school. Specifically, in *Sweatt v. Painter* (1950) and a companion case, *McLaurin v. Oklahoma State Regents* (1950), the Court ruled that a black applicant had been denied the equal protection of the laws when he was refused admission to the University of Texas School of Law though offered an opportunity to attend a law school that Texas had recently created specifically for blacks.[63] In its ruling, the Court stated that even had the facilities in both schools been materially equal, a constitutionally cognizable level of inequality would remain, for the white school, older and more established, necessarily would possess "to a far greater degree those qualities which are incapable of objective measurement but which make for greatness in a law school."[64] These "intangible considerations" included the "reputation of the faculty, experience of the administration, position and influence of the alumni, standing in the community, traditions and prestige."[65]

This doctrinal acknowledgment of "intangible" factors enabled the NAACP to challenge *Plessy* directly in *Brown* and to argue that segregation was per se a violation of the Fourteenth Amendment. The case began as a series of four lawsuits challenging Jim Crow in primary and secondary schools in South Carolina, Virginia, Kansas, and Delaware.[66] Significantly, four of the schools provided facilities and curricula that were largely equal to those of nearby white schools; they were separate, though ostensibly equal. But by extending the intangible doctrine of *Sweat* and *McLaurin*, the NAACP argued that the mere fact of segregation necessarily made the two schools unequal, with the black inferior to the white—and not simply because black Americans were unnecessarily touchy, as had been the implication in *Plessy*, but rather as an objective fact about the world that, in turn, should be reflected in constitutional law.[67] To bring such intangible inequality into sharp relief, NAACP attorney Thurgood Marshall, future Supreme Court justice, sought to show at trial that segregated schools inflicted an actual psychological injury upon his clients and prevented them from learning at their full potential. Here, he relied not only on legal argument, but also on modern social science research, presenting social scientists as expert witnesses at trial and, when the four cases were consolidated as *Brown v. Board of Education* on appeal to the Supreme Court, attaching a "social science statement" to the NAACP appellate brief that spelled out the psychological harm caused by Jim Crow.[68] Many hands went into this statement, at once celebrated and notorious, but one man in particular became associated most closely with its argument, Kenneth B. Clark, whose doll studies were to become an icon of the *Brown* decision itself.

Like Myrdal in *An American Dilemma*, for which he had provided scholarly assistance, Clark had academic roots that blended the Boasian intellectual tradition with liberal policymaking and state building. After graduating from Howard University in 1931, Clark chose to pursue graduate studies so that he could become part of a developing area of work in psychology exemplified by one of Boas's students. Determining that he "wanted to go into the field that Otto Klineberg was in," he enrolled at Columbia University in 1938, studying under Klineberg himself and, at the same time, consciously seeking to emulate another scholar he deeply admired, Ruth Benedict.[69] The place within the liberal policy consensus of the work Clark pursued at Columbia is evident in one of the early organizational settings in which it was presented, and which served as the publisher or the subject of the first two works the Court cited in footnote eleven, the Midcentury White House Conference on Children and Youth.[70] The fifth in a series of theme-oriented meetings about the young inaugurated in 1909 by Theodore Roosevelt, the 1950 conference was to consider the status of youth in the postwar era by using all of the "outstanding advances in the last 50 years" in the social sciences, particularly "the developments in the field of human behavior and the relationship of people to each other and to their environment."[71] The theme of this "truly Midcentury Conference," begun as "individual happiness and responsible citizenship," was later changed simply to "the healthy personality," focusing attention on issues of social adjustment and suggesting that to be a happy and responsible citizen was itself to be fully robust in psychological being.[72] "What we desire in these days of strain and crisis," wrote the organizers in their post-Conference report, "is that young people shall have both [happiness and civic responsibility], so that, among other things, they may produce a social order in which the chance for happiness will be greatly improved. . . . For it is the thesis of this [conference] that by putting to use what is currently known about conditions favoring or obstructing the healthy development of personality we can rear a generation of happy, responsible individuals who will be better able to 'take' modern life." "Quite aside from the individual, humanitarian aspects" of the issue, continued the organizers, society "now more than ever stands in need of efficient workers, clear thinkers, loyal citizens, who are strong enough to protect its way of life."[73]

The first two academic works the Court would cite in footnote eleven of *Brown* began as a report assigned to Clark by the conference session on racial discrimination in youth.[74] Titled "Effect of Prejudice and Discrimination on Personality Development," the report drew on studies that Clark and his wife, Mamie Phipps Clark, had conducted beginning in 1939 to determine the effect of racism on the self-concept of black children. These studies relied on projective tests, a scientific tool central to the culture-and-personality school, in which an ambiguous stimulus is presented to a test subject, whose recorded reactions are by definition subjective, thereby offering a window onto the symbolic patterns an individual has incorporated from its culture.[75] In their work, Clark showed black children two dolls, one brown, the other white.[76] He then asked the children a series of questions that led them into an American psychological dilemma. First, they were asked to show Clark the "nice" doll; then, to point out the doll that looked "bad"; then, they were asked to indicate the dolls that looked "like a white child" and "like a colored child"— and, finally, to point out the doll that "looks like you." With this final question, the children were thrown into a deep psychological conflict, for pointing out the doll that looked like them would be, at that point, a self-reproach. The reaction of the children was heartbreaking, and sometimes they became completely distraught. From these studies, Clark drew a conclusion that he presented to the Midcentury Conference and that also became part of liberal American common wisdom: that segregation led to a "basic confusion" in black self-image and diminished black self-esteem.[77] For Clark, as for Myrdal, a self-contradiction within the law, the institution of Jim Crow, registered as an injury within the self; like Myrdal's white Americans, Clark's children did not fully know themselves as themselves.[78] It was this psychological self-contradiction that the Court in *Brown* would heal through its rejection of the doctrine of separate-but-equal.

To do so, the Court would need not only to reevaluate past constitutional doctrine, in the course of which it would cite Clark's work for the Midcentury White House Conference, but also to consolidate its own institutional authority. In this effort, the opinion of the Court reflected in both argument and form the judicial approach of its Chief Justice, Earl Warren. A Californian, Warren was born in Los Angeles in 1891 to a Norwegian immigrant father, and he attended both the University of California-Berkeley and Boalt Hall School of Law. He came to the Court after a career in politics that culminated in his election as governor of California in 1942. Assuming the office of Chief Justice after Chief Justice Fred Vinson died of a heart attack in 1953, Warren brought his political skills to the Court when they were most needed. For while most members of the Court appeared essentially sympathetic to the goals of the NAACP, their support of its legal claim was by no means certain or straightforward. Chief Justice Vinson, for instance, had been troubled by the break with long-established precedent that would be required to declare that segregation in public schools was in itself a violation of the Fourteenth Amendment. Justice Stanley Reed actively favored sustaining *Plessy*. And most of the Justices were concerned with the nature of the injunctive relief they might grant in the event the Court declared Jim Crow education unconstitutional; a demand that Jim Crow schools be dismantled immediately might be ignored or resisted in the South, leading to a constitutional crisis in which the Court's public legitimacy and power would be greatly eroded. A skilled negotiator and politician, Justice Warren understood that such resistance would be encouraged if the Court were itself disunited. Summoning his abilities as a persuader and negotiator, he convinced Justice Robert Jackson not to write a planned separate concurrence, and after much argument, he persuaded Justice Reed not to file a lone dissent, promising in exchange that desegregation would occur at a measured pace.

The unanimous opinion that the Court issued on May 17, 1954 also reflected the link characteristic of the jurisprudence of the Warren Court, and of postwar liberalism generally, between a thick conception of national identity and an abiding concern for the subjective life of the solitary individual citizen. Although as attorney general in California, Warren supported the wartime removal of Japanese to relocation camps, while on the Court he famously presided over a marked extension of individual rights, inaugurating a new era of noneconomic substantive due process jurisprudence. That fundamental concern for the self lay at the heart of *Brown*, resting at the same time on an equally powerful interest in strengthening a common national civic identity. The first section of the opinion examines whether the drafters of the Fourteenth Amendment intended its provisions to apply to public education, and generally the extent to which the historical record cast light on the challenge to the separate-but-equal doctrine. Although the question of original intent was of basic interest, and substantial argument had been devoted to the issue in the course of the *Brown* litigation, the research of Justice Felix Frankfurter's clerk Alexander Bickel had convinced the Justices that historical investigation of original intent was "not enough to resolve the problem with which we are faced."[79] The historical record of the Fourteenth Amendment proved "inconclusive" on the matter.[80] In the second section of its opinion, therefore, the Court turned to an issue that could provide interpretive guidance in the absence of historical clarity: the status of public education in the United States as an agent of individual achievement and socio-political coherence. Calling education "perhaps the most important function of state and local governments," and recognizing its "importance . . . to our democratic society," the Court noted that education was "the very foundation of good citizenship." Required "in the performance of our most basic public responsibilities, even service in the armed forces," education prepared children for "later professional training," helped them "adjust normally to [their] environment," and played a central part in the inculcation of "cultural values" (the first time the phrase had been used in a published state or federal court decision).[81] It was the foundation of "succe[ss] in life," the Court asserted, and "where the state has undertaken to provide it, is a right which must be made available to all on equal terms."[82]

Could such an important, nationalizing cultural process be provided on equal terms to whites and blacks under the conditions of Jim Crow, even if the facilities provided to the races were materially the same? In answering that question, in the third section of its opinion, the Court turned to the self and the way it mirrored its socio-legal environment. Citing its opinions in *Sweatt* and *McLaurin*, the Court noted that whether racially separate educational institutions were equal depended not simply on tangible factors, such as material facilities and curricula, but also on "intangible considerations." Those considerations, the Court argued, included the psychological effect on black children of the fact of separation itself, especially "when it has the sanction of the law." Racial separation as sanctioned by the separate-but-equal doctrine, the Court asserted, in its one rhetorical flight, "generates a feeling of inferiority as to their status in the community that may affect their hearts and minds in a way unlikely ever to be undone."[83] That sense of inferiority, that racial self-hatred, in turn, decreased the motivation of black children to learn, retarded their "educational and mental development," and so "deprive[d] [black children] of some of the benefits they would receive in a racially integrated school system." By definition, then, as the NAACP had claimed, segregation was itself a violation of the Fourteenth Amendment. "Separate educational facilities," the Court announced, "are inherently unequal."[84] It was in the context of this argument about law and black subjectivity that the Court contradicted what it called the "psychological knowledge" available at the time of *Plessy* by citing the modern social scientific research of footnote eleven, including *An American Dilemma* and the Mid-century White House Conference studies of Kenneth Clark.[85] In conference, Warren had indicated that a hereditarian ideology of racial hierarchy was a thing of the past, and the social science in footnote eleven confirmed that point.[86] But citation of the work also reaffirmed the point about law, self, and society that the Court already had argued as a matter of constitutional law: that the "inherent" contradiction of the separate-but-equal doctrine registered as a split within the black psyche, within the "hearts and minds" of Negro children, who were embedded within a network of institutions dedicated to national progress and cultural coherence.

That pattern was central to the modern liberal program of which *Brown* itself was to become a symbol, and its cultural force drew on the same simultaneous break with and extension of the social and political past with which liberalism defines our own historical moment. The historic departure of *Brown* sounds most deeply in the field of juridical racialism. For in healing the nation by bringing the inherent contradiction of separate-but-equal to an end, the decision announced through the constitutive language of constitutionalism the nationalization of the concept of law as an element of the modern boundaries of citizenship. And in doing so through a recognition of the way in which jurisprudential ideals defined racial identity within the world of Jim Crow, and speaking with the psychological inflection that the Boasian tradition impressed upon modern civic discourse, the decision was animated by juridical-racial principles at the same time that it brought the juridical-racial tradition largely to an end. Nevertheless, as with the previous developments within the juridical-racial tradition, from the mid-nineteenth century forward, this closing transformation furthered the same historical processes juridical racialism served and from which, indeed, it first arose. The continuation of those processes, and at times their attainment of a particularly high degree of efficiency, was evident in the immediate and lasting sociolegal wake of 1954. For in dismantling the world of separate-but-equal, healing the nation and the black self at once, the decision in *Brown* came to require the ongoing, intimate assertion of federal power over individuals and local governments in a process of nationalization and state development underscored by *Brown v. Board of Education II* (1955) but rooted ultimately in the Civil War.[87] That assertion of national power, moreover, not only brought about the moral and political transformation of American society, but also furthered its commercial growth. Thus, tellingly, the moral and economic programs of modern liberalism were fused yet again in the jurisprudential grounding of federal anti-discrimination law, which put the spirit of *Brown* into statutory form: the power of Congress to enact those laws, whose constitutionality was upheld in *Heart of Atlanta Motel* (1964) and *Katzenbach v. McClung* (1964), was justified in terms of its authority to regulate interstate commerce.[88] In this, the story of *Brown* traced some of the same civic patterns earlier sketched by *Kagama* and the Dawes General Allotment Act—and in breaking with the past through a new structure of juridical-racial thought, *Brown* and the movement it helped foster were part of an ongoing American story of citizenship, state power, and economic development.

Conclusion

The opinion of the Court in *Brown v. Board of Education* effectively signaled the end of the juridical-racial tradition in American cultural history. With its reinterpretation of the meaning of the Fourteenth Amendment, the Court established new terms for the civic inclusion of racial minorities in American constitutional law and facilitated a thoroughgoing change in popular racial thought, ferrying the United States to an era that I have described elsewhere as one "after caste."[1] The closing of the juridical-racial tradition had both specific and far-reaching sources. Most immediately, its roots traced to the intellectual transformation of anthropology, whose institutional emergence in the previous century had marked the birth of juridical racialism as a discourse distinct from ethno-legal thought. The establishment of the modern concept of culture as one of the main tenets of the field changed the way human difference was understood and so also the way the relation between race and law could be discussed in public life and implicitly used as a guide in judicial decision-making. The culture concept shattered juridical racialism's intellectual structure. In addition, it should be noted, by drawing scholarly attention to symbolic themes running throughout and unifying social experience, the culture concept established the very basis for understanding juridical racialism. The same intellectual change that brought the tradition of juridical racialism to a close also provided the academic perspective and interpretive tools for comprehending and studying its history. This study, accordingly, has explored its subject by highlighting rhetorical homologies between judicial doctrine and the work of anthropologists, revealing photographic cross-sections of patterned ideas, mapping the territory of American civic belonging through a culturalist view of the past.

Where the intellectual transformation of anthropology provided the specific mechanism for the passing of the tradition of juridical racialism, its first source lay in the broad historical process the tradition furthered, that of economic and state development. The same trajectory of commercial growth and increased national administrative capacities that was advanced through the juridical-racial vision of citizenship in the late-nineteenth and early-twentieth centuries, and which rested on parallel conceptions and practices of the self, in turn prompted the dismantling of that racial civic vision as the twentieth century rounded its midpoint. This book thus has followed the course of a history in which law, social science, and the self were linked on the field of economic and state modernization. In chapter 1, I suggested how legal decisions animated by a form of juridical-racial vision resonant with evolutionary anthropology restricted American Indian civic membership and, by expanding federal power over native affairs, constitutionally enabled the later mass redistribution of tribal lands. In chapter 2, I explored how judicial opinions whose jurisprudence paralleled the principles of the Teutonic origins thesis of American government limited Puerto Rican and Filipino national belonging and facilitated access to overseas markets by establishing the constitutional doctrine of territorial incorporation. In chapter 3, I considered how legal cases resting on principles of the contracting self central to both eugenicist thought and natural law jurisprudence closed the door on Asian immigration and naturalization by advancing or reasserting federal plenary immigration authority, thereby helping to stabilize domestic labor in the West. And in chapter 4, I examined how a vision of law, culture, and the self paralleling that of the Boasian school of anthropology underlay the logic of *Brown v. Board of Education*, which expanded the power of American national government over the states and, in consequence, released the economic energies stifled by Jim Crow.

This is not to say that ethno-legal principles are never invoked today in public discourse. As Adda Bozeman explained many years ago in *The Future of Law in a Multicultural World* (1971), the peoples of the globe are divided by fundamentally contrasting visions of the nature of law, with Occidental systems of legality standing in basic, perhaps irreconcilable contrast to those of Oriental, African, and Islamic societies.[2] Given these actual jurisprudential differences, it would be surprising if at least some Americans did not continue to describe social groups in terms of their capacity or incapacity for legal behavior, as peoples with or without law (public concerns about the association of black Americans with lawlessness also continue to place limits on their full civic assimilation).[3]

Such depictions of ethno-legal character have assumed a special salience in debates over the exercise of American military power in the Islamic world, particularly in Iraq and Afghanistan, with doubts expressed as to the appropriateness of extending Western notions of individual human rights and democratic governance to societies said to be unprepared for them; these concerns have been evident especially among liberals, inheritors of the group-based thinking central to earlier periods of American state development. Ethno-legalism of this kind notably also has found some academic sustenance from the political culture debate in political science and its complex explanation of differential group capacities for the liberal rule of law.[4] But the field lacks deep cultural authority of the kind that long bound legal and anthropological thought so closely together; moreover, public concerns about the absence of group legal capacity in the international arena have been associated most powerfully with a strain of isolationism opposed to the liberal state-building with which juridical racialism was intertwined as a principle of state rationality. In contrast to the nineteenth and early-twentieth centuries, today the strain of ethno-legalism present in public political debate is an ideological pole away from which nearly every economically globalizing, militarily expansive trend in American power is directed.

In the place of juridical racialism, American concepts of law and civic life have been linked less to anthropology or historical political science than to the academic field with the most powerful influence in American public life today, economics. For the closing of the juridical-racial tradition with *Brown v. Board of Education* in turn opened a cultural space for the ascendancy of the brand of legal economic thought whose tendency toward market liberalization has become the central contemporary paradigm for conceiving of the nation and its citizens, as well as a basic feature of the proclaimed importance of securing liberal rights overseas. It will take many years to tell what this new legal and civic language, formed through the coupling of law and the reigning social scientific discipline of our own time, will hold for the shape of the American nation and its dependencies. Surely its full understanding will be possible only after another fundamental shift in social thought displaces economics itself from its preeminent social position, just as culture once displaced race as an explanatory scholarly principle. In the meantime, one can only wait and watch the next stage in the unfolding drama of development in which the American state and its evolving concept of law will continue to play their united part.

Notes

INTRODUCTION

1. Ludwig Wittgenstein, *Philosophical Investigations*, trans. G. E. M. Anscombe (Oxford: Basil Blackwell, 1958), 8e.

2. The most significant of the *Insular Cases*, which include approximately twenty-three separate decisions not grouped under a single citation, are *DeLima v. Bidwell*, 182 U.S. 1 (1901), *Downes v. Bidwell*, 182 U.S. 244 (1901), the subject of my discussion, *Hawaii v. Mankichi*, 190 U.S. 197 (1903), and *Dorr v. United States*, 195 U.S. 138 (1904).

3. Madison Grant, *The Passing of the Great Race; or, The Racial Basis of European History* (New York: C. Scribner, 1916); *Takao Ozawa v. United States*, 260 U.S. 178 (1922).

4. Gunnar Myrdal, *An American Dilemma: The Negro Problem and Modern Democracy*, 2 vols., intro. Sissela Bok (New Brunswick: Transaction Publishers, 1996 [1944]); *Brown v. Board of Education*, 347 U.S. 483 (1954).

5. Karl Marx, *Capital: A Critique of Political Economy*, trans. Ben Fowkes (New York: Vintage Books, 1977), vol. 1, p. 873–940.

6. Peter Fitzpatrick, *The Mythology of Modern Law* (London: Routledge, 1992), 140.

7. Fitzpatrick, *Mythology of Modern Law*, 140. See also, generally, Michel Foucault, *The Foucault Effect: Studies in Governmentality*, ed. Graham Burchell et al. (Chicago: The University of Chicago Press, 1991).

8. Benedict R. O'G. Anderson, *Imagined Communities: Reflections on the Origin and Spread of Nationalism* (London: Verso, 1983).

9. Rogers M. Smith, *Civic Ideals: Conflicting Visions of Citizenship in U.S. History* (New Haven: Yale University Press, 1997) and *Stories of Peoplehood: The Politics and Morals of Political Membership* (New York: Cambridge University Press, 2003).

10. Fredric Jameson, *The Political Unconscious: Narrative as a Socially Symbolic Act* (Ithaca: Cornell University Press, 1981), 87–88. On the concept of mythemes, from which Jameson's analysis derives, see Claude Lévi-Strauss, *The View from Afar*, trans. Joachim Neugroschel and Phoebe Hoss (New York: Basic Books, 1985), 144–47.

11. Major works in the political science literature, which has been a traditional locus of studies of citizenship, include Kenneth L. Karst, *Belonging to America: Equal Citizenship and the Constitution* (New Haven: Yale University Press, 1989); James H. Kettner, *The Development of American Citizenship, 1608–1870* (Chapel Hill: University of North Carolina Press, 1978); Will Kymlicka, *Multicultural Citizenship: A Liberal Theory of Minority Rights* (Oxford: Clarendon Press, 1995); Martha Minow, *Making All the Difference: Inclusion, Exclusion, and American Law* (Ithaca: Cornell University Press, 1990); Judith N. Sklar, *American Citizenship: The Quest for Inclusion* (Cambridge: Harvard University Press, 1991); and Smith, *Civic Ideals.*

12. David A. Hollinger, *Postethnic America: Beyond Multiculturalism* (New York: Basic Books, 1995), 9.

13. Edmund S. Morgan, *American Slavery, American Freedom: The Ordeal of Colonial Virginia* (New York: Norton, 1975).

14. David A. Hollinger, "How Wide the Circle of 'We'? American Intellectuals and the Problem of the Ethnos since World War II," *American Historical Review* 98 (2) (April 1993): 317–37.

15. The term itself draws on the formulation "juridical nationalism," Donald R. Kelley, "History, English Law and the Renaissance," chapter 11 in *History, Law and the Human Sciences* (London: Variorum Reprints, 1984), 25, citing Vittorio de Capariis, *Propaganda e pensiero politico in Francia durante le guerre di religione* (Naples, 1959), 261, and Vincenzo Piano Mortari, *Diritto romano e diritto nazionale in Francia nel secolo XVI* (Milan, 1962), 79. On "[t]he ability of law and the ideology of legality to express and represent the nation state," see also Paul Gilroy, *'There Ain't No Black in the Union Jack': The Cultural Politics of Race and Nation* (London: Hutchinson, 1987), 74. On the mutually constitutive theory of law, see Christine Harrington, "Moving from Integrative to Constitutive Theories of Law," *Law & Society Review* 22 (1988): 963–68; John Brigham and Christine Harrington, "Realism and Its Consequences: An Inquiry into Contemporary Socio-Legal Research, *International Journal of the Sociology of Law* 17 (1989): 41–62; and John Brigham, *The Constitution of Interests: Beyond the Politics of Rights* (New York: New York University Press, 1996).

16. On Durkheim, see Roger Cotterrell, *Émile Durkheim: Law in a Moral Domain* (Stanford: Stanford University Press, 1999).

17. For a more extended discussion of the history and significance of the concept of a "people of law," see Mark S. Weiner, *Black Trials: Citizenship from the Beginnings of Slavery to the End of Caste* (New York: Alfred A. Knopf, 2004), 9–13.

18. Max Horkheimer and Theodor W. Adorno, *Dialectic of Enlightenment*, trans. John Cumming (New York: Continuum, 1993 [1944]), 64–69.

19. Maureen Cain and Carol Smart, summarizing Fitzpatrick's argument in their "Series Editors' Preface" to Fitzpatrick, *Mythology*, xiii.

20. Fitzpatrick, *Mythology*, 45, 73, 75–76, citing Thomas Hobbes, *Leviathan* (Chicago: Encyclopaedia Britannica, 1952), 87–88.

21. John Locke, *Two Treatises of Government*, ed. and intro. Peter Laslett (Cambridge: Cambridge University Press, 1988), II: 49, p. 319; see also Michel de Montaigne, "Of Cannibals," *The Essays of Michel de Montaigne*, trans. and ed. Jacob Zeitlin (New York: Alfred A. Knopf, 1934), vol. 1, p. 178–90.

22. For a discussion of *bricolage*, a term that has no English equivalent but that generally denotes creating from whatever materials are at hand, see Marcel Hénaff, *Claude Lévi-Strauss and the Making of Structural Anthropology*, trans. Mary Baker (Minneapolis: University of Minnesota Press, 1998), 144–47.

23. See Talcott Parsons, *The System of Modern Societies* (Englewood Cliffs: Prentice Hall, 1971).

24. On the development of anthropology from history and the general social sciences, see Fred W. Voget, *A History of Ethnology* (New York: Holt, Rinehart and Winston, 1975), 114–64, and the work of George W. Stocking, Jr., cited below in n. 26.

25. Raymond Williams, "Culture," *Keywords: A Vocabulary of Culture and Society* (New York: Oxford University Press, 1983), 87–93.

26. On Tylor and Arnold, see George W. Stocking, Jr., "Matthew Arnold, E. B. Tylor, and the Uses of Invention" and "'Cultural Darwinism' and 'Philosophical Idealism' in E. B. Tylor," *Race, Culture and Evolution: Essays in the History of Anthropology* (Chicago: The University of Chicago Press, 1968), 69–90, 91–109.

27. Matthew Arnold, *Culture and Anarchy and Other Writings*, ed. Stefan Collini (Cambridge: Cambridge University Press, 1993), 61, 190.

28. Edward B. Tylor, *Primitive Culture: Researches into the Development of Mythology, Philosophy, Religion, Art, and Custom* (London: J. Murray, 1871), vol. 1, p. 1.

29. Carolus Linnaeus, *Systema Naturae* (Lyons, 1735). On Linnaeus, see Gunnar Broberg, "Homo sapiens: Linnaeus's Classification of Man," in Tore Frängsmyr, ed., *Linnaeus: The Man and His Work* (Berkeley: University of California Press, 1983), 156–94. In the Linnaean scheme, notably, races were differentiated in part by their system of governance: *Homo Asiaticus* as governed by caprice; *Homo Americanus* as regulated by custom; *Homo Afer* as driven by passion; and *Homo Europaeus* as ruled by law. On Blumenbach, see *The Anthropological Treatises of Johann Friedrich Blumenbach*, ed. and trans. Thomas Bendyshe et. al., (London: Longman, Green, Roberts, and Green, 1865).

30. On race, see, generally, Thomas F. Gossett, *Race: The History of an Idea in America*, New Edition (New York: Oxford University Press, 1997). For discussions of race and anthropology, see Elazar Barkan, *The Retreat from Scientific Racism: Changing Concepts of Race in Britain and the United States Between the World Wars* (Cambridge: Cambridge University Press, 1992); Carl N.

Degler, *In Search of Human Nature: The Decline and Revival of Darwinism in American Social Thought* (New York: Oxford University Press, 1991); Audrey Smedley, *Race in North America: Origin and Evolution of a Worldview* (Boulder: Westview Press, 1993); William Ragan Stanton, *The Leopard's Spots: Scientific Attitudes Toward Race in America, 1815–59* (Chicago: The University of Chicago Press, 1960); and Vernon J. Williams, Jr., *Rethinking Race: Franz Boas and His Contemporaries* (Lexington: The University Press of Kentucky, 1996).

31. Clifford Geertz, "The Impact of the Concept of Culture on the Concept of Man," and "The Growth of Culture and the Evolution of Mind," *The Interpretation of Cultures: Selected Essays* (New York: Basic Books, 1973), 33–54, 55–83.

32. On the Boasian culture concept, see George W. Stocking, Jr., "The Basic Assumptions of Boasian Anthropology," in Franz Boas, *A Franz Boas Reader: The Shaping of American Anthropology, 1883–1911*, ed. George W. Stocking, Jr. (Chicago: The University of Chicago Press, 1974), 1–20.

33. On Boas, see Walter Rochs Goldschmidt, ed., *The Anthropology of Franz Boas: Essays on the Centennial of His Birth* (San Francisco: American Anthropology Association, 1959); Melville J. Herskovits, *Franz Boas: The Science of Man in the Making* (New York: Charles Scribner's Sons, 1953); Marshall Hyatt, *Franz Boas, Social Activist: The Dynamics of Ethnicity* (New York: Greenwood Press, 1990); Stocking, "Franz Boas and the Culture Concept in Historical Perspective," *Race, Culture and Evolution*, 195–233 and "Anthropology as *Kulturkampf*: Science and Politics in the Career of Franz Boas," *The Ethnographer's Magic* (Madison: The University of Wisconsin Press, 1992), 92–113; and Leslie A. White, *The Ethnography and Ethnology of Franz Boas* (Austin: Texas Memorial Museum, 1963).

34. Herskovits, *Franz Boas*, 120–21; Margaret Mead, "The Years as Boas' Left Hand," in Margaret Mead, ed., *An Anthropologist at Work: Writings of Ruth Benedict* (Boston: Houghton Mifflin Company, 1959), 341–55, 355.

35. On the limits of Boas's vision in relation to black Americans, see Stocking, ed., *A Franz Boas Reader*, 308.

36. See Franz Boas, "Changes in Bodily Form of Descendants of Immigrants" [1910], in *Race, Language and Culture* (Chicago: University of Chicago Press, 1982 [1940]), 60–75.

37. On the professionalization of the American social sciences, see, generally, Dorothy Ross, *The Origins of American Social Science* (Cambridge: Cambridge University Press, 1991).

38. Madison Grant, *The Passing of the Great Race; or, The Racial Basis of European History*; Franz Boas, *The Mind of Primitive Man* (New York: The Macmillan Company, 1911). Boas's views on culture changed over time. See Stocking, "Franz Boas and the Culture Concept," *Race, Culture, and Evolution*, 202–3. On debates with Powell, see Stocking, "From Physics to Ethnology,"

Race, Culture, and Evolution, 155 and "Franz Boas and the Culture Concept," *Race, Culture, and Evolution*, 205. On differences with Brinton, see Franz Boas, "Human Faculty as Determined by Race," *Proceedings of the American Association for the Advancement of Science* 43 (1894): 301–27, reprinted in Stocking, ed., *Franz Boas Reader*, 221–42; Daniel G. Brinton, "The Aims of Anthropology," *Proceedings of the American Association for the Advancement of Science* 44 (1895): 1–17; and Franz Boas, "The Limitations of the Comparative Method of Anthropology," *Science*, n.s., 4 (103) (Dec. 18, 1896): 901–908, reprinted in Boas, *Race, Language and Culture*, 270–80.

39. Ruth Benedict, *Patterns of Culture* (Boston: Houghton Mifflin, 1934). See also Ruth Benedict, *Race: Science and Politics*, Revised Edition, with *The Races of Mankind* (New York: Viking Press, 1943). For other Boasian critics of American culture, see Richard Handler, "Boasian Anthropology and the Critique of American Culture," *American Quarterly* 42 (2) (June 1990): 252–73.

40. *Muller v. Oregon*, 208 U.S. 412 (1908). See Alpheus T. Mason, "The Case of the Overworked Laundress," in John A. Garraty, ed., *Quarrels that Have Shaped the Constitution* (New York: Harper & Row, 1975), 176–90. On the Brandeis brief, see, generally, Philippa Strum, *Brandeis: Beyond Progressivism* (Lawrence: University of Kansas Press, 1993), 59–64.

41. *Lochner v. New York*, 198 U.S. 45 (1905).

42. On Brandeis, see Strum, *Brandeis: Beyond Progressivism* and *Louis D. Brandeis: Justice for the People* (Cambridge: Harvard University Press, 1984). See also Leonard Baker, *Brandeis and Frankfurter: A Dual Biography* (New York: Harper & Row, 1984); Thomas K. McCraw, *Prophets of Regulation: Charles Francis Adams, Louis D. Brandeis, James M. Landis, Alfred E. Kahn* (Cambridge: Belknap Press of Harvard University Press, 1984); and Melvin I. Urofsky, *Louis D. Brandeis and the Progressive Tradition* (Boston: Little, Brown, 1981).

43. Strum, *Brandeis: Beyond Progressivism*, 13–14.

44. For criticism, see, e.g., Derrick Bell, *Faces at the Bottom of the Well* (New York: Basic Books, 1992) and *And We Are Not Saved: The Elusive Quest for Racial Justice* (New York: Basic Books, 1987), and Austin Sarat, ed., *Race, Law, and Culture: Reflections on* Brown v. Board of Education (New York: Oxford University Press, 1997). For an example of its centrality, see Owen M. Fiss, *The Troubled Beginnings of the Modern State, 1888–1910* (New York: Macmillan, 1993), 395.

45. For a notable attack, see Ernest van den Haag and Ralph Ross, *The Fabric of Society: An Introduction to the Social Sciences* (New York: Harcourt, Brace and Company, 1957).

46. For a classic approach, see Paul L. Rosen, *The Supreme Court and Social Science* (Urbana: University of Illinois Press, 1972). See also Herbert Hovenkamp, "Social Science and Segregation Before *Brown*," *Duke Law Journal* 3/4

(1985): 624–72 and "Evolutionary Models of Jurisprudence," *Texas Law Review* 64 (1985): 645–85. While Hovenkamp in many respects moves beyond the model of the Brandeis brief in his concern for "bias," his work nevertheless is largely concerned with explicit citations of social science within the law.

47. Peter Goodrich, *Legal Discourse: Studies in Linguistics, Rhetoric, and Legal Analysis* (New York: St. Martin's Press, 1987), 212.

48. Robert W. Gordon, "Introduction: J. Willard Hurst and the Common Law Tradition in American Legal Historiography," *Law & Society Review* (Fall, 1975): 9–55, 10, 11.

49. See, e.g., James Willard Hurst, *The Growth of American Law: The Law Makers* (Boston: Little, Brown, 1950).

50. See Alan Hunt, *Explorations in Law and Society: Towards a Constitutive Theory of Law* (New York: Routledge, 1993). "Contemporary legal theory," asserts Hunt, "is still haunted by the ghost of realism. It arose as the most powerful challenge within Anglo-American legal scholarship to the self-referentiality of legal positivism or analytical jurisprudence. But the question to pose is: did legal realism break with self-referentiality?" (304).

51. Geertz, "Ritual and Social Change: A Javanese Example," *The Interpretation of Cultures*, 142–69, 145. "The nature of the distinction between culture and social system is brought out more clearly," writes Geertz, "when one considers the contrasting sorts of integration characteristic of each of them. This contrast is between what Sorokin has called 'logico-meaningful integration' and what he has called 'causal-functional integration.' By logico-meaningful integration, characteristic of culture, is meant the sort of integration one finds in a Bach fugue, in Catholic dogma, or in the general theory of relativity; it is a unity of style, of logical implication, of meaning and value. By causal-functional integration, characteristic of the social system, is meant the kind of integration one finds in an organism, where all the parts are united in a single causal web; each part is an element in a reverberating causal ring which 'keeps the system going.' And because these two types of integration are not identical, because the particular form one of them takes does not directly imply the form the other will take, there is an inherent incongruity and tension between the two and between them and a third element, the pattern of motivational integration within the individual which we usually call personality structure" (145, citing Pitirim Sorokin, *Social and Cultural Dynamics*, 3 vols. [New York: American Book Company, 1937]).

52. Geertz, "Thick Description: Toward an Interpretive Theory of Culture," *Interpretation of Cultures*, 3–30, 5.

53. E. E. Evans-Pritchard, "Anthropology and History," *Social Anthropology and Other Essays* (New York: Free Press, 1962), 190, "history must choose between being social anthropology or being nothing"; F. W. Maitland, "The Body Politic," *Selected Essays*, ed. H. D. Hazeltine et al. (Cambridge: Cambridge Uni-

versity Press, 1936), 249, "by and by anthropology will have the choice between being history and being nothing."

CHAPTER 1

1. Margaret Mead, "Introduction," in Margaret Mead and Ruth L. Bunzel, eds., *The Golden Age of American Anthropology* (New York: George Braziller, 1960), 1–12, 4–5.

2. On civil service reform, see Stephen Skowronek, *Building a New American State: The Expansion of National Administrative Capacities, 1877–1920* (Cambridge: Cambridge University Press, 1982). See also Ari Arthur Hoogenboom, *Outlawing the Spoils: A History of the Civil Service Reform Movement, 1865–1883* (Urbana: University of Illinois Press, 1968).

3. For a general social and cultural overview, see Alan Trachtenberg, *The Incorporation of America: Culture and Society in the Gilded Age* (New York: Hill and Wang, 1982).

4. On the assimilationist era, see works cited below. The era can be divided into two periods, an initial "idealistic" phase, on which I focus here, and a second period, in which reformers became less sanguine about the possibilities of native assimilation and reflected that skepticism in their legal and political advocacy. See Frederick E. Hoxie, *A Final Promise: The Campaign to Assimilate the Indians, 1880–1920* (Lincoln: University of Nebraska Press, 1984).

5. See Hoxie, *Final Promise*, 62–70. On the BIA, see, generally, Theodore W. Taylor, *The Bureau of Indian Affairs* (Boulder: Westview Press, 1984).

6. See H. Craig Miner, *The Corporation and the Indian: Tribal Sovereignty and Industrial Civilization in Indian Territory, 1865–1907* (Columbia: University of Missouri Press, 1976).

7. General Allotment Act, 24 Stat. 388 (1887). For relevant excerpts, see Francis Paul Prucha, ed., *Documents of United States Indian Policy*, 2nd Edition, Expanded (Lincoln: University of Nebraska Press, 1990), 171–74.

8. *Ex parte Crow Dog*, 109 U.S. 556 (1883); *United States v. Kagama*, 118 U.S. 375 (1886).

9. Henry E. Fritz, *The Movement for Indian Assimilation, 1860–1890* (Philadelphia: University of Pennsylvania Press, 1963), 217 (referring to *Kagama*).

10. On federal policy toward American Indians in the assimilationist era, see Brian W. Dippie, *The Vanishing American: White Attitudes and U.S. Indian Policy* (Middletown: Wesleyan University Press, 1982); Loring Benson Priest, *Uncle Sam's Stepchildren: The Reformation of United States Indian Policy, 1865–1887* (New York: Octagon Books, 1969); and, especially, Francis Paul Prucha, *The Great Father: The United States Government and the American Indians*, vol. 2 (Lincoln: University of Nebraska Press, 1984), 609–757, *Indian Policy in the*

United States: Historical Essays (Lincoln: University of Nebraska Press, 1981), and *American Indian Policy in Crisis: Christian Reformers and the Indian, 1865–1900* (Norman: University of Oklahoma Press, 1976). For brief or general histories, see Robert F. Berkhofer, Jr., *The White Man's Indian: Images of the American Indian from Columbus to the Present* (New York: Vintage, 1978); Frederick E. Hoxie, ed., *Indians in American History: An Introduction* (Arlington Heights: Harlan Davidson, 1988); William T. Hagan, *American Indians* (Chicago: The University of Chicago Press, 1961); and Prucha, *The Great Father*, Abridged Edition (Lincoln: University of Nebraska Press, 1984). A general overview of legal issues can be found in Wilcomb E. Washburn, *Red Man's Land/White Man's Law: A Study of the Past and Present Status of the American Indian*, Second Edition (Norman: University of Oklahoma Press, 1971). On the colonial background to some of the juridical-racial issues discussed here, see Robert A. Williams, Jr., *The American Indian in Western Legal Thought: The Discourses of Conquest* (New York: Oxford University Press, 1990). See also the suggestive comments on Vattel and the law of nations in Roy Harvey Pearce, *The Savages of America: A Study of the Indian and the Idea of Civilization*, Revised Edition (Baltimore: Johns Hopkins University Press, 1965), 70–71, and the remarks on law and conceptions of race and property in William Cronon, *Changes in the Land: Indians, Colonists, and the Ecology of New England* (New York: Hill and Wang, 1983), 63.

11. On the role of the Supreme Court in the Cherokee removal, see Jill Norgren, *The Cherokee Cases: The Confrontation of Law and Politics* (New York: McGraw Hill, 1996).

12. Prucha, *American Indian Policy in Crisis*, 30. For Grant's statement of the peace policy, see the extract from his second annual message to Congress (5 December 1870), reprinted in Prucha, *Documents of United States Indian Policy*, 135.

13. See Francis Paul Prucha, ed., *Americanizing the American Indians: Writings by 'Friends of the Indian,' 1880–1900* (Cambridge: Harvard University Press, 1973).

14. Hoxie, *Final Promise*, ix.

15. Few Americans at the time took up the cause of the "Indians' right to be an Indian." See Prucha, *American Indian Policy in Crisis*, 165–6.

16. See William T. Hagan, *The Indians Rights Association: The Herbert Welsh Years, 1882–1904* (Tucson: University of Arizona Press, 1985); Frederick E. Hoxie, "The Curious Story of Reformers and the American Indians," in Hoxie, ed. *Indians in American History*, 205–28; Robert M. Utley, *The Indian Frontier of the American West, 1846–1890* (Albuquerque: University of New Mexico Press, 1984), 203–26.

17. "Annual Report of the Commissioner of Indian Affairs," in *Report of the Secretary of the Interior* (Washington: Government Printing Office, 1888), vol.

2, p. lxxxix. On Oberly, see Robert M. Kvasnicka and Herman J. Viola, eds., *The Commissioners of Indian Affairs, 1824–1977* (Lincoln: University of Nebraska Press, 1979), 189–91. "But if he will not learn?" continues Oberly, "If he shall continue to persist in saying, 'I am content; let me alone?' Then the Guardian must act for the Ward, and do for him the good service he protests shall not be done—the good service that he denounces as a bad service. The Government must then, in duty to the public, compel the Indian to come out of his isolation into the civilized way that he does not desire to enter—into citizenship—into assimilation with the masses of the Republic—into the path of national duty; and in passing along that path he will find not only pleasure in personal independence and delight in individual effort in his own interest, but also the consummation of that patriotic enjoyment which is always to be found in the exercise of the high privilege of contributing to the general welfare" (lxxxix).

18. On Christian reform and the movement for Indian assimilation, see Robert H. Keller, Jr., *American Protestantism and United States Indian Policy, 1869–82* (Lincoln: University of Nebraska Press, 1983). See also Francis Paul Prucha's study of the differing Protestant and Catholic visions of Indian schooling, a central component of assimilationist policy, *The Churches and the Indian Schools, 1888–1912* (Lincoln: University of Nebraska Press, 1979), and Michael C. Coleman's analysis of missionary rhetoric and the coexistence of radical egalitarianism and cultural intolerance among "cultural revolutionary" Christian missionaries, *Presbyterian Missionary Attitudes toward American Indians, 1837–1893* (Jackson: University Press of Mississippi, 1985). See also, generally, Robert Winston Mardock, *The Reformers and the American Indian* (Columbia: University of Missouri Press, 1971).

19. See Miner, *The Corporation and the Indian*, passim. For other relevant works, see Ira G. Clark, *Then Came the Railroads: The Century from Steam to Diesel in the Southwest* (Norman: University of Oklahoma Press, 1958), 119–30 and the bibliographic essay and works cited in 321–22.

20. See, e.g., Thomas Jefferson, *Notes on the State of Virginia*, ed. William Peden (New York: W. W. Norton, 1982), 92–107. On the roots of Indian policy in the thought and practice of the Jeffersonian period, see Bernard W. Sheehan, *Seeds of Extinction: Jeffersonian Philanthropy and the American Indian* (Chapel Hill: The University of North Carolina Press, 1973).

21. The place of professional anthropology in Indian administration and its use in governmental policy as "applied science" has generated a considerable literature. See, e.g., Huntington Cairns, *Law and the Social Sciences* (New York: Harcourt, Brace and Company, 1935), 7–47, a straightforward account of law and the social sciences generally, with some specific attention paid to anthropology as a discipline; Felix S. Cohen, "Anthropology and the Problems of Indian Administration," *The Southwestern Social Science Quarterly* 18 (2) (1937): 171–80, which looked forward to a coming rapprochement between anthropol-

ogy and Indian administrators; Vine Deloria, Jr., "Anthropologists and Other Friends," *Custer Died for Your Sins: An Indian Manifesto* (New York: Avon, 1969), 78–100, which contains a now-classic, scathing account of the relation of anthropologists and their Indian subjects; Edward A. Kennard and Gordon MacGregor, "Applied Anthropology in Government: United States," in A. L. Kroeber, ed., *Anthropology Today: An Encyclopedic Inventory* (Chicago: University of Chicago Press, 1953), 832–40, a discussion of the practical application of anthropology in American government; and Prucha, "Scientific Racism and Indian Policy," *Indian Policy in the United States*, 180–97, which doubts the influence of the American School on earlier, Jacksonian-era Indian administration.

22. Utley, *The Indian Frontier*, 223, 225.

23. See Utley, *The Indian Frontier*, 219–23. For an overview of one important aspect of this legal campaign, see William T. Hagan, *Indian Police and Judges: Experiments in Acculturation and Control* (New Haven: Yale University Press, 1966). For an example of assimilationist-era views of Indian law, see Henry S. Pancoast, *The Indian Before the Law* (Philadelphia: Indian Rights Association, 1884).

24. Carl Schurz, "Annual Report of the Secretary of the Interior," in *Report of the Secretary of the Interior* (Washington: Government Printing Office, 1879), vol. 1, p. 12. "In the last three annual reports of this office urgent appeals have been made for the enactment of laws for Indian reservations," wrote the Commissioner of Indian Affairs Ezra A. Hayt in the same report: "A civilized community could not exist as such without law, and a semi-civilized and barbarous people are in a hopeless state of anarchy without its protection and sanctions. . . . The most intelligent among them ask for the laws of the white man to enable them to show that Indians can understand and respect law" (105–106). Similarly, see "Annual Report of the Secretary of the Interior," in *Report of the Secretary of the Interior* (Washington: Government Printing Office, 1883), vol. 1, p. x–xv.

25. W[illiam] J[ustin] Harsha, "Law for the Indians," *North American Review* 134 (March 1882): 272–92, 272. Harsha takes a critical stance toward Schurz in his analysis.

26. On John Wesley Powell, see William Culp Darrah, *Powell of the Colorado* (Princeton: Princeton University Press, 1951), and Wallace Stegner, *Beyond the Hundredth Meridian: John Wesley Powell and the Second Opening of the West* (Boston: Houghton Mifflin, 1954). See also William C. Darrah, "John Wesley Powell and an Understanding of the West," *Utah Historical Quarterly* 37 (1969): 146–51, and Paul Meadows, *John Wesley Powell: Frontiersman of Science* (Lincoln: University of Nebraska Press, 1952). The collection of John Wesley Powell primary and secondary materials in the Library of Congress and the Museum of Natural History yield little material not readily available in these works.

27. On the connection in Methodism between the patriotic self-sacrifice, organizational discipline, and inner sentimentalism that would characterize Powell's career, see A. Gregory Schneider, "Discipline and the Rhetoric of Separation," *The Way of the Cross Leads Home: The Domestication of American Methodism* (Bloomington: Indiana University Press, 1993), 78–91.

28. Darrah, *Powell of the Colorado*, 47–72.

29. For an example that mirrors Powell's systematizing impulse, see J. G. Barnard and W. F. Barry, *Report of the Engineer and Artillery Operations of the Army of the Potomac* (New York: D. Van Nostrand, 1863). Powell himself was critical of the U.S. Army Corps of Engineers for their "meandering methods." See Todd A. Shallat, *Structures in the Stream: Water, Science, and the Rise of the U.S. Army Corps of Engineers* (Austin: University of Texas Press, 1994), 190.

30. Stegner, *Beyond the Hundredth Meridian*, 17.

31. George M. Fredrickson, *The Inner Civil War: Northern Intellectuals and the Crisis of the Union* (Urbana: University of Illinois Press, 1993 [1965]).

32. Fredrickson, *Inner Civil War*, 211.

33. Oliver Wendell Holmes, Jr., "The Soldier's Faith," in Julius J. Marke, ed., *The Holmes Reader* (New York: Oceana, 1955), 148–56, 150–51.

34. Stegner, *Beyond the Hundredth Meridian*; John Wesley Powell, *The Exploration of the Colorado River and its Canyons* (New York: Dover Publications, 1961 [1895]).

35. See, e.g., illustrations in Powell, *Exploration*, 250, 169.

36. On the USGS, see Thomas G. Manning, *Government in Science: The U.S. Geological Survey, 1867–1894* (Lexington: University of Kentucky Press, 1967). On Powell's work with the USGS, in addition to the writings of Darrah and Stegner cited above, see Thomas G. Alexander, "John Wesley Powell, the Irrigation Survey, and the Inauguration of the Second Phase of Irrigation Development in Utah," *Utah Historical Quarterly* 37 (1969): 190–206; Robert N. Olsen, Jr., "The Powell Survey of the Kanab Base Line," *Utah Historical Quarterly* 37 (1969): 261–68; and Robert Brewster Stanton, *Colorado River Controversies* (New York: Dodd, Mead & Company, 1932). For an example of Powell's work, see his *Report on the Lands of the Arid Region of the United States* (Washington: Government Printing Office, 1878).

37. On BAE history, see Regna Diebold Darnell, "The Development of American Anthropology, 1879–1920: From the Bureau of American Ethnology to Franz Boas" (Doctoral dissertation, University of Pennsylvania, 1969); Regna Darnell, "The Professionalization of American Anthropology: A Case Study in the Sociology of Knowledge," *Social Science Information* 10 (1971): 83–103; Curtis M. Hinsley, Jr., *Savages and Scientists: The Smithsonian Institution and the Development of American Anthropology, 1846–1910* (Washington: Smithsonian Institution Press, 1981) and "Anthropology as Science and Politics: The Dilemma of the Bureau of American Ethnology, 1879 to 1904," in Walter Gold-

schmidt, ed., *The Uses of Anthropology* (Washington: American Anthropological Association, 1979); Neil M. Judd, *The Bureau of American Ethnology: A Partial History* (Norman: University of Oklahoma Press, 1967); and V. Hull McKimmon Noelke, "The Origin and Early History of the Bureau of American Ethnology, 1879–1910" (Doctoral dissertation, University of Texas, Austin, 1974). For Powell's understanding of government science, see John Wesley Powell, *On the Organization of Scientific Work of the General Government* (Washington: Government Printing Office, 1885).

38. John Wesley Powell, "Introductory," *First Annual Report of the Bureau of Ethnology* (Washington: Government Printing Office, 1881), xi–xv, xiv.

39. Darrah, *Powell of the Colorado*, 255–56.

40. See Robert E. Bieder, *Science Encounters the Indian, 1820–1880: The Early Years of American Ethnology* (Norman: University of Oklahoma Press, 1986), 16–54.

41. Darrah, *Powell of the Colorado*, 267; John Wesley Powell, *Introduction to the Study of Indian Languages* (Washington: Government Printing Office, 1877); Fredrick Webb Hodge, ed., *Handbook of American Indians North of Mexico*, Bureau of American Ethnology, Bulletin 30 (Washington: Government Printing Office, 1907–10).

42. A. Irving Hallowell, "The Beginnings of Anthropology in America," in Frederica de Laguna, ed., *Selected Papers from the American Anthropologist, 1888–1920* (Evanston: Row, Peterson and Company, 1960), 1–104, 57.

43. See Powell, *Introduction to the Study of Indian Languages*.

44. J[ohn] W[esley] Powell, *Report on the Methods of Surveying the Public Domain, to the Secretary of the Interior, at the Request of the National Academy of Sciences* (Washington: Government Printing Office, 1878), 15–16. The report was presented to Secretary of the Interior Carl Schurz.

45. For a summary, see Idus L. Murphree, "The Evolutionary Anthropologists: The Progress of Mankind. The Concepts of Progress and Culture in the Thought of John Lubbock, Edward B. Tylor, and Lewis H. Morgan," *Proceedings of the American Philosophical Society* 105 (3) (June 1961): 265–300.

46. John W[esley] Powell, "Darwin's Contributions to Philosophy," *Proceedings of the Biological Society of Washington* 1 (Washington: Smithsonian Institution, 1882): 60–70, 64, italics in original. See also, Powell, "Human Evolution," *Transactions of the Anthropological Society of Washington* 2 (1883): 176–208, and "The Three Methods of Evolution," *Bulletin of the Philosophical Society of Washington* 6 (1884): 27–52. Powell took pains to distinguish human cultural evolution from the biological evolution of animals.

47. Franz Boas, "The Occurrence of Similar Inventions in Areas Widely Apart," *Science* 9 (May 20, 1887): 485–86. See also Franz Boas, "Museums of Ethnology and their Classification," *Science* 9 (228) (June 17, 1887): 587–89

and (June 24, 1887): 614; and Franz Boas, "The Limitations of the Comparative Method of Anthropology," *Science*, n.s., 4 (103) (Dec. 18, 1896): 901–908, reprinted in Franz Boas, *Race, Language and Culture* (Chicago: University of Chicago Press, 1982 [1940]), 270–80. On Powell's response, see John Wesley Powell, "Museums of Ethnology and their Classification," *Science* 9 (229) (June 24, 1887): 612–14. For Mason's views, see O[tis] T. Mason, "The Occurrence of Similar Inventions in Areas Widely Apart," *Science* 9 (226) (June 3, 1887): 534–35. For a review of the debate, see George W. Stocking, Jr., ed., *The Shaping of American Anthropology, 1883–1911: A Franz Boas Reader* (Chicago: University of Chicago Press, 1974), 1–20.

48. See Bieder, *Science Encounters the Indian*, 194–246. On Morgan, see also Carl Resek, *Lewis Henry Morgan, American Scholar* (Chicago: University of Chicago Press, 1960), and Bernhard J. Stern, *Lewis Henry Morgan, Social Evolutionist* (Chicago: University of Chicago Press, 1931). On Morgan, law, and political theory, see Elizabeth Colson, *Tradition and Contract: The Problem of Order* (Chicago: Aldine, 1974).

49. Lewis Henry Morgan, *League of the Ho-dé-no-sau-nee, or Iroquois* (Rochester: Sage and Brother, 1851); *Systems of Consanguinity and Affinity of the Human Family* (Washington: Smithsonian Institution, 1871); *Ancient Society: Researches in the Lines of Human Progress from Savagery through Barbarism to Civilization* (New York: Henry Holt, 1907 [1877]).

50. Friedrich Engels, *The Origin of Family, Private Property, and the State, in Light of the Researches of Lewis H. Morgan*, intro. Eleanor Burke Leacock (New York: International Publishers, 1972).

51. Morgan, *Ancient Society*, vi. On Morgan and the concept of progress, see Murphree, "The Evolutionary Anthropologists," 266–300. For a lively debate on Morgan's relation to doctrines of unilinear evolution, see Robert Heinrich Lowie, "Evolution in Cultural Anthropology: A Reply to Leslie White," *American Anthropologist* 48 (2) (1946): 223–33.

52. The question of the origin of property was a significant one in scholarly debate at the time. See my discussion in chapter 3. For a contemporaneous example, see, e.g., Frederic Seebohm, *The English Village Community Examined in Its Relations to the Manorial and Tribal Systems and to the Common or Open Field System of Husbandry. An Essay in Economic History* (London: Longmans, Green, and Co., 1883).

53. Morgan, *Ancient Society*, 527, 528.

54. Morgan, *Ancient Society*, 531.

55. Morgan, *Ancient Society*, 535.

56. Morgan, *Ancient Society*, 527.

57. Peter Fitzpatrick, *The Mythology of Modern Law* (London: Routledge, 1992).

58. Morgan, *Ancient Society*, 525.

59. For Powell's esteem of Morgan, see John Wesley Powell, "Sketch of Lewis Henry Morgan," *Popular Science Monthly* 18 (1881): 114–21.

60. Stern, *Lewis Henry Morgan*, 193–94: "Since its reading," Powell continued, "I found that I have many facts which fall properly into the system which you have laid out: the bearing of these facts I did not understand before. Had I more fully appreciated your system, I believe I could have given you much additional data. . . . After reading your book, I believe you have discovered the true system of social and governmental organization among the Indians."

61. Bieder, *Science Encounters the Indian*, 243. On aspects of John Wesley Powell's developmentalist anthropological thought, see Don D. Fowler and Catherine S. Fowler, "John Wesley Powell, Anthropologist," *Utah Historical Quarterly* 37 (1969): 152–72.

62. See Harry Gershenowitz, "John Wesley Powell: Staunch Neo-Lamarckian," *Indian Journal of History of Science* 16 (2) (1981): 130–38.

63. For one example, see Paul Starr, *The Social Transformation of American Medicine* (New York: Basic Books, 1982).

64. Major J[ohn] W[esley] Powell, "On Primitive Institutions," *Report of the Nineteenth Annual Meeting of the American Bar Association* 19 (1896): 573–93.

65. John Wesley Powell, "Are Our Indians Becoming Extinct?" *The Forum* 15 (May 1893): 343–54, 352–54.

66. Cited in Hoxie, *Final Promise*, 24. But see Dippie, *The Vanishing American*, 168–71, which argues that Powell was cautious, like other social evolutionists, though also notes that "[o]ccasionally, it seemed as though the social evolutionists wanted to have it both ways" (170).

67. General Allotment Act, 25 U.S.C.A. § 331 (1887). On the Dawes Act and its aftermath, see Leonard A. Carlson, *Indians, Bureaucrats, and Land: The Dawes Act and the Decline of Indian Farming* (Westport: Greenwood Press, 1981); Janet A. McDonnell, *The Dispossession of the American Indian, 1887–1934* (Bloomington: Indiana University Press, 1991); D. S. Otis, *The Dawes Act and the Allotment of Indian Lands*, intro. and ed. Francis Paul Prucha (Norman: University of Oklahoma Press, 1973); and Wilcomb E. Washburn, *The Assault on Indian Tribalism: The General Allotment Law (Dawes Act) of 1887* (Philadelphia: J. B. Lippincott, 1975).

68. Theodore Roosevelt, cited in Bruce Elliott Johansen, ed., *The Encyclopedia of Native American Legal Tradition* (Westport: Greenwood Press, 1998), 16.

69. *Cherokee Nation v. Georgia*, 30 U.S. (5 Pet.) 1 (1831); *Worcester v. Georgia*, 31 U.S. (6 Pet.) 515 (1832).

70. For an example in practice, see John Phillip Reid, "A Right to Vengeance," *The Law of Blood: The Primitive Law of the Cherokee Nation* (New York: New York University Press, 1970), 73–84.

71. "Brief and Argument of Defendant in Error," G. M. Lambertson, 1–18,

18, in "Transcript of Record, Supreme Court of the United States, October Term, 1884, No. 27, Elk v. Wilkins," *U.S. Supreme Court Records and Briefs*, Part IV, 111 U.S. 770–112 U.S. 123 (1884), Reel No. 27, Shelf No. CL-043. The brief continues, quoting Longfellow, "'Every human heart is human / That even in savage bosoms, / There are longings, yearnings, strivings / For the good they comprehend not.'/ / This is a most striking instance of an Indian savage or 'noble red man' striving and yearning 'for the good hecomprehends [*sic*] not.'"

72. James Bradley Thayer, "A People without Law," *Atlantic Monthly* 68 (Oct.-Nov. 1891), 540–51, 676–87. See also James Bradley Thayer, "The Dawes Bill and the Indians," *Atlantic Monthly* 61 (March 1888): 315–22, which raises serious concerns about the Dawes Act vis-à-vis Indian welfare and the power of the federal government. An interesting juridical-racial expression of this view is present in Harsha, "Law for the Indians," which reveals the depth of its juridical-racial vision in the circuity of its argument. Noting that it might be difficult to enforce law among Indians through United States courts because of "prejudice against the red men," Harsha writes, "But if our position is well taken,—that this very prejudice owes its origin to the absence of law,—it might be expected quite rapidly to disappear, now that law would be present. The same complications have been observed to exist in several instances in the past—in the early days of the Anglo-Saxon race, as well as in the case of the black and yellow races in our own land; but as these have disappeared, or give promise of so doing, it needs but the same public sentiment to accomplish a like result for the red man" (275).

73. For an institutional analysis of the Office of Indian Affairs, see Laurence F. Schmeckebier, *The Office of Indian Affairs: Its History, Activities, and Organization* (Baltimore: The Johns Hopkins Press, 1927). For an overview of the BIA from both historical and contemporary perspectives, see Taylor, *Bureau of Indian Affairs*. On those ultimately responsible for BIA administration, and specifically on John D. C. Atkins, commissioner from 1885 to 1888, and Thomas Jefferson Morgan, 1889 to 1893, see Kvasnicka and Viola, eds., *The Commissioners of Indians Affairs*, 181–88, 193–203.

74. "Annual Report of the Secretary of the Interior," in *Report of the Secretary of the Interior* (Washington: Government Printing Office, 1866), 17.

75. See Hagan, *Indian Police and Judges*.

76. *United States v. Clapox*, 35 Fed. Rep. 575 (1888) at 577. The opinion here refers to the courts of Indian offenses, "by which the government of the United States is endeavoring to improve and elevate the condition of these dependent tribes to whom it sustains the relation of guardian." "In fact," the opinion continues, "the reservation itself is in the nature of a school, and the Indians are gathered there, under the charge of an agent, for the purpose of acquiring the habits, ideas, and aspirations which distinguish the civilized from the uncivilized

man," citing *Kagama*. The case later refers to "this laudable effort to accustom and educate these Indians in the habit and knowledge of self-government" (579).

77. See also in this regard Committee on Indian Legislation, *American Bar Association Annual Report* (1893), 351–63, which stresses the importance of property laws and cites Thayer, "A People without Law"; and William B. Hornblower, "The Legal Status of the Indians," *American Bar Association Annual Report* (1891): 261–77, which refers to the "horde of savages," and notes: "As we have already said, that which once was a fact has now become fiction. The Indian nations have become wretched remnants, hanging on the outskirts of civilization, or living on reservations and surrounded by civilized communities and dependent, in whole or in part, for their support upon the Government in whose jurisdiction they reside. Let the fiction be abolished. Let us enact laws suitable for the present situation, and place the legal status of the Indian upon a rational and practical basis" (262, 277).

78. See, generally, Sidney L. Harring, *Crow Dog's Case: American Indian Sovereignty, Tribal Law, and United States Law in the Nineteenth Century* (Cambridge: Cambridge University Press, 1994).

79. For a treatment, see George E. Hyde, *Spotted Tail's Folk: A History of the Brulé Sioux*, New Edition (Norman: University of Oklahoma Press, 1974).

80. The General Crimes Act (Federal Enclaves Act), 18 U.S.C. § 1152 (1817).

81. *United States v. Kan-Gi-Shun-Ca*, "Judgment," in "Petition and Transcript of Record, Ex Parte: In the Matter of Kan-Gi-Shun-Ca, Otherwise Known as Crow Dog, Petitioner," *United States Supreme Court Records and Briefs*, Part 4, 109 U.S. 513–641 (1883), Reel 214, Shelf LL-043, 13.

82. Alexis de Tocqueville, *Democracy in America*, trans. Henry Reeve, rev. Francis Bowen, ed. Phillips Bradley, intro. Daniel J. Boorstin (New York: Vintage, 1990), vol. 1, p. 340, 354–55.

83. 19 Stat. 254–64 (28 February 1877). On the Treaty of 1876, the conditions of duress under which it was signed, and its consequences for Sioux land-holding, see Edward Lazarus, *Black Hills, White Justice: The Sioux Nation versus the United States, 1775 to the Present* (New York: Harper Collins, 1991), 3–149. See also Francis Paul Prucha, *American Indian Treaties: The History of a Political Anomaly* (Berkeley: University of California Press, 1994), 316–18.

84. See Leonard Crow Dog and Richard Erdoes, *Crow Dog: Four Generations of Sioux Medicine Men* (New York: Harper Perennial, 1995).

85. *Marbury v. Madison*, 5 U.S. (1 Cranch) 137 (1803).

86. Louis Filler, "Stanley Matthews," in *The Justices of the United States Supreme Court, 1789–1978: Their Lives and Major Opinions*, eds. Leon Friedman and Fred L. Israel (New York: Chelsea House, 1980), vol. 2, p. 1351–61, 1360. On the juridical-racial views of Presbyterian missionaries, see Coleman, *Presbyterian Missionary Attitudes toward American Indians*, 129–32. "American republican law and institutions possessed something close to divine sanction

for these Presbyterians," writes Coleman, "a secular-religious fusion encapsulated in the vision of the Christian civilization. Obviously Indians possessed no such law before sustained contact with Americans. . . . Indian societies and cultures appeared to lack any law at all" (129–30).

87. The provision stated that "if bad men among the Indians shall commit a wrong or depredation upon the person or property of any one, white, black or Indian, subject to the authority of the United States and at peace therewith, the Indians herein named solemnly agree that they will, upon proof made to their agent and notice by him, deliver up the wrong-doer to the United States, to be tried and punished according to its laws" (cited in *Crow Dog*, 109 U.S. at 567). "But it is quite clear from the context," wrote Justice Matthews, "that this does not cover the present case of an alleged wrong committed by one Indian upon the person of another of the same tribe" (*Crow Dog*, 109 U.S. at 567).

88. *Crow Dog*, 109 U.S. at 568–9.

89. *Crow Dog*, 109 U.S. at 571.

90. See, e.g., "Report of the Commissioner of Indian Affairs," in *Report of the Secretary of the Interior* (Washington: Government Printing Office, 1884), 10–12, which cites other examples of legal disorder and writes, "The average Indian may not be ready for the more complex questions of civil law, but he is sufficiently capable to discriminate between right and wrong, and should be taught by the white man's law to respect the persons and property of his race" (11).

91. *Congressional Record*, 48th Congress, 2nd Session (Jan. 22, 1885), 934. "I do not believe we shall ever succeed in civilizing the Indian race," argued Cutcheon, "until we teach them regard for law, and show them that they are not only responsible to the law, but amenable to its penalties."

92. Major Crimes Act, § 9, 23 U.S.C. 385 (1885), cited in Prucha, ed., *Documents of United States Indian Policy*, 168: "[I]mmediately upon and after the date of the passage of this act all Indians, committing against the person or property of another Indian or other person any of the following crimes, namely, murder, manslaughter, rape, assault with intent to kill, arson, burglary, and larceny within any Territory of the United States, and either within or without an Indian reservation, shall be subject therefor to the laws of such Territory relating to said crimes, and shall be tried therefor in the same courts and in the same manner and shall be subject to the same penalties as are all other persons charged with the commission of said crimes."

93. Pancoast, *Indian Before the Law*, 15, 28.

94. On the story of *Kagama*, see Harring, *Crow Dog's Case*, 142–74. See also "Transcript of Record, United States vs. Kagama," *United States Supreme Court Records and Briefs*, Part 4, 118 U.S. 211–389 (1885–6), Reel 258, Shelf LL-043, and *United States v. Kan-Gi-Shun-Ca*, 3 Dak. 106 (1882). For an analysis, see also David E. Wilkins, *American Indian Sovereignty and the U.S. Supreme Court: The Masking of Justice* (Austin: University of Texas Press, 1997), 67–81.

95. On Miller, see T. C. Crawford, "Rural Doctor and Jurist. The Very Interesting Story of Senior Justice Miller's Life," *New York World* (1886): 17; Charles Fairman, *Mr. Justice Miller and the Supreme Court, 1862–1890* (New York: Russell & Russell, 1966 [1939]); and Charles Noble Gregory, *Samuel Freeman Miller* (Iowa City: The State Historical Society of Iowa, 1907).

96. William Gillette, "Samuel Miller," in Friedman and Israel, eds., *Justices of the United States Supreme Court, 1789–1978*, vol. 2, p. 1011–1024, 1014.

97. *Hepburn v. Griswold*, 75 U.S. 603 (1870) (Miller dissenting); *Knox v. Lee*, 79 U.S. (12 Wall.) 457 (1871). *Wabash v. Illinois*, 118 U.S. 557 (1886).

98. Crawford, "Rural Doctor and Jurist," 17.

99. *United States Constitution*, Art. I, Sec. 8, Cl. 3. "This clause is relied on in the argument in the present case," writes Justice Miller, "the proposition being that the statute under consideration is a regulation of commerce with the Indian tribes. But we think it would be a very strained construction of this clause, that a system of criminal laws for Indians living peaceably in their reservations, which left out the entire code of trade and intercourse laws justly enacted under that provision, and established punishments for the common-law crimes of murder, manslaughter, arson, burglary, larceny, and the like, without any reference to their relation to any kind of commerce, was authorized by the grant of power to regulate commerce with the Indian tribes" (*Kagama*, 118 U.S. at 378–9).

100. James Kent, "Of Parent and Child," *Commentaries on American Law*, vol. 2 (New York: O. Halsted, 1827), 159–200.

101. For a similarly expansive, extra-constitutional view of federal power over Indians, see G. F. Canfield, "The Legal Position of the Indian," *American Law Review* 15 (Jan. 1881): 21–37. See also Austin Abbott, "Indians and the Law," *Harvard Law Review* 2 (Nov. 1888): 167–79, which reviews Indian law and advances the views of James Bradley Thayer.

102. *Kagama*, 118 U.S. at 384. "These Indian Tribes *are* the wards of the Nation," emphasized Miller, "They are communities *dependent* on the United States. Dependent largely for their daily food. Dependent for their political rights" (383–84), italics in original.

103. *Lone Wolf v. Hitchcock*, 187 U.S. 553 (1903).

104. Kent, "Of Parent and Child," *Commentaries*, 169. "The exposition of infants," he wrote, with delicate directness, "was the horrible and stubborn vice of almost all antiquity. *Gibbon's Hist.* vol. 8, p. 55–57. *Noodt de Partus Expositione et Nece apud veteres*; and which is considered to be a singular work of great accuracy on this subject" (169, n. A).

105. Robert M. Cover, "Nomos and Narrative," in *Narrative, Violence, and the Law: The Essays of Robert Cover*, eds. Martha Minow et al. (Ann Arbor: University of Michigan Press, 1992), 95–172.

106. *Brown v. Board of Education*, 347 U.S. 483 (1954).

CHAPTER 2

1. On the ideological origins of American imperialism in the experience of Indian policy, see Walter L. Williams, "United States Indian Policy and the Debate Over Philippine Annexation: Implications for the Origins of American Imperialism," *The Journal of American History* 66 (4) (1980): 810–31.

2. See, e.g., Henry Cabot Lodge, *Congressional Record*, 56th Congress, 1st Session (March 7, 1900), 2618.

3. Albert J. Beveridge, *Cong. Rec.*, 56th Congress, 1st Session (Jan. 9, 1900), 704–12, 710.

4. The *Insular Cases* included approximately twenty-three separate decisions and are not grouped under a single citation. The most significant are *DeLima v. Bidwell*, 182 U.S. 1 (1901), *Downes v. Bidwell*, 182 U.S. 244 (1901), discussed below, *Hawaii v. Mankichi*, 190 U.S. 197 (1903), and *Dorr v. United States*, 195 U.S. 138 (1904). See Christina Duffy Burnett, "A Note on the *Insular Cases*," in *Foreign in a Domestic Sense: Puerto Rico, American Expansion, and the Constitution*, eds. Christina Duffy Burnett and Burke Marshall (Durham: Duke University Press, 2001), 389–92. On the *Insular Cases*, see, generally, the essays collected in Burnett and Marshall, eds., *Foreign in a Domestic Sense*.

5. While the Teutonic origins thesis of American government does not typically hold a place in the history of American anthropology, and is associated primarily with the disciplines of political science and history, or more widely with "historico-politics," see Dorothy Ross, *The Origins of American Social Science* (Cambridge: Cambridge University Press, 1991), 64–77, it not only was based on the comparative method developed within anthropology, but also consciously was proclaimed by its advocates as "ethnological" in character.

6. *Downes*, 182 U.S. (1901).

7. For a concise treatment, see Joseph Smith, *The Spanish-American War: Conflict in the Caribbean and the Pacific, 1895–1902* (London: Longman, 1994). See also H. Wayne Morgan, *America's Road to Empire: The War with Spain and Overseas Expansion*, ed. Robert A. Divine (New York: John Wiley and Sons, 1965).

8. Smith, *The Spanish-American War*, 1.

9. Smith, *The Spanish-American War*, 1–2.

10. Smith, *The Spanish-American War*, 19.

11. Smith, *The Spanish-American War*, 11.

12. Smith, *The Spanish-American War*, 19.

13. On the military aspects of the Spanish-American conflict, see David F. Trask, *The War with Spain in 1898* (New York: Macmillan, 1981), passim.

14. For a discussion of Lodge's place in the history of American foreign policy, see William C. Widenor, *Henry Cabot Lodge and the Search for an American Foreign Policy* (Berkeley: University of California Press, 1980).

15. For Lodge on Roosevelt, see Henry Cabot Lodge, "Theodore Roosevelt," *The Senate of the United States and Other Essays and Addresses Historical and Literary* (New York: Charles Scribner's Sons, 1921), 113–58.

16. Alfred Thayer Mahan, *The Influence of Sea Power upon History* (New York: Hill and Wang, 1960 [1890]).

17. On anti-imperialism, see Robert L. Beisner, *Twelve Against Empire: The Anti-Imperialists, 1898–1900* (New York: McGraw-Hill, 1968). On the complexities of immigrant responses to the Spanish-American War in this regard, see Matthew Frye Jacobson, *Special Sorrows: The Diasporic Imagination of Irish, Polish, and Jewish Immigrants in the United States* (Cambridge: Harvard University Press, 1995), 177–216.

18. For an overview of motivations, see David Healy, *US Expansionism: The Imperialist Urge in the 1890s* (Madison: The University of Wisconsin Press, 1970).

19. See Martin J. Sklar, *The Corporate Reconstruction of American Capitalism, 1890–1916: The Market, the Law, and Politics* (Cambridge: Cambridge University Press, 1988).

20. Alan Trachtenberg, *The Incorporation of America: Culture and Society in the Gilded Age* (New York: Hill and Wang, 1982).

21. For an early estimate of Philippine market opportunities, see Philippine Commission [Taft Commission], "Market for American Products," *Reports of the Taft Philippine Commission* (Washington: Government Printing Office, 1901), 57–62.

22. John A. Garraty, *Henry Cabot Lodge: A Biography* (New York: Alfred A. Knopf, 1965), 3. For other biographical material on Lodge, see Widenor, *Henry Cabot Lodge*, and Henry Cabot Lodge, *Early Memories* (New York: Charles Scribner's Sons, 1913).

23. Garraty, *Henry Cabot Lodge*, 9.

24. On Lodge's "filiopietism," see Edward N. Saveth, *American Historians and European Immigrants, 1875–1925* (New York: Russell & Russell, 1965), 30, 201–3.

25. Henry Cabot Lodge, *Life and Letters of George Cabot* (Boston: Little, Brown, and Company, 1877), v, 578.

26. Henry Cabot Lodge, "Critical Notice of Henry Dexter's *As to Roger Williams and his Banishment from the Massachusetts Plantation*," *North American Review* 123 (Oct. 1876): 474–77; "Critical Review of Von Holst's *Constitutional and Political History of the United States*," *North American Review* 123 (Oct. 1876): 328–61; "Notice of George Shea's *Alexander Hamilton*," *The Nation* 24 (May 10, 1877): 283–4; "New England Federalism," *The Nation* 26 (Jan. 3, 1878): 11–12.

27. Henry Cabot Lodge, *A Short History of the English Colonies in America* (New York: Harper and Brothers, 1882); ed., *The Federalist* (New York: G. P.

Putnam's Sons, 1888); *Historical and Political Essays* (Freeport: Books for Libraries Press, 1972 [1892]); *Certain Accepted Heroes and Other Essays in Literature and Politics* (New York: Harper and Brothers, 1897); *Alexander Hamilton* (Boston: Houghton, Mifflin and Company, 1882); *Daniel Webster* (Boston: Houghton, Mifflin and Company, 1883); *George Washington* (Boston: Houghton, Mifflin and Company, 1889); Theodore Roosevelt and Henry Cabot Lodge, *Hero Tales From American History; or the Story of Some Americans Who Showed that They Knew How to Live and How to Die* (New York: The Century Co., 1903 [1895]).

28. Lodge, "Why Patronage in Offices is Un-American," *Historical and Political Essays*, 114–37, 123.

29. Lodge, *Early Memories*, 211. "The other fact in regard to them which seems to me obvious is their lawlessness," writes Lodge, "their disregard of the rights of others, especially of others about whom they are not informed, and as they know only money, their information is limited. I do not mean by this to say merely that they are arrogant; that is an old characteristic of the type. I use the word 'lawless' in its exact sense. They pay no regard to the laws of the land or the laws and customs of society if the laws are in their way."

30. See Ross, *The Origins of American Social Science*, passim.

31. See Ernest Samuels, *Henry Adams* (Cambridge: Harvard University Press, 1989), 100.

32. For Adams's approach to the seminar, see Ernest Samuels, *The Young Henry Adams* (Cambridge: Harvard University Press, 1948), 245, 247–58.

33. [Henry Adams], ed., *Essays in Anglo-Saxon Law* (Boston: Little, Brown, and Company, 1876).

34. Lodge, *Early Memories*, 239.

35. Frederick Pollock, *The Land Laws, The English Citizen* (London: Macmillan, 1883), 190–96, 190. Lodge dodges Pollock's criticism of his scholarly presentism in *Early Memories*, 263.

36. Lodge, "The Anglo-Saxon Land Law," in Adams, ed., *Essays in Anglo-Saxon Land Law*, 56.

37. On the Teutonic origins thesis, see Reginald Horsman, *Race and Manifest Destiny: The Origins of American Racial Anglo-Saxonism* (Cambridge: Harvard University Press, 1981). For a treatment focusing on historians, see Saveth, *American Historians and European Immigrants*. See also Ross, *The Origins of American Social Science*.

38. See Cornelius Tacitus, *Tacitus on Britain and Germany: A Translation of the 'Agricola' and the 'Germania'*, trans. Harold Mattingly (Baltimore: Penguin Books, 1948).

39. See the discussion of James Bryce in Richard A. Cosgrove, *Our Lady the Common Law: An Anglo-American Legal Community, 1870–1930* (New York: New York University Press, 1987), 59–94.

40. Among other scholarly studies of the period, see George Laurence Gomme, *Primitive Folk-Moots; or, Open-Air Assemblies in Britain* (London: Sampson Low, Marston, Searle & Rivington, 1880); Frederic Seebohm, *Tribal Custom in Anglo-Saxon Law* (New York: Longmans, Green, and Co., 1911 [1902]); and John M. Stearns, ed., *The Germans and Developments of the Laws of England, Embracing the Anglo-Saxon Laws Extant . . .* (New York: Banks & Brothers, 1889). See also Sir Henry Sumner Maine, *Village-Communities of the East and West*, Second Edition (London: John Murray, 1872) and *Lectures on the Early History of Institutions* (London: John Murray, 1875 [1874]), 225–305.

41. See Ross, *The Origins of American Social Science*, passim.

42. For a study that places such ideas in intellectual context, see Peter Stein, *Legal Evolution: The Story of an Idea* (Cambridge: Cambridge University Press, 1980).

43. Sir Henry Sumner Maine, *Ancient Law: Its Connection with the Early History of Society and Its Relation to Modern Ideas* (London: John Murray, 1861); Lewis Henry Morgan, *Ancient Society: Researches in the Lines of Human Progress from Savagery through Barbarism to Civilization* (New York: Henry Holt, 1907 [1877]).

44. Albert Kocourek and John Henry Wigmore, eds., *Sources of Ancient and Primitive Law* (Boston: Little, Brown and Company, 1915); *Primitive and Ancient Legal Institutions* (Boston: Little, Brown and Company, 1915); *Formative Influences of Legal Development* (Boston: Little, Brown and Company, 1918).

45. Henry Adams, "The Anglo-Saxon Courts of Law," in Adams, ed., *Essays in Anglo-Saxon Law*, 1–54, 1.

46. On the transformation of the Teutonic origins thesis between 1815 and 1850 from a descriptive statement of the nature of Anglo-Saxon life to a proscriptive theory advocating Anglo-Saxon world domination, see Horsman, *Race and Manifest Destiny*, 62–77.

47. See Thomas Bendyshe et al., ed. and trans., *The Anthropological Treatises of Johann Friedrich Blumenbach* (London: Longman, Green, Roberts, and Green, 1865).

48. Kocourek and Wigmore, "Preface," *Primitive and Ancient Legal Institutions*, v–vi, v.

49. Daniel G. Brinton, "The Aims of Anthropology," *Proceedings of the American Association for the Advancement of Science* 44 (Aug.-Sept. 1895): 1–17, 12. On Brinton, see Regna Darnell, *Daniel Garrison Brinton: The "Fearless Critic" of Philadelphia* (Philadelphia: Department of Anthropology, University of Pennsylvania, 1987). For Boas's response, see Franz Boas, "Human Faculty as Determined by Race," *Proceedings of the American Association for the Advancement of Science* 43 (1894): 301–27, reprinted in George W. Stocking, Jr., ed., *A Franz Boas Reader* (Chicago: University of Chicago Press, 1974),

221–42 and "The Limitations of the Comparative Method of Anthropology," *Science*, n.s., N.S. 4 (103) (Dec. 18, 1896): 901–908, reprinted in Franz Boas, *Race, Language and Culture* (Chicago: University of Chicago Press, 1940), 270–80.

50. *Cong. Rec.*, 54th Congress, 1st Session (March 16, 1896), 2817–20, 2819.

51. *Cong. Rec.*, 54th Congress, 1st Session (March 16, 1896), 2819.

52. *Cong. Rec.*, 54th Congress, 1st Session (March 16, 1896), 2818. For Lodge, these descendants included not only successive waves of Germans and Danes, but also Normans, who in his view were Germanic people who spoke French.

53. *Cong. Rec.*, 54th Congress, 1st Session (March 16, 1896), 2819, 2820.

54. *Cong. Rec.*, 56th Congress, 1st Session (March 7, 1900), 2621.

55. Theodore Roosevelt to Henry Cabot Lodge, Sep. 11, 1899, in *Selections from the Correspondence of Theodore Roosevelt and Henry Cabot Lodge, 1884–1918* (New York: Charles Scribner's Sons, 1925), vol. 1, p. 420–21, 421. Albert J. Beveridge, "Our Philippine Policy," *The Meaning of the Times and Other Speeches* (Indianapolis: Bobbs-Merrill, 1908), 58–88, 71. For another expression of this position, written after the decision in the primary *Insular Cases*, see Albert J. Beveridge, "The Development of a Colonial Policy for the United States," *Annals of the American Academy of Political and Social Science* 30 (July-Dec. 1907), 3–15. See also Louis Livingston Seaman, "The Problem of the Philippines," *Annals of the American Academy of Political and Social Science* 30 (July-Dec. 1907), 130–34, which, like Beveridge's essays and speeches, also makes comparisons between Filipino inferiority and the recent national "attempted elevation of the blacks" (134).

56. Beveridge, "Institutional Law," *Meaning of the Times*, 101–17, 113. On Beveridge, see John Braeman, *Albert J. Beveridge: American Nationalist* (Chicago: The University of Chicago Press, 1971); see also Claude G. Bowers, *Beveridge and the Progressive Era* (New York: The Literary Guild, 1932).

57. Beveridge, "Institutional Law," 106–7.

58. For a study of social engineering in the Philippines, paying special attention to educational issues, see Glenn Anthony May, *Social Engineering in the Philippines: The Aims, Execution, and Impact of American Colonial Policy, 1900–1913* (Westport: Greenwood Press, 1980). On law, see, generally, Winfred Lee Thompson, *The Introduction of American Law in the Philippines and Puerto Rico, 1898–1905* (Fayetteville: University of Arkansas Press, 1989). See also Peter W. Stanley, *A Nation in the Making: The Philippines and the United States, 1899–1921* (Cambridge: Harvard University Press, 1974), 81–138. For a contemporary description of activities, see, e.g., United States Philippine Commission, *Report* (Dec. 1901) (Washington: Government Printing Office, 1901), 76–91. See also Philippine Commission, *Report* (January 1900), 122–26,

137–41. "And so it has come to pass," stated James T. Young at the eleventh annual meeting of the American Academy of Political and Social Science, "that we Americans went into the Spanish tropics as the political champions of oppressed peoples, with the Declaration of Independence in one hand, the United States Constitution in the other and something of a halo round our heads, but we have folded up the Declaration for possible future use and laid aside our halo to settle down to the business task of building railroads, introducing law and order, putting up telegraph poles, settling people on the farms, studying the possibilities of the soil, developing new crops, digging harbors, paving streets, suppressing disease and building school houses. We went to the tropics to preach political liberty and remained to work" (James T. Young, Remarks at the eleventh annual meeting of the American Academy of Political and Social Science, in *Annals of the American Academy of Political and Social Science* 30 [July-Dec. 1907]: 138–39, 138).

59. Arnold H. Leibowitz, *Defining Status: A Comprehensive Analysis of United States Territorial Relations* (Boston: Martinus Nijhoff, 1989), 6. See also Earl S. Pomeroy, *The Territories and the United States, 1861–1890: Studies in Colonial Administration* (Seattle: University of Washington Press, 1969 [1947]).

60. On the exceptions, see, e.g., the work of Ferdinand Blumentritt, or the more popular Homer C. Stuntz, *The Philippines and the Far East* (Cincinnati: Jennings and Pye, 1904). On the Ifugao, see the classic R. F. Barton, *Ifugao Law* (Berkeley: University of California Press, 1919). On the perceptions of the Igorots by the West, see John Henry Scott, *The Discovery of the Igorots: Spanish Contacts with the Pagans of Northern Luzon* (Quezon City: New Day Publishers, 1974). On the Ilongot, see Renato Rosaldo, *Ilongot Headhunting, 1883–1974* (Stanford: Stanford University Press, 1980), and Michelle Z. Rosaldo, *Knowledge and Passion: Ilongot Notions of Self and Social Life* (Cambridge: Cambridge University Press, 1980).

61. C. H. Forbes-Lindsay, *The Philippines under Spanish and American Rules* (Philadelphia: The John C. Winston Co., 1906), 102, a book dedicated to William H. Taft, first civil governor of the Philippines. The work of Forbes-Lindsay, observed one contemporary reviewer, "'stands pat' with the present American administration" (Carl C. Plehn, review, *Annals of the American Academy of Political and Social Science* 30 [July-Dec. 1907]: 179–80, 180).

62. For a contemporaneous view on the development of criminal law, see Richard R. Cherry, *Lectures on the Growth of Criminal Law in Ancient Communities* (London: Macmillan, 1890).

63. These surveys also formed the basis for a large exhibition about the Philippines at the Louisiana Purchase Exposition of 1904. See Philippine Commission, *Report of the Philippine Exposition Board* (Washington: Bureau of Insular Affairs, War Department, 1905). See, especially, Albert E. Jenks, "Ethno-

logical Exhibit," *Report of the Philippine Exposition Board*, 19–20, and photographs, passim.

64. On the great respect held by Justice Brown for Taft, see H. B. Brown to Theodore Roosevelt (Jan. 6, 1903), Theodore Roosevelt Papers, Library of Congress, Washington, D.C.

65. These and other studies are listed by Merton L. Miller in his "Report of the Ethnological Survey," in the *Annual Report of the War Department* [*Report of the Philippine Commission*] (Washington: Government Printing Office, 1905), vol. 2, part 2, p. 417–27, 421–22.

66. See, e.g., David P. Barrows, "Report of the Chief of the Bureau of Nonchristian [*sic*] Tribes," in *Annual Report of the War Department* [*Report of the Philippine Commission*] (Washington: Government Printing Office, 1902), vol. 10, part 1, p. 679–77, 685–86.

67. See, e.g., Dean C. Worcester, "Report of the Secretary of the Interior," in *Annual Report of the War Department* (1905), vol. 2, part 2, p. 1–62, 56–57. See also his congressional testimony in "Statement," in *Government of the Philippines: Hearings before the Committee on the Philippines, United States Senate*, 63rd Congress, 3rd Session [on H.R. 18459] (Washington: Government Printing Office, 1915), 264–361. On Worcester, see Arthur S. Pier, *American Apostles to the Philippines* (Boston: Beacon Press, 1950), 69–82.

68. See, e.g., Otto Scheerer, "The Igorrotes of Benguet," in Taft Philippine Commission, *Report* (Washington: Government Printing Office, 1901), 149–61. And see, generally, Philippine Commission [The Schurmann Commission], *Report*, Volume 3 (Washington: Government Printing Office, 1901).

69. Philippine Commission, *Report*, Volume 1 (Washington: Government Printing Office, 1900), 11.

70. On the legislative history of the act, see José A. Cabranes, *Citizenship and the American Empire: Notes on the Legislative History of the United States Citizenship of Puerto Ricans* (New Haven: Yale University Press, 1979).

71. Despite his argument in favor of Downes as a matter of law, Coudert later expressed sympathy with the Court, noting years after that the doctrine of territorial incorporation arising from the case "has been sufficiently elastic to permit of a government which, while maintaining the essentials of modern civil liberty, has not attempted to impose upon the new peoples certain ancient Anglo-Saxon institutions for which their history has not adapted them" (Frederic R. Coudert, "The Evolution of the Doctrine of Territorial Incorporation," *Columbia Law Review* 26 [Nov. 1926]: 823–50, 850). Nevertheless, Coudert reviled the thought that the United States might have "subjects" under its jurisdiction, preferring instead the term "American national" (Frederic R. Coudert, Jr., "Our New Peoples: Citizens, Subjects, Nationals or Aliens," *Columbia Law Review* 3 [1903]: 13–32).

72. U.S. Constitution, Art. I, Sec. 8, Cl. 1.

73. *Downes*, 182 U.S. at 249.

74. C[hristopher] C[olumbus] Langdell, "The Status of Our New Territories," *Harvard Law Review* 12 (1899): 365–92; James Bradley Thayer, "Our New Possessions," *Harvard Law Review* 12 (1898–99): 464–85.

75. Simeon E. Baldwin, "The Constitutional Questions Incident to the Acquisition and Government by the United States of Island Territory," *Harvard Law Review* 12 (1899): 393–416; Carman F. Randolph, "Constitutional Aspects of Annexation," *Harvard Law Review* 12 (1898): 291–315; Abbott Lawrence Lowell, "The Status of Our New Possessions—A Third View," *Harvard Law Review* 13 (1899): 155–76.

76. Langdell, "The Status of Our New Territories," 386; Baldwin, "Constitutional Questions," 415; Lowell, "The Status of Our New Possessions," 176; A[bbott] Lawrence Lowell, "The Colonial Expansion of the United States," *Atlantic Monthly* (Feb. 1899): 145–54, 152. Similarly, Randolph argued that the United States "ought not to annex a country evidently and to all appearances irredeemably unfit for statehood because of the character of its people," because of the "inferior estate" of its inhabitants ("Constitutional Aspects of Annexation," 304–5).

77. For a related classification of the Court, see Coudert, "Evolution of the Doctrine of Territorial Incorporation," 825–26, which divides the body into "fundamentalists and modernists," as well as "strict constructionists" and "opportunists" or "latitudinarians."

78. *Downes*, 182 U.S. at 380 (Harlan, J., dissenting).

79. *Downes*, 182 U.S. at 372 (Fuller, C. J., dissenting).

80. *Downes*, 182 U.S. at 384 (Harlan, J., dissenting).

81. *Loughborough v. Blake*, 18 U.S. (5 Wheat.) 317 (1820), 319.

82. Henry Billings Brown, "Memoranda for Biographical Sketch," in Charles A. Kent, *Memoir of Henry Billings Brown* (New York: Duffield and Company, 1915), 1–33, 1. On Justice Brown, see Joel Goldfarb, "Henry Billings Brown," in *The Justices of the United States Supreme Court, 1789–1978: Their Lives and Major Opinions*, eds. Leon Friedman and Fred L. Israel (New York: Chelsea House, 1980), vol. 2, p. 1553–74, and Kent, *Memoir of Henry Billings Brown*. See also Robert J. Glennon, Jr., "Justice Henry Billings Brown: Values in Tension," *University of Colorado Law Review* 44 (1973), 553–604.

83. *Downes*, 182 U.S. at 286–87.

84. *Downes*, 182 U.S. at 306 (White, J., concurring). According to Coudert, based on a conversation after the conclusion of the case, Justice White "was much preoccupied by the danger of racial and social questions" in his decision-making process (Coudert, "Evolution of the Doctrine of Territorial Incorporation," 832).

85. *Downes*, 182 U.S. at 282.

86. *Downes*, 182 U.S. at 287.

87. *Cong. Rec.*, 56th Congress, 1st Session (March 16, 1896), 2820.

88. *Downes*, 182 U.S. at 280. Responding to this juridical-racial assertion, Justice Harlan wrote: "The wise men who framed the Constitution, and the patriotic people who adopted it, were unwilling to depend for their safety upon what, in the opinion referred to, is described as 'certain principles of natural justice inherent in Anglo-Saxon character which need no expression in constitutions or statutes to give them effect or to secure dependencies against legislation manifestly hostile to their real interests.' They proceeded upon the theory—the wisdom of which experience has vindicated—that the only safe guarantee against governmental oppression was to withhold or restrict the power to oppress. They well remembered that Anglo-Saxons across the ocean had attempted, in defiance of law and justice, to trample upon the rights of Anglo-Saxons on this continent and had sought, by military force, to establish a government that could at will destroy the privileges that inhere in liberty" (*Downes*, 182 U.S. at 381 [Harlan, J., dissenting]).

89. In this light, on the close policy relationship between Theodore Roosevelt and Justice White, see Theodore Roosevelt to E. D. White (Oct. 19, 1903) and E. D. White to Theodore Roosevelt (1907), Theodore Roosevelt Papers.

90. *Dorr v. United States*, 195 U.S. 138 (1904). Similar and related holdings were later expressed in *Rasmussen v. United States*, 197 U.S. 516 (1905) and *Dowdell v. United States*, 221 U.S. 325 (1911).

91. For an overview of the Philippines in the wake of the Treaty of Paris, see Smith, *The Spanish-American War*, 216–31. For an introduction to American history in the Philippines, extending through World War II and to the present, see Stanley Karnow, *In Our Image: America's Empire in the Philippines* (New York: Random House, 1989).

92. For one soldier's view of the process, see the anonymous "For Future Reference," published in the patriotic collection of poetry in *The Story of Our Wonderful Victories, Told by Dewey, Schley, Wheeler, and Other Heroes: A True History of Our War with Spain by the Officers and Men of Our Army and Navy* (Philadelphia: American Book and Bible House, 1899), 509–608, 531–32: "Say, Aguinaldo, / You measly / Malay moke, / What's the matter with you? / Don't you know enough / To know / That when you don't see / Freedom, / Inalienable rights, / The American Eagle, / The Fourth of July, / The Star Spangled Banner, / And the Paladium of your Liberties, / All you've got to do is to ask for them? / Are you a natural born chump / Or did you catch it from the Spaniards? / You ain't bigger / Than a piece of soap / After a day's washing, / But, by gravy, you / Seem to think / You're a bigger man / Than Uncle Sam. / You ought to be shrunk / Young fellow; / And if you don't / Demalayize yourself / At an early date, / And catch on / To your golden glorious opportunities, / Something's going to happen to you / Like a Himalaya / Sitting down kerswot / On a gnat. / If you ain't / A yel-

low dog / You'll take in your sign / And scatter / Some Red, White and Blue / Disinfectant / Over yourself. / What you need, Aggie, / Is civilizing. / And goldarn / Your yaller percoon-skin, / We'll civilize you / Dead or alive. / You'd better / Fall into the / Procession of Progress / And go marching on to glory, / Before you fall / Into a hole in the ground. / Understand? / That's us— / U.S." The editors of the collection, who write that the War, "inspired poetry, much of it of a very high degree of excellence," seem not to have caught the irony of the poem (509).

93. See, e.g., William R. Wood, "The Saxons," in *The Story of Our Wonderful Victories*, 554, which is more typical of the collection cited above: "We sing the fame of Saxon name, / And the spell of its world-wide power, / Of its triumphs vast in the glorious past, / And the might of the rising hour; / And our bosoms glow, for we proudly know / With the flag of right unfurled, / That the strength and skill of the Saxon will / Is bound to rule the world. . . . In days of yore from the Saxon shore / Our sea-born fathers came. / They conquered then by the might of men / And sword, and spear, and flame; / But to us 'tis given by the voice of Heaven, / With the peace flag far unfurled, / In our Union's might, by the power of Right, / To rule, 'neath God, the world. . . . 'Tis a mighty dower, this earth-wide power, / And a mighty task involves; / With our hearts steel-true, let us hold in view / The might of our high resolves; / Let us stand for Right in our race's might, / With our fearless flag unfurled; / For the might of Love from our God above / Is bound to rule the world."

94. Stuart Creighton Miller, *"Benevolent Assimilation": The American Conquest of the Philippines, 1899–1903* (New Haven: Yale University Press, 1982), 195, 187.

95. Brian M. Linn, "The Struggle for Samar," in James C. Bradford, ed., *Crucible of Empire: The Spanish-American War and Its Aftermath* (Annapolis: Naval Institute Press, 1993), 158–82, 158. For discussions of the notorious Samar campaign, see Joseph L. Schott, *The Ordeal of Samar* (Indianapolis: Bobbs-Merrill, 1965). Samar assumed particular importance during the Philippine Insurrection because it was a critical supplier of commercial hemp. For an analysis that reveals the variety of military responses to the conflict in the Philippines, and suggests that military men acted with more than simple racist brutality, see Brian McAllister Linn, *The U.S. Army and Counterinsurgency in the Philippine War, 1899–1902* (Chapel Hill: University of North Carolina Press, 1989).

96. On the raid and the man who led it, see Pier, "Frederick Funston," *American Apostles to the Philippines*, 13–26.

97. For an analysis of anti-imperialist opinion in this regard, see Daniel B. Schirmer, *Republic or Empire: American Resistance to the Philippine War* (Cambridge: Schenkman, 1972), and Richard E. Welch, Jr., *Response to Imperialism: The United States and the Philippine-American War, 1899–1902* (Chapel Hill: University of North Carolina Press, 1979).

98. Miller, *"Benevolent Assimilation,"* 169–70.

99. See Miller, *"Benevolent Assimilation,"* 212–18, 239–45.

100. Arthur MacArthur, "Testimony of Arthur MacArthur," in Henry F. Graff, ed., *American Imperialism and the Philippine Insurrection: Testimony taken from Hearings on Affairs in the Philippine Islands Before the Senate Committee on the Philippines—1902* (Boston: Little, Brown and Company, 1969), 135–45, 136.

101. Miller, *"Benevolent Assimilation,"* 245.

CHAPTER 3

1. 43 Stat. 153 (1924).

2. My perspective on masculinity is informed by Gail Bederman, *Manliness & Civilization: A Cultural History of Gender and Race in the United States, 1880–1917* (Chicago: University of Chicago Press, 1995); Carole Pateman, *The Sexual Contract* (Stanford: Stanford University Press, 1988); and George M. Fredrickson, *The Inner Civil War: Northern Intellectuals and the Crisis of the Union* (Urbana: University of Illinois Press, 1993 [1965]).

3. *The Chinese Exclusion Case. Chae Chan Ping v. United States*, 130 U.S. 581 (1889).

4. *Takao Ozawa v. United States*, 260 U.S. 178 (1922).

5. On the history of American immigration law, see Peter H. Schuck, "The Transformation of Immigration Law," *Columbia Law Review* 84 (1) (Jan. 1984): 1–90; E. P. Hutchinson, *Legislative History of American Immigration Policy, 1798–1965* (Philadelphia: University of Pennsylvania Press, 1981); George M. Stephenson, *A History of American Immigration, 1820–1924* (New York: Russell & Russell, 1964); and Robert A. Divine, *American Immigration Policy, 1924–1952* (New Haven: Yale University Press, 1957). See also Roger Daniels, *Coming to America: A History of Immigration and Ethnicity in American Life* (New York: HarperCollins, 1990).

6. On fear of economic competition as a driving force behind immigration policy, see Kitty Calavita, *U.S. Immigration Law and the Control of Labor, 1820–1924* (London: Academic Press, 1984). For a contemporaneous view of some of the forces animating exclusion, see George F. Seward, *Chinese Immigration, in its Social and Economical Aspects* (New York: Charles Scribner's Sons, 1881).

7. On racial segregation in San Francisco schools, from a perspective from the time, see Gilbert Thomas Stephenson, "Exclusion of Japanese from Public Schools of San Francisco," *Race Distinctions in American Law* (New York: D. Appleton and Company, 1910), 159–63.

8. Basic biographical information about Grant may be found in John Higham, *Strangers in the Land: Patterns of American Nativism, 1860–1925*

(New York: Atheneum, 1973 [1955]), 155–56; Kenneth M. Ludmerer, *Genetics and American Society: A Historical Appraisal* (Baltimore: Johns Hopkins University Press, 1972), 22–31; and Allan Chase, *The Legacy of Malthus: The Social Costs of the New Scientific Racism* (New York: Alfred A. Knopf, 1977), 163–75. Grant's personal papers passed through his brother Deforest and then to the private possession of a descendant of Deforest and anti-Boasian anthropologist Daniel Brinton. More extensive Grant material may be found in the Henry Fairfield Osborn Papers in the American Museum of Natural History, New York; the Immigration Restriction League Papers in the Houghton Library, Harvard University; the archives division of the Bronx Zoo; and the Bancroft Library, University of California, Berkeley, which houses Grant material in the Papers of the Save the Redwoods League.

9. See "Madison Grant, 71, Zoologist, is Dead; Head of New York Zoological Society Since 1925; Sponsored the Bronx River Parkway; Saved Redwood Trees; Discovered Many Mammals While Exploring American Frontier—Wrote Several Books," *New York Times* (May 31, 1937): 15 (5). On the need to place public intellectuals in the New York urban context, see Eric J. Sandeen, "Civic Culture and the American Metropolis: Why American Studies Scholars Need to Return to New York City," *American Quarterly* 40 (2) (1988): 259–65. On New York intellectual history, see Thomas Bender, *New York Intellect: A History of Intellectual Life in New York City, from 1750 to the Beginnings of Our Own Time* (New York: Knopf, 1987).

10. D. G. Brinton Thompson, "A Personal Memory of Madison Grant" (n.d., unpublished manuscript from papers of Madison Grant, in possession of the author), 7.

11. Julius Goebel, Jr., dir., *A History of the School of Law, Columbia University* (New York: Columbia University Press, 1955), 90–132.

12. Grant acquired the majority of his wealth after the death of his mother in 1916, the same year as the publication of *The Passing of the Great Race*, as well as of Deforest Grant's marriage to Emilia Brinton Thompson. See Thompson, "A Personal Memory," 6.

13. Madison Grant, *The Rocky Mountain Goat* (New York: Office of the [New York Zoological] Society, 1905); "The Vanishing Moose," *Century Magazine* 47 (1893–94): 345–56. See also Madison Grant, *Early History of Glacier National Park, Montana* (Washington: Government Printing Office, 1919).

14. Fairfield Osborn, "Grant, Madison," in *Dictionary of American Biography*, Supplement 2 (New York: Scribner, 1946–), 256. Grant also has been described, *The National Cyclopedia of American Biography* 29 (Clifton: J. T. White, 1893–), 319–20, 320, as having possessed "a deep sense of honor." On Grant and Roosevelt, note also, Thompson, "A Personal Memory," 4: "One of his first gifts to me," writes Thompson of his uncle, "was Roosevelt's *Winning of the West*."

15. The Major [Madison Grant], *Hank: his lies and his yarns* (New York: privately printed, 1931), 11, 114. Titles of chapters in the humorous yet muscular work include: "The Debtor," "Insurance," "Chicago," "Fecundity," "That Bear Charge," "That Black Heart," "They Always Charge," "Before Prohibition," "Art in the Woolly West," "The Marcus," "White Men," "I am a Dunkard," "The Inch of Cowardice," "The Road Agent," "An Ideal Country," "Queenie," "Klondike in 1907," "The Touch of Midas," "The Sons of Boreas," "The Sourdough," "The Man who Understood Women," and "The Umatilla." The work has been overlooked in scholarship concerning Grant. On the Boone & Crockett Club and the relation between hunting and zoology, see Helen L. Horowitz, "Animal and Man in the New York Zoological Park," *New York History* 56 (1975): 425–55.

16. See Thompson, "A Personal Memory," 2: "It is doubtful if either one held a deeper affection than that which existed between the two," writes Thompson of Madison and Deforest. "He often visited my mother and stepfather in Maine in the summer and once we traveled to western Canada together. From 1926 until Madison Grant's death in 1937, my stepfather and his brother had connecting apartments at 320–330 Park Avenue, New York." On Deforest Grant, see *National Cyclopedia of American Biography* (48), 315 and (F), 249–50. See also his obituary, *New York Times* (Feb. 17, 1960): 37 (5). Grant's relation with his brother has gone unmentioned in the historical literature, and no scholarly treatment of Deforest appears to exist. There were two other siblings in the Grant clan: Katherine Manice, who died young in 1909, and Norman, who was employed by Deforest as vice-president of The Atlantic Terra Cotta Company. Grant and his family are buried in Sleepy Hollow Cemetery, Sleepy Hollow, New York, plot 2119, on the corner of Rockwood Road and Summit Avenue.

17. On the history of terra cotta in New York, see Susan Tunick, "Architectural Terra Cotta: Its Impact on New York," *Sites* 18 (1986): 4–39. On the history of terra cotta, generally, see the partial reprint of *"The Story of Terra Cotta* (Chapters 16 and 17)," *Sites* 18 (1986 [1920]): 42–57.

18. Deforest remarried after the death in 1952 of his first wife; his second wife died in 1958. Deforest passed away in Tucson in 1960. On Daniel Brinton, see Regna Darnell, *Daniel Garrison Brinton: The "Fearless Critic" of Philadelphia* (Philadelphia: Department of Anthropology, University of Pennsylvania, 1987). On Brinton's differences with Franz Boas, see Franz Boas, "Human Faculty as Determined by Race," *Proceedings of the American Association for the Advancement of Science* 43 (Aug. 1894): 301–27, reprinted in George W. Stocking, Jr., ed., *A Franz Boas Reader* (Chicago: University of Chicago Press, 1974), 221–42; "The Limitations of the Comparative Method of Anthropology," *Science*, n.s., 4 (103) (Dec. 18, 1896): 901–8, reprinted in Franz Boas, *Race, Language and Culture* (Chicago: University of Chicago Press, 1982 [1940]), 270–80;

and Daniel G. Brinton, "The Aims of Anthropology," *Proceedings of the American Association for the Advancement of Science* 44 (Aug.-Sept. 1895): 1–17.

19. On the National Industrial Conference Board, see David F. Noble, *America By Design: Science, Technology, and the Rise of Corporate Capitalism* (New York: Knopf, 1977), and David Montgomery, *The Fall of the House of Labor: The Workplace, the State, and American Labor Activism, 1865–1925* (Cambridge: Cambridge University Press, 1989 [1987]).

20. George Francis Knerr, "The Mayoral Administration of William L. Strong, New York City, 1895 to 1897" (Doctoral dissertation, New York University, 1957), 39. On Strong, see also Richard L. McCormick, *From Realignment to Reform: Political Change in New York State, 1893–1910* (Ithaca: Cornell University Press, 1981) and Richard Skolnik, "1895—A Test for Municipal Nonpartisanship in New York City," *Essays in the History of New York City: A Memorial to Sidney Pomerantz*, ed. Irving Yellowitz (Port Washington: Kennikat Press, 1978), 132–44.

21. On the Bronx River Parkway, see *Report of the Bronx Parkway Commission* (New York: State of New York, 1922), which contains fascinating before-and-after photographs revealing another aspect of Grant's conservation work, as well as the relation of that work to masculinity (see photographs of Boy Scouts and baseball game, p. 87, 18) and Grant's concerns about consumerism (p. 10, 12, 18).

22. Henry James, "The Bowery and Thereabouts," *The American Scene* (Bloomington: Indiana University Press, 1968), 194–208.

23. On the history of the Immigration Restriction League, see Barbara Miller Solomon, *Ancestors and Immigrants: A Changing New England Tradition* (Boston: Northeastern University Press, 1956). See also Higham, *Strangers in the Land*.

24. Madison Grant, *The Passing of the Great Race* (New York: Charles Scribner's Sons, 1916); *Conquest of a Continent; Or the Expansion of Races in America* (New York: Charles Scribner's Sons, 1933). See also Madison Grant and Charles Stewart Davison, eds., *The Alien in Our Midst; Or "Selling Our Birthright for a Mess of Pottage"* (New York: The Galton Publishing Co., 1930), and Grant, "Introduction," in Lothrop Stoddard, *The Rising Tide of Color Against White World-Supremacy* (New York: Charles Scribner's Sons, 1920), xi–xxxii. In considering Grant, it is best to use the second edition of *Passing of the Great Race*, first published in 1917; the edition includes an appendix supporting Grant's racial assertions with extensive citations to anthropological literature.

25. On the place of hereditarian and eugenicist scholars in American science, their progressivist social vision, and their contest with Boasians, see Ludmerer, *Genetics and American Society*, 1–43, 75–85. On Boas and the rise of the culture concept in American anthropology, see George W. Stocking, Jr., *Race, Culture*

and Evolution: Essays in the History of Anthropology (Chicago: University of Chicago Press, 1968). See also, generally, Fred W. Voget, *A History of Ethnology* (New York: Holt, Rinehart and Winston, 1975), and Carl N. Degler, *In Search of Human Nature: The Decline and Revival of Darwinism in American Social Thought* (New York: Oxford University Press, 1991).

26. On the melting-pot ideal, see Philip Gleason, "The Melting Pot: Symbol of Fusion or Confusion?" *American Quarterly* 16 (1) (1964): 20–46; "Minorities (Almost) All: The Minority Concept in American Social Thought," *American Quarterly* 43 (3) (1991): 392–424. On the intellectual background of modern liberal cosmopolitans, see David A. Hollinger, "Ethnic Diversity, Cosmopolitanism and the Emergence of the American Liberal Intelligentsia," *American Quarterly* 27 (2) (1975): 133–51.

27. Franz Boas, "Changes in Bodily Form of Descendants of Immigrants" [1910], in *Race, Language and Culture*, 60–75. Boas undertook his study as part of the Dillingham Commission's celebrated mandate to study problems in immigration and industry, and it was originally published in Washington by the Government Printing Office in 1910. The comprehensive social scientific investigation of the Commission encompasses multiple volumes. See *Reports of the Immigration Commission*, vols. 1–2, *Abstracts of Reports of the Immigration Commission* (New York: Arno, 1970 [1911]).

28. Letter of Madison Grant to Percy Stickney Grant (April 8, 1912), Box 2, "CA 1910 O-P-R-S" Folder, Immigration Restriction League Papers.

29. Franz Boas, "Inventing a Great Race," *New Republic* (Jan. 13, 1917): 305–7, 305. On Boas's view of Grant and the Nordic doctrine, see also Melville J. Herskovits, *Franz Boas: The Science of Man in the Making* (New York: Charles Scribner's Sons, 1953), 117.

30. On Grant and the Nordic doctrine, see Charles C. Alexander, "Prophet of American Racism: Madison Grant and the Nordic Myth," *Phylon* 23 (Spring 1962): 73–90. See also Joseph S. Roucek, "The Roots of Racism of the American Social Scientists," *Indian Sociological Bulletin* 6 (3) (1969): 165–77; Frank H. Hankins, *The Racial Basis of Civilization: A Critique of the Nordic Doctrine* (New York: Alfred A. Knopf, 1931); and Ernest Barker, *National Character and the Factors in its Formation* (New York: Harper and Brothers, 1927). Although the Nordic doctrine bears much similarity to racial science employed in Nazi Germany, Grant was highly critical of what is sometimes known as the Teutonic doctrine, and his intellectual relation to German racial science was deeply ambivalent. See, for instance, Stefan Kühl, *The Nazi Connection: Eugenics, American Racism, and German National Socialism* (New York: Oxford University Press, 1994), 131, fn. 35. Grant has been mischaracterized as calling for the "total annihilation of the Jews" (see, e.g., Chase, *The Legacy of Malthus*, 164). On the other hand, while Grant "[w]ith satisfaction . . . claimed that Hitler had banned his book" (Thompson, "A Personal Memory," 4), this assertion appears

to have no basis in fact, editions of *Passing of the Great Race* appearing in German translation well into the war period, and none of Grant's publications apparently included on lists of books banned under the Reich.

31. Grant, *Passing of the Great Race*, 227.

32. Grant, *Passing of the Great Race*, 167.

33. Grant, *Conquest of a Continent*, 64, italics in original. For further adumbration of the connection between Jews and Asians in Grant's worldview, see Grant, "Introduction," in Stoddard, *Rising Tide of Color*, xxxi: "Now that Asia, in the guise of Bolshevism with Semitic leadership . . . is organizing an assault upon western Europe." On the place of Grant's thought in the history of anti-Semitism, see Leonard Dinnerstein, *Antisemitism in America* (New York: Oxford University Press, 1994).

34. Letter of Madison Grant to Percy Stickney Grant (April 8, 1912).

35. Grant, "Closing the Floodgates," in Grant and Davison, eds., *The Alien in Our Midst*, 13–24, 15. See also Grant's working-class appeals in Grant, "Introduction," in Stoddard, *Rising Tide of Color*, xxx–xxxi: "The great hope of the future here in America lies in the realization of the working class that the competition of the Nordic with the alien is fatal, whether the latter be the lowly immigrant from southern or eastern Europe or whether he be the obviously more dangerous Oriental against whose standards of living the white man cannot compete. In this country we must look to such of our people—our farmers and artisans—as are still of American blood to recognize and meet this danger."

36. An unconscionable contract typically involves "gross overall one-sidedness"; it is an agreement "so grossly unfair to one of the parties because of stronger bargaining powers of the other party [and thus is] usually held to be void against public policy. An unconscionable bargain or contrast is one which no man in his senses, not under delusion, would make . . . and which no fair and honest man would accept" (*Black's Law Dictionary*, Sixth Edition [St. Paul: West Publishing Co., 1990], 1524–25).

37. On Grant's sense of triumph, see the revised fourth edition of Grant, *Passing of the Great Race* (New York: C. Scribner's Sons, 1922 [1921]), xxviii. On Johnson's, see Alfred J. Hillier, "Albert Johnson, Congressman," *The Pacific Northwest Quarterly* 36 (1945): 193–212. See also Albert Johnson, "Foreword," in Roy L. Garis, *Immigration Restriction: A Study of the Opposition to and Regulation of Immigration into the United States* (New York: The Macmillan Company, 1927), vii–viii. For Grant's influence on Johnson, see Higham, *Strangers in the Land*, 313.

38. See, generally, Carey McWilliams, *Prejudice: Japanese Americans, Symbol of Racial Intolerance* (Boston: Little, Brown and Company, 1944), and Roger Daniels, *The Politics of Prejudice: The Anti-Japanese Movement in California and the Struggle for Japanese Exclusion* (Gloucester: Peter Smith, 1966). For primary material, see the testimony of V. S. McClatchy Before the House Immigra-

tion Committee reprinted in *Our New Racial Problem: Japanese Immigration and its Menace* (Sacramento: The Sacramento Bee, 1920); V. S. McClatchy, *Japanese Immigration and Colonization: Brief Prepared for Consideration of the State Department* (Sacramento: News Printing and Publishing Co., 1921); the opinions cited in *The Verdict of Public Opinion on the Japanese-American Question* (New York: Cornelius Vanderbilt, Jr., 1921); and arguments in favor of exclusion advanced by the variety of authors in *Chinese and Japanese in America, Annals of the American Academy of Political and Social Science* 34 (2) (1909): 3–51 and *Present-Day Immigration, with Special Reference to the Japanese, Annals of the American Academy of Political and Social Science* 93 (1921). Dual national allegiance under Japanese law played a role in Western concern as well. On fears of dual allegiance, see State Board of Control of California, "Citizenship," *California and the Oriental: Japanese, Chinese, and Hindus* (Sacramento: California State Printing Office, 1920), 177–91. See also Charles E. Martin, *An Introduction to the Study of the American Constitution* (New York: Oxford University Press, 1926), 169–73; K. K. Kawakami, *The Real Japanese Question* (New York: The Macmillan Company, 1921), 172–88; and T. Iyenaga and Kenoske Sato, *Japan and the California Problem* (New York: G. P. Putnam's Sons, 1921).

39. On Johnson and expert testimony, see "One Who Must be Shown," *Saturday Evening Post* (May 19, 1923): 92, 97. For an example of Johnson's hearings, see, for instance, *Restriction of Immigration: Hearings Before the Committee on Immigration and Naturalization*, 68th Congress, 1st Session (Washington: Government Printing Office, 1924). For an example of Senate hearings, see *Selective Immigration Legislation: Hearings Before the Committee on Immigration, United States Senate*, 68th Congress, 1st Session [on S. 2365 and S. 2576] (Washington: Government Printing Office, 1924).

40. Harry H. Laughlin, *An Analysis of the Metal and Dross in America's Modern Melting-Pot, Hearings Before the Committee on Immigration and Naturalization*, 67th Congress, 3rd Session (Washington: Government Printing Office, 1923). See also, *Biological Aspects of Immigration: Hearings Before the Committee on Immigration and Naturalization, Statement of Harry H. Laughlin*, 68th Congress, 7th Session (Washington: Government Printing Office, 1921) and *Immigration and Conquest* (New York: Committee on Immigration and Naturalization of the Chamber of Commerce of the State of New York, 1939). On Laughlin, see Frances Janet Hassencahl, "Harry H. Laughlin, 'Expert Eugenics Agent' for the House Committee on Immigration and Naturalization, 1921 to 1931" (Doctoral dissertation, Case Western Reserve University, 1970).

41. On Gulick's culturalist views, see Sandra C. Taylor, *Advocate of Understanding: Sidney Gulick and the Search for Peace with Japan* (Kent: Kent State University Press, 1984). Among Gulick's works on Asian-American citizenship, see *American Democracy and Asiatic Citizenship* (New York: Charles Scribner's

Sons, 1918); *Evolution of the Japanese, Social and Psychic* (New York: F. H. Revell Company, 1903); *Should Congress Enact Special Laws Affecting Japanese? A Critical Examination of the "Hearings Before the Committee on Immigration and Naturalization," Held in California, July 1920* (New York: National Committee on American Japanese Relations, 1922); and the Gulick-Hall exchange in the Immigration Restriction League Papers, Box 1, "Gulick, Sidney" Folder, Immigration Restriction League Papers.

42. 43 Stat. 153 (1924). The Immigration and Nationality Act of 1952, also known as the McCarran-Walter Act, established small quotas for Asian immigrants; the strong restrictions on Asian immigration were not dismantled until the Hart-Celler Act of 1965. See generally Hyung-Chan Kim, *Asian Americans and Congress: A Documentary History* (Westport: Greenwood Press, 1996).

43. Hillier, "Albert Johnson," 208.

44. See Rogers M. Smith, *Civic Ideals: Conflicting Visions of Citizenship in U.S. History* (New Haven: Yale University Press, 1997), 357–69.

45. U.S. Const., Art. I, Sec. 8, Cl. 3.

46. *Henderson v. Mayor of New York*, 92 U.S. 259 (1875).

47. On Field, see Carl Brent Swisher, *Stephen J. Field: Craftsman of the Law* (Washington: The Brookings Institution, 1930), and Charles W. McCurdy, "Stephen J. Field and the American Judicial Tradition," in Philip J. Bergan, Owen M. Fiss, and Charles W. McCurdy, eds. *The Fields and the Law: Essays* (New York: United States District Court for the Northern District of California Historical Society/Federal Bar Council, 1986), 5–20. See also John Norton Pomeroy, intro. and ed., *Some Account of the Work of Stephen J. Field as a Legislator, State Judge, and Judge of the Supreme Court of the United States* (New York: B. S. Smith, 1881).

48. *Slaughter-House Cases*, 83 U.S. (16 Wall.) 36 (1873), 83–111 (Field, J., dissenting). On the theoretical consolidation of principles of private property, contract, commercial exchange, and individual freedom at common law, see, generally, Daniel J. Boorstin, *The Mysterious Science of the Law: An Essay on Blackstone's Commentaries* (Chicago: University of Chicago Press, 1941). In this light, see Field's substantive view of the racial character of American identity. In "Stephen J. Field and the American Judicial Tradition," 17, for instance, Charles McCurdy quotes Field as writing, "You know I belong to the class who repudiate the doctrine that this country was made for the people of all races. . . . On the contrary, I think it is for our race—the Caucasian race. . . . [The Chinese ought to be excluded from the Untied States, for] [t]he manners, habits, mode of living, and everything connected with the Chinese prevent the possibility of their ever assimilating with our people. They are a different race, and, even if they could assimilate, assimilation would not be desirable.'"

49. 22 Stat. 58, 61 (1882). On enforcement of exclusion laws, Chinese legal challenges, and the development of modern immigration law, generally, see Lucy

E. Salyer, *Laws Harsh as Tigers: Chinese Immigrants and the Shaping of Modern Immigration Law* (Chapel Hill: University of North Carolina Press, 1995). On the effect of immigration laws on Asian Americans, see Bill Ong Hing, *Making and Remaking Asian America through Immigration Policy, 1850–1990* (Stanford: Stanford University Press, 1993). On the forces behind and against exclusion, see also Philip S. Foner and Daniel Rosenberg, eds., *Racism, Dissent, and Asian Americans from 1850 to the Present: A Documentary History* (Westport: Greenwood Press, 1993). For a contemporary discussion, see *Report of the Joint Special Committee to Investigate Chinese Immigration*, 44th Congress, 2nd Session, Report 689 (Washington: Government Printing Office, 1877).

50. *The Chinese Exclusion Case. Chae Chan Ping v. United States*, 130 U.S. 581 (1889) at 609.

51. Sec. 13(c), 43 Stat. 161 (1924).

52. 1 Stat. 103 (1790), 16 Stat. 250 (1870).

53. On naturalization decisions, or "racial prerequisite cases," see Ian F. Haney López, *White by Law: The Legal Constructions of Race* (New York: New York University Press, 1996). See also, Jerome C. Shear, *Syllabus-Digest of Decisions Under the Laws of Naturalization of the United States, September, 1906 to August, 1913* (Collingswood: I. L. Shear, 1913), and Frederick Van Dyne, *Citizenship of the United States* (Rochester: The Lawyers' Co-Operative Publishing Co., 1904). For a contemporary comparison of Japanese and American laws of naturalization, see Masuji Miyakawa, *Powers of the American People: Congress, President, and Courts*, second edition (New York: Baker & Taylor, 1908), 99–112.

54. On laws concerning Asian landholding, see generally Milton R. Konvitz, *The Alien and the Asiatic in American Law* (Ithaca: Cornell University Press, 1946), 148–70. See also Frank F. Chuman, *The Bamboo People: The Law and Japanese-Americans* (Del Mar: Publisher's Inc., 1976), and Moritoshi Fukuda, *Legal Problems of Japanese-Americans: Their History and Development in the United States* (Tokyo: Keio Tushin Co., 1980).

55. Benjamin B. Ringer, *"We the People" and Others: Duality and America's Treatment of Its Racial Minorities* (New York: Tavistock Publications, 1983), 720; Eliot Grinnell Mears, "California's Attitude Towards the Oriental," *Annals of the American Academy of Political and Social Science* [The Far East], 122 (211) (Nov. 1925): 199–213, 200.

56. Yuji Ichioka, "Japanese Immigrant Response to the 1920 California Alien Land Law," in Charles McCain, ed., *Japanese Immigrants and American Law: The Alien Land Laws and Other Issues* (New York: Garland, 1994), 229–50, 230, 234. See also Bruce A. Castleman, "California's Alien Land Laws," *Western Legal History* 7 (1) (1994): 24–68.

57. On fear of Asian landholding in California, see State Board of Control of California, "Land," *California and the Oriental*, 43–73. In defense of the Japan-

ese, see Fred C. Robertson, "The Power of the Federal Government to Fix the Rights of Aliens within the States," *Proceedings of the Washington State Bar Association* (1913): 153–73. For contemporary arguments concerning the background and constitutionality of land laws, see Thomas Reed Powell, "Alien Land Cases in the United States Supreme Court," *California Law Review* 12 (4) (1924): 259–82; Justin Miller, "Alien Land Laws," *George Washington Law Review* 8 (1) (1939): 1–20; Harriette M. Dilla, "The Constitutional Background of the Recent Japanese Anti-Alien Land Bill Controversy," *Michigan Law Review* 12 (7) (1914): 573–84; and Charles Wallace Collins, "Will the California Alien Land Law Stand the Test of the Fourteenth Amendment?" *Yale Law Journal* 23 (1914): 330–38. See also Eliot Grinnell Mears, *Resident Orientals on the American Pacific Coast: Their Legal and Economic Status* (New York: Institute of Pacific Relations, 1927). And see, generally, Jun Furuya, "Gentlemen's Disagreement: The Controversy between the United States and Japan over the California Alien Land Law of 1913" (Doctoral dissertation, Princeton University, 1989); Daniels, *Politics of Prejudice*; and McWilliams, *Prejudice*.

58. Yuji Ichioka, "Japanese Immigrant Response," 235. On the status of alien property at common law, see Chester G. Vernier, asst. by Richard A. Frank, *American Family Laws*, vol. 5: *Incompetents and Dependents* (Stanford: Stanford University Press, 1938), 302–40, 346–70. At common law, aliens could take title to real property by purchase, gift, or devise, but not by operation of law. Aliens could not transmit title by descent, as they did not possess "inheritable blood" (346). When aliens died intestate, their property would escheat to the sovereign.

59. U.S. Const., Art. 1, Sec. 8, Cl. 4.

60. For an impassioned argument that Japanese should have been considered "white persons" under the law, written by one of the foremost legal thinkers of the period, see John H. Wigmore, "American Naturalization and the Japanese," *American Law Review* 28 (1894): 818–27. Wigmore recently had returned from Japan, where he held his first teaching position. See William R. Roalfe, *John Henry Wigmore: Scholar and Reformer* (Evanston: Northwestern University Press, 1977), and Kenneth W. Abbott, "Wigmore: The Japanese Connection," in Albert Kocourek and Kurt Schwerin, eds., *John Henry Wigmore: An Annotated Bibliography, Northwestern University Law Review* 75 (6) (1981, Supplement): 10–16. See also, *In re Saito*, 62 Fed. Rep. 126 (1894) (ruling Japanese not white under § 2169, instigating Wigmore article).

61. See, generally, Haney López, *White by Law*.

62. On Blumenbach, whose work formed the basis for "most nineteenth century anthropometrical studies" (studies that significantly saw their watershed in the activities of the United States Sanitary Commission during the Civil War), see John S. Haller, *Outcasts from Evolution: Scientific Attitudes of Racial Inferiority, 1859–1900* (Urbana: University of Illinois Press, 1971), 4. See also Haller's

discussion, 4, of the Linnaean 1735 system of classification, which divided humans into four groups: *Homo Americanus* (a race that, among other characteristics, was said to be regulated by custom); *Homo Asiaticus* (said to be ruled by opinions), *Homo Afer* (governed by caprice); *Homo Europaeus* (governed by law).

63. *United States v. Cartozian*, 6 F. 2d 919 (1925). See "Deposition of Dr. Franz Boas" (April 11, 1924), "Deposition of Dr. James L. Barton" (April 9, 1924), and "Depositions on Behalf of Defendant" (April 1924), all in *United States v. Cartozian* Case Files, National Archives—Pacific Northwest Region, Seattle, Washington. See also Phillip E. Lothyan, "A Question of Citizenship," *Prologue* 21 (3) (Fall 1989): 267–73.

64. Yuji Ichioka, "The Early Japanese Immigrant Quest for Citizenship: The Background of the 1922 Ozawa Case," in McCain, ed., *Japanese Immigrants and American Law*, 397–418, 407.

65. See, generally, Ichioka, "The Early Japanese Immigrant Quest for Citizenship."

66. On the state of social scientific and specifically anthropological knowledge about Japan around the time of *Ozawa*, see works cited in "Catalogue of the Library of the Asiatic Society of Japan, 1919," *Transactions of the Asiatic Society of Japan* 47 (1919): 1–57; L. H. Dudley Buxton, *The Peoples of Asia* (New York: Alfred A. Knopf, 1925), 205–19, 250–59; Edward A. Ackerman et al., *Japan's Prospect* (Cambridge: Harvard University Press, 1946), 419–38; and "A List of Books on Japan," *Annals of the American Academy of Political and Social Science* [The Far East], 122 (211) (Nov. 1925): 227–40. On Asians in American social science generally, see Henry Shuen Ngei Yu, "Thinking about Orientals: Modernity, Social Science, and Asians in Twentieth-Century America" (Doctoral dissertation, Princeton University, 1995). For comments on the developing state of law in Japan, a subject bearing upon the perception that Japanese were or were not capable of republican self-government, see Basil Hall Chamberlain, "Law," *Japanese Things: Being Notes on Various Subjects Connected with Japan* (Rutland: Charles E. Tuttle, 1905 [1890]), 278–84, 284: "Dutifully obedient to authority and not naturally litigious, the Japanese are nevertheless becoming a nation of lawyers"; Rokuichiro Masujima, "The Present Position of Japanese Law and Jurisprudence," *New York Bar Association Proceedings* (1903): 116–97; and B. K. Miller, "The Japanese Codes," *Wisconsin State Bar Association Proceedings* (1901): 139–60.

67. David L. Withington, "Brief for Petitioner," in The Consulate-General of Japan, *Documental History of Law Cases Affecting Japanese in the United States, 1916–1924* (San Francisco: Consulate-General of Japan, 1925), 17–51, 42.

68. Ozawa and his attorney particularly cited the work of Japanologist Gordon Munro. See Neil Gordon Munro, *Prehistoric Japan* (Yokohama, 1908).

69. Takao Ozawa, *Naturalization of a Japanese Subject in the United States of America* (Honolulu: 1922), 16–17, italics in original (quoting M. Fishbery [Maurice Fishberg]). Ozawa's brief was not included in the briefs compiled by the Consulate-General of Japan in the useful *Documental History*. It can be found, among other locations, bound together with pamphlets concerning Japan in *New Japan Problems, 1907–1924*, in Yale University's Sterling Memorial Library. Ozawa apparently sent a personal message to Chief Justice Taft with his brief to the Court, but it seems to have been destroyed. See William Howard Taft to George Sutherland (Oct. 8, 1922), William Howard Taft Papers, "My dear Justice Sutherland: You have the Japanese case, so that I suppose you ought to have this informal communication, though I presume that it is not important . . . Enclosures. Letter from Takao Ozawa, 3737 Park Avenue, Kaimuki, Honolulu."

70. See Committee on the Territories, *Nonassimilability of Japanese in Hawaii and the United States: Hearings Before the Committee on the Territories, House of Representatives, Sixty-Seventh Congress, Second Session, Regarding Anthropological and Historical Data Affecting Nonassimilability of Japanese in the Territory of Hawaii and the United States, July 17, 1922* (Washington: Government Printing Office, 1922), 1–65. On Hrdlička generally, see Frank Spencer, "Aleš Hrdlička, M.D., 1869–1943: A Chronicle of the Life and Work of an American Physical Anthropologist" (Doctoral dissertation, University of Michigan, 1979). On Hrdlička and Boas, see "Hrdlička's Journal and Other Schemes for the Development of American Physical Anthropology, 1916–1918" and "The Boasian Siege and Hrdlička's Trojan Horse, 1919–1930" in Spencer, "Aleš Hrdlička," 624–750. For a more critical view of Hrdlička, see Michael L. Blakey, "Skull Doctors: Intrinsic Social and Political Bias in the History of American Physical Anthropology, With Special Reference to the Work of Aleš Hrdlička," *Critique of Anthropology* 7 (2) (1987): 7–35.

71. Committee on the Territories, *Nonassimilability of Japanese in Hawaii and the United States*, 2.

72. For a discussion of an alternative view of *Ozawa*, see Mark S. Weiner, "'Naturalization' and Naturalization Law: Some Empirical Observations," *Yale Journal of Law & the Humanities* 10 (Summer 1998): 657–66.

73. On George Sutherland, see Joel Francis Paschal, *Mr. Justice Sutherland: A Man Against the State* (Princeton: Princeton University Press, 1951) and *Proceedings of the Bar and Officers of the Supreme Court of the United States in Memory of George Sutherland, December 18, 1944* (Washington: Supreme Court of the United States, 1944). See also Hadley Arkes, *The Return of George Sutherland: Restoring a Jurisprudence of Natural Rights* (Princeton: Princeton University Press, 1994). Justice Sutherland's personal papers are housed in the Library of Congress; examination revealed almost no explicit discussion of racial issues.

74. *Adkins v. Children's Hospital*, 261 U.S. 525 (1923).

75. On Sutherland's place in the history of the Supreme Court's use of social science, see Paul L. Rosen, *The Supreme Court and Social Science* (Urbana: University of Illinois Press, 1972), 50–51, 91–92. For a poetic indication of Justice Sutherland's concerns about interpretive contingency, see George Sutherland, "The ground it is a lovely thing," Box 6, Undated Folder, George Sutherland Papers: "The ground it is a lovely thing / To catch us when we fall / For if it didn't, goodness knows, / We mightn't stop at all." The poem is written in Sutherland's mature hand. For a use by Sutherland of the metaphor of falling specifically in relation to progressive social legislation and natural law, see George Sutherland, "The Courts and the Constitution: An Address by Hon. George Sutherland Before the American Bar Association at Milwaukee," 62nd Congress, Senate Document 970 (Washington: 1912), 6.

76. Louis Brandeis to George Sutherland (Nov. 6, 1915); George Sutherland to Louis Brandeis (Nov. 8, 1915); Louis Brandeis to George Sutherland (Nov. 18, 1915), Box 2, Folder November 1915, George Sutherland Papers, Library of Congress, Washington, D.C.

77. See, e.g., George Sutherland to E. M. Allison (Feb. 7, 1908), Box 2, Folder 1908–9, George Sutherland Papers.

78. *United States v. Curtiss-Wright Export Corp.*, 299 U.S. 304 (1936).

79. George Sutherland, *Constitutional Power and World Affairs* (New York: Columbia University Press, 1919), 48, 55.

80. George Sutherland to Nicholas Murray Butler, Columbia University [Director of Carnegie Endowment for International Peace] (Jan. 13, 1923), Box 5, Folder January-March 1923, George Sutherland Papers.

81. Dictionaries of the period suggest that by 1922, the term did not have a generally scientific meaning, but instead was used more or less as an equivalent for a person of European descent. See William Dwight Whitney and Benjamin E. Smith, eds., *The Century Dictionary* (New York: The Century Co., 1911), 866; Ernest Weekley, *An Etymological Dictionary of Modern English* (London: John Murray, 1921), 266; Hulbert G. Emery and K. G. Brewster, eds., *The New Century Dictionary of the English Language* (New York: The Century Co., 1927), 224; Henry Cecil Wyld, ed., *The Universal Dictionary of the English Language* (New York: E. P. Dutton, 1932), 162; and John B. Opdycke, *Don't Say It: A Cyclopedia of English Use and Abuse* (New York: Funk and Wagnalls, 1939), 158.

82. *Takao Ozawa v. United States*, 260 U.S. 178 (1922) at 208, italics in original.

83. *Ozawa*, 260 U.S. at 196–97.

84. "Law and Common Sense," newspaper clipping (n.d.), Box 7, Folder General Miscellany-Newspaper Clippings, 1906–1938, George Sutherland Papers. See also James W. Garner, "Recent Decisions of the United States Supreme Court Affecting the Rights of Aliens," *Journal of Comparative Legislation and International Law*, third series, vol. 6 (1924): 210–14, 210–11.

85. *Terrace v. Thompson,* 263 U.S. 197 (1923); *Porterfield v. Webb,* 263 U.S. 225 (1923). Consulate-General of Japan, *Documental History,* vol. 2, p. 25: "It is obvious that the objection on the part of Congress is not due to color, as color, but only to color as an evidence of a type of civilization which it characterizes. The yellow or brown racial color is the hallmark of the Oriental despotisms, or was at the time the original naturalization law was enacted. It was deemed that the subjects of those despotisms, with their fixed and ingrained pride in the type of their civilization, which works for its welfare by subordinating the individual to the personal authority of the sovereign, as the embodiment of the state, were not fitted and suited to make for the success of a republican form of government. Hence, they were denied citizenship." On Justice Butler, see Francis Joseph Brown, *The Social and Economic Philosophy of Pierce Butler* (Washington: Catholic University of America Press, 1945).

86. See *Chang Chan v. Nagle,* 268 U.S. 346 (1925).

87. On Justice McReynolds, see David Burner, "James C. McReynolds," in Leon Friedman and Fred L. Israel, eds., *The Justices of the United States Supreme Court, 1789–1978: Their Lives and Major Opinions* (New York: Chelsea House, 1980), vol. 3, p. 2023-33.

88. *Chung Fook v. White,* 264 U.S. 443 (1924), 446; *Commissioner of Immigration v. Gottlieb,* 265 U.S. 310 (1924), 313.

CHAPTER 4

1. *Adkins v. Children's Hospital,* 261 U.S. 525 (1923).

2. *Brown v. Board of Education,* 347 U.S. 483 (1954); *Plessy v. Ferguson,* 163 U.S. 537 (1896).

3. *Brown,* 347 U.S. at 494, n. 11: "K.B. Clark, Effect of Prejudice and Discrimination on Personality Development (Midcentury White House Conference on Children and Youth, 1950); Witmer and Kotinsky, Personality in the Making (1952), c. VI; Deutscher and Chein, The Psychological Effects of Enforced Segregation: A Survey of Social Science Opinion, 26 J. of Psychol. 259 (1948); Chein, What are the Psychological Effects of Segregation Under Conditions of Equal Facilities?, 3 Int. J. Opinion and Attitude Res. 229 (1949); Brameld, Educational Costs, in Discrimination and National Welfare (McIver, ed., 1949), 44–48; Frazier, The Negro in the United States (1949), 674–681. And see generally Myrdal, An American Dilemma (1944)." On the significance of Boasian anthropology for the *Brown* decision, see also David A. J. Richards, *Conscience and the Constitution: History, Theory, and Law of the Reconstruction Amendments* (Princeton: Princeton University Press, 1993), 158–59, 166–67, 257.

4. Gunnar Myrdal, *An American Dilemma: The Negro Problem and Modern Democracy,* 2 vols., intro. Sissela Bok (New Brunswick: Transaction Publishers, 1996 [1944]).

5. For an analysis resting on the assumption of the logical necessity of footnote eleven, see Paul L. Rosen, *The Supreme Court and Social Science* (Urbana: University of Illinois Press, 1972). For some contemporaneous reaction to the use of social science in Brown, see Edmond Cahn, "Jurisprudence," *New York University Law Review* 30 (Jan. 1955): 150–69; Ernest van den Haag, "Social Science Testimony in the Desegregation Cases—A Reply to Professor Kenneth Clark," *Villanova Law Review* 6 (Fall 1960): 69–79; Ernest van den Haag and Ralph Ross, *The Fabric of Society: An Introduction to the Social Sciences* (New York: Harcourt, Brace and Company, 1957); and Herbert Wechsler, "Toward Neutral Principles of Constitutional Law," *Harvard Law Review* 73 (1) (Nov. 1959): 1–35. Wechsler notes correctly that the *Brown* opinion "is often read with less fidelity by those who praise it than by those by whom it is condemned" (32). To a large degree, scholarly understanding of the historical significance of footnote eleven has not advanced far beyond the positions suggested in the immediate aftermath of the decision, particularly in its largely proscriptive policy concerns.

6. See, e.g., van den Haag, "Social Science Testimony in the Desegregation Cases."

7. For a representative analysis, see Chief Justice Earl Warren's discussion of footnote eleven, "It was only a note, after all," in Richard Kluger, *Simple Justice: The History of* Brown v. Board of Education *and Black America's Struggle for Equality* (New York: Vintage Books, 1977 [1975]), 706. See also the significance of the theme of laughter in Charles L. Black, Jr., "The Lawfulness of the Segregation Decisions," *Yale Law Journal* 69 (1960): 421–30, and Louis H. Pollock, "Racial Discrimination and Judicial Integrity: A Reply to Professor Wechsler," *University of Pennsylvania Law Review* 108 (1) (Nov. 1959): 1–34.

8. Walter A. Jackson, *Gunnar Myrdal and America's Conscience: Social Engineering and Racial Liberalism, 1938–1987* (Chapel Hill: University of North Carolina Press, 1990), 40.

9. Jackson, *Gunnar Myrdal*, 41.

10. Jackson, *Gunnar Myrdal*, 52.

11. Gunnar Myrdal, *Monetary Equilibrium* (London: William Hodge & Company, 1939 [based on a series of lectures delivered in 1931]). For Myrdal's treatment of economic and social scientific methodology, a subject also of lifelong concern, see Myrdal, *The Political Element in the Development of Economic Theory* (New York: Simon and Schuster, 1969 [1954]).

12. Gunnar Myrdal, "Socialpolitkens dilemma," *Spektrum* 2 (3–4) (1932): 1–31.

13. The English edition can be found in Alva Myrdal, *Nation and Family: The Swedish Experiment in Democratic Family and Population Policy* (New York: Harper & Brothers, 1941 [1934]). See, generally, Allan Carlson, *The Swedish Experiment in Family Politics: The Myrdals and the Interwar Population Crisis* (New Brunswick: Transaction Publishers, 1990).

14. Jackson, *Gunnar Myrdal*, 86.

15. Gunnar Myrdal, *Population: A Problem for Democracy; The Godkin Lectures, 1938* (Cambridge: Harvard University Press, 1940). The terms of Myrdal's employment were good by any standard, designed to compensate for the loss of what he described as a "rather comfortable European upper class level [of income], with our own house, two servants, etc." (quoted in Jackson, *Gunnar Myrdal*, 86). According to David W. Southern, *Gunnar Myrdal and Black-White Relations: The Use and Abuse of* 'An America Dilemma,' *1944–1969* (Baton Rouge: Louisiana State University Press, 1987), 14–15, Myrdal was to receive $19,800 for an expected two years of work (approximately $257,000 in contemporary figures in terms of the Consumer Price Index), to which the Corporation added $11,000 to supplement the cost of living in New York. Moreover, Myrdal and his staff were given what amounted to carte blanche in their research—and, not surprisingly, the study significantly overran its budget. The trustees had appropriated $25,000 to the project in 1938, with an estimated total cost of $75,000. By the summer of 1939, Myrdal had proposed a budget of over $166,000 to run simply through August 1940. Eventually, as Jackson notes, the study would cost the Corporation over $300,000, or almost four million 2005 dollars compared with their 1938 value, or about $3.1 million compared with their value in 1944 (*Gunnar Myrdal*, 34).

16. Jackson, *Gunnar Myrdal*, 106–16.

17. Myrdal, *American Dilemma*, lxii–lxiv.

18. Myrdal, *American Dilemma*, 78.

19. Sissela Bok, "Introduction to the Transaction Fiftieth Anniversary Edition," in Myrdal, *American Dilemma*, xxi–xxxii, xxi–xxii (relating story told by her sister Kaj Fölster). For two important critiques of *An American Dilemma*, see Stanford M. Lyman, *The Black American in Sociological Thought: A Failure of Perspective* (New York: Capricorn Books, 1972), and Herbert Aptheker, *The Negro Problem in America: A Critique of Gunnar Myrdal's* 'An American Dilemma' (New York: International Publishers, 1946).

20. Myrdal, *American Dilemma*, 1003, 114, italics in original. For the similar opinion of Franz Boas himself on Madison Grant, see Melville J. Herskovits, *Franz Boas: The Science of Man in the Making* (New York: Charles Scribner's Sons, 1953), 117.

21. Myrdal, *American Dilemma*, 91, 92.

22. Myrdal, *American Dilemma*, 1216, 150; see also 90, 1202–03, 1217; but see criticism of Boas, 146, for suggesting some psychic differences are innate and vary by race.

23. Otto Klineberg, ed., *Characteristics of the American Negro* (New York: Harper & Brothers, 1944); Melville J. Herskovits, *The Myth of the Negro Past* (New York: Harper & Brothers, 1941). Myrdal, *American Dilemma*, lxii.

24. Myrdal, *American Dilemma*, 110, italics in original (citing Ruth Benedict, *Race: Science and Politics* [New York: Modern Age Books, 1940], 237).

25. See Ruth Benedict, *Patterns of Culture* (New York: Mentor Books, 1959 [1934]) and *The Chrysanthemum and the Sword: Patterns of Japanese Culture* (Boston: Houghton Mifflin, Co., 1946); and Margaret Mead, *Sex and Temperament in Three Primitive Societies* (New York: W. Morrow & Co., 1935); *Growing Up in New Guinea* (New York: Blue Ribbon Books, 1930); and *Coming of Age in Samoa: A Psychological Study of Primitive Youth for Western Civilisation* (New York: W. Morrow & Co., 1928). On Ruth Benedict, see Margaret M. Caffrey, *Ruth Benedict: Stranger in This Land* (Austin: University of Texas Press, 1989); Judith Schachter Modell, *Ruth Benedict: Patterns of a Life* (Philadelphia: University of Pennsylvania Press, 1983); Christopher Shannon, *A World Made Safe for Differences: Cold War Intellectuals and the Politics of Identity* (Lanham: Rowman and Littlefield, 2001), 1–13; and Margaret Mead, *Ruth Benedict* (New York: Columbia University Press, 1974). On Margaret Mead, see Margaret Mead, *Blackberry Winter: My Earlier Years* (Gloucester: Peter Smith, 1989 [1972]); Jane Howard, *Margaret Mead: A Life* (New York: Fawcett Crest, 1984); and Robert Cassidy, *Margaret Mead: A Voice for the Century* (New York: Universe Books, 1982). Although many of the important studies of the culture-and-personality school were undertaken in the 1930s and 1940s, popular acclaim came particularly after World War II; in many respects, *Patterns of Culture* should be understood as a work of the postwar period.

26. For a discussion of the relation of legal structure and individual personality, see Yehudi A. Cohen, "Institutional Integrations," *Social Structure and Personality: A Casebook* (New York: Holt, Rinehart and Winston, 1961), 225–54. See also James L. Gibbs, Jr., "Law and Personality: Signposts for a New Direction," in Laura Nader, ed., *Law in Culture and Society* (Chicago: Aldine, 1969), 176–207.

27. For an overview of this aspect of the culture-and-personality school, see Philip K. Bock, *Continuities in Psychological Anthropology: A Historical Introduction* (San Francisco: W. H. Freeman, 1980), esp. 60–62. For the immediate background to liberal democratic thought in the postwar United States, see Edward A. Purcell, Jr., *The Crisis of Democratic Theory: Scientific Naturalism & the Problem of Value* (Lexington: University Press of Kentucky, 1973). For a critical analysis of one of the leading exponents of the school, see Shannon, *World Made Safe*, 1–13, and Christopher Shannon, "A World Made Safe for Differences: Ruth Benedict's *The Chrysanthemum and the Sword*," *American Quarterly* 47 (4) (Dec. 1995): 659–80. See also Christopher Lasch, *Haven in a Heartless World: The Family Besieged* (New York: Basic Books, 1977), 62–96.

28. Myrdal, *American Dilemma*, lix.

29. Myrdal, *American Dilemma*, 42; see also, generally, Myrdal, *American Dilemma*, 26–49.

30. Southern, *Gunnar Myrdal and Black-White Relations*, 26. In a similar vein, during one interview with a white supremacist, who spoke vehemently against miscegenation, Myrdal asked "if she was aware of psychological theories that people with . . . sexual phobias secretly desired that which they professed to abhor" (Jackson, *Gunnar Myrdal*, 124).

31. Myrdal, *American Dilemma*, 58, italics in original; see also, generally, Myrdal, *American Dilemma*, 50–60.

32. Myrdal, *American Dilemma*, lxxix. See also Myrdal, *American Dilemma*, lxxxiii.

33. Myrdal, *American Dilemma*, 3, italics in original.

34. See, for example, Louis Hartz, *The Liberal Tradition in America: An Interpretation of American Political Thought since the Revolution* (New York: Harcourt Brace, 1955).

35. See Myrdal, *American Dilemma*, 75–78.

36. Myrdal, *American Dilemma*, 8.

37. On Myrdal's belief in individual rationality, see, e.g., Myrdal, *American Dilemma*, 1003.

38. Myrdal, *American Dilemma*, 89, italics in original.

39. Myrdal, *American Dilemma*, 75.

40. Myrdal, *American Dilemma*, 12.

41. For Myrdal, these ideals also came, in part, from the teachings of "various lower class Protestant sects, split off from the Anglican Church," which brought to the Creed a democratic spirit and an "emotional temper" of charity and generosity (Myrdal, *American Dilemma*, 9, 11).

42. Myrdal, *American Dilemma*, 1182, 8.

43. Myrdal, *American Dilemma*, 12.

44. Myrdal, *American Dilemma*, 14.

45. Myrdal, *American Dilemma*, 12, 14.

46. Myrdal, *American Dilemma*, 16.

47. See Lee Coleman, "What is American? A Study of Alleged American Traits," *Social Forces* 19 (4) (1941): 492–99, a survey of contemporary social scientists that shows consensus that "disregard of law" has been a basic feature of American life throughout U.S. history (498). See also Francis L. K. Hsu, "American Core Value and National Character," in Francis L. K. Hsu, ed., *Psychological Anthropology* (Cambridge: Schenkman Publishing Company, 1972), 241–62.

48. James Truslow Adams, "Our Lawless Heritage," *Atlantic Monthly* 142 (Dec. 1928): 732–40; Roscoe Pound, "Criminal Justice in the American City—A Summary," in Roscoe Pound and Felix Frankfurter, dirs. and eds., *Criminal Justice in Cleveland* (Cleveland: The Cleveland Foundation, 1922), 557–652, 573.

49. Myrdal, *American Dilemma*, 18.

50. See Southern, *Gunnar Myrdal and Black-White Relations*, 187–259 and passim.

51. Ralph Ellison, "*An American Dilemma*: A Review," in John F. Callahan, ed., *The Collected Essays of Ralph Ellison* (New York: The Modern Library, 1995), 328–40, 337.

52. See, generally, Michel Foucault, *The Foucault Effect: Studies in Governmentality*, ed. Graham Burcell, Colin Gordon, and Peter Miller (London: Harvester Wheatsheaf, 1991).

53. On Myrdal's global vision of development, see, for instance, Gunnar Myrdal, *An International Economy: Problems and Prospects* (New York: Harper & Brothers, 1956), and *Development and Under-development* (Cairo: National Bank of Egypt, 1956).

54. See, e.g., *Schechter Poultry Corp. v. United States*, 295 U.S. 495 (1935); *Carter v. Carter Coal Co.*, 298 U.S. 238 (1936).

55. *West Coast Hotel Co. v. Parrish*, 300 U.S. 379 (1937); *Adkins*, 261 U.S. (1923); *NLRB v. Jones and Laughlin Steel Corp.*, 301 U.S. 1 (1937).

56. *United States v. Darby Lumber Co.*, 312 U.S. 100 (1941); *Wickard v. Filburn*, 317 U.S. 111 (1942).

57. *United States v. Carolene Products Co.*, 304 U.S. 144 (1938).

58. *Carolene Products*, 304 U.S. at 152.

59. *Carolene Products*, 304 U.S. at 152 n.4.

60. *Plessy v. Ferguson*, 163 U.S. 537 (1896).

61. *Plessy*, 163 U.S. at 551. On racial discrimination in jury service, see *Strauder v. West Virginia*, 100 U.S. 303 (1880).

62. Kenneth L. Karst, "Separate But Equal Doctrine," *Encyclopedia of the American Constitution* (New York: Free Press, 1986), vol. 4, p. 1649–50, 1649.

63. *McLaurin v. Oklahoma State Regents for Higher Education*, 339 U.S. 637 (1950); *Sweatt v. Painter*, 339 U.S. 629 (1950).

64. *Sweatt*, 339 U.S. at 634.

65. *Brown*, 347 U.S. at 493; *Sweatt*, 339 U.S. at 634.

66. The cases were *Briggs v. Elliott*, 98 F. Supp. 529 (E.D. S.C. 1951), remanded 342 U.S. 350 (1952), on remand 103 F. Supp. 920 (E.D. S.C. 1952), decision on merits, 347 U.S. 483 (1954), on remand 132 F. Supp. 776 (E.D. S.C. 1955); *Davis v. County School Board of Prince Edward County*, 103 F. Supp. 337 (E.D. Va. 1952), decision on merits, 347 U.S. 483 (1954); *Brown v. Board of Education of Topeka*, 98 F. Supp. 797 (D. Kansas 1951), interim order, 344 U.S. 141 (1952), second interim order, 344 U.S. 1 (1952), decision on merits, 347 U.S. 483 (1954); *Belton v. Gebhart*, 87 A.2d 862 (Del. Ch.), affirmed, 91 A.2d 137 (Del. Sup. Ct. 1952), decision on merits, 347 U.S. 483 (1954).

67. For a discussion of NAACP legal strategy, see Mark V. Tushnet, *The NAACP's Legal Strategy against Segregated Education, 1925–1950* (Chapel

Hill: University of North Carolina Press, 1987) and *Making Civil Rights Law: Thurgood Marshall and the Supreme Court, 1936–1961* (New York: Oxford University Press, 1994).

68. See "Appendix to Appellant's Briefs: The Effects of Segregation and the Consequences of Desegregation," in Kenneth B. Clark, *Prejudice and Your Child* (Boston: Beacon Press, 1963), 166–84. For the history of the use of social science in desegregation cases both before and after *Brown*, see Mark A. Chesler, Joseph Sanders, and Debra S. Kalmuss, *Social Science in Court: Mobilizing Experts in the School Desegregation Cases* (Madison: University of Wisconsin Press, 1988). For the use of social science in the wake of *Brown*, see Betsy Levin and Willis D. Hawley, eds., *The Courts, Social Science, and School Desegregation* (New Brunswick: Transaction Books, 1975).

69. Ben Keppel, *The Work of Democracy: Ralph Bunche, Kenneth B. Clark, Lorraine Hansberry, and the Cultural Politics of Race* (Cambridge: Harvard University Press, 1995), 102–3.

70. On the place of Clark's work within the larger history of social scientific studies of black psychology, see Daryl Michael Scott, *Contempt and Pity: Social Policy and the Image of the Damaged Black Psyche, 1880–1996* (Chapel Hill: University of North Carolina Press, 1997).

71. Edward A. Richards, ed., *Proceedings of the Midcentury White House Conference on Children and Youth* (Report of Conference Sessions, Washington D.C., December 3–7, 1950) (Raleigh: Health Publications Institute, 1951), 16. For proceedings of some pre-Conference activities, see Milton J. E. Senn, ed., *Symposium on the Healthy Personality* (New York: Josiah Macy, Jr. Foundation, 1950) and *Problems of Infancy and Childhood* (New York: Josiah Macy, Jr. Foundation, 1951).

72. Helen Leland Witmer and Ruth Kotinsky, eds., *Personality in the Making: The Fact-Finding Report of the Midcentury White House Conference on Children and Youth* (New York: Harper & Brothers, 1952), xvi–xviii. The Court in *Brown* specifically cited chapter 6, "The Effects of Prejudice and Discrimination," p. 135–58, which was based on Clark's research, as its second reference in note eleven.

73. Witmer and Kotinsky, eds., *Personality in the Making*, xviii, xvi. See also the similar perspective on social adjustment taken by Erik H. Erikson in *Childhood and Society* (New York: W. W. Norton, 1993 [1950]); the Midcentury Conference based its view of the human personality on Erikson's work.

74. A series of drafts of the report, which was published in mimeograph form, are available from the library of the University of Michigan. See Kenneth B. Clark, "Effect of Prejudice and Discrimination on Personality Development; CONFIDENTIAL DRAFT for the use of The Technical Committee on Fact Finding" (ca. 1950).

75. On projective tests, see Bock, *Continuities in Psychological Anthropol-*

ogy. See also David H. Spain, "On the Use of Projective Tests for Research in Psychological Anthropology," in Hsu, ed., *Psychological Anthropology*, 267–308; John Bushnell and Donna Bushnell, "Projective Doll Play Reconsidered: The Use of a Group Technique with Rural Mexican Children," in Thomas R. Williams, ed., *Psychological Anthropology* (The Hague: Mouton, 1975), 163–220.

76. On Clark's method, see Keppel, *Work of Democracy.* For earlier Clark studies, see Kenneth B. Clark and Mamie K. Clark, "The Development of Consciousness of Self and the Emergence of Racial Identification in Negro Preschool Children," *The Journal of Social Psychology* 10 (1939): 591–99; "Segregation as a Factor in the Racial Identification of Negro Pre-School Children: A Preliminary Report," *Journal of Experimental Education* 8 (2) (Dec. 1939): 161–63; "Skin Color as a Factor in Racial Identification of Negro Preschool Children," *The Journal of Social Psychology* 11 (1940): 159–69; "Racial Identification and Preference in Negro Children," in Eleanor E. Maccoby et al., eds., *Readings in Social Psychology* (New York: Henry Holt and Company, 1958), 602–11. For a study of racial identification in youth from which the Clarks drew inspiration, see Ruth E. Horowitz, "Racial Aspects of Self-Identification in Nursery School Children," *The Journal of Psychology* 7 (1939): 91–99.

77. Testimony of Kenneth Clark, *Briggs v. Elliot,* reprinted in Mark Whitman, ed., *Removing a Badge of Slavery: The Record of* Brown v. Board of Education (Princeton: Markus Wiener Publishing, 1993), 50. This finding is now complicated by contemporary social science. For a review of the literature on black motivation and self-esteem, see Sandra Graham, "Motivation in African Americans," *Review of Educational Research* 64 (1) (Spring 1994): 55–117.

78. Notably, like Myrdal's white Americans, a specter of sexual pathology implicitly hung over Clark's children as well, and in terms of a striking literary parallel. According to the White House Conference, one of the basic problems of personality development in adolescence was "self-diffusion"—represented by the character Biff in Arthur Miller's *Death of a Salesman*; similarly, one of the basic reactions to prejudice, discrimination, and racial self-hate was "open hostility"—represented especially by the "fictional case history" of Bigger Thomas in Richard Wright's *Native Son* (Witmer and Kotinsky, eds., *Personality in the Making*, 21, 143).

79. Bickel later published his research as Alexander M. Bickel, "The Original Understanding and the Segregation Decision," *Harvard Law Review* 69 (1) (Nov. 1955): 1–65.

80. *Brown*, 347 U.S. at 489.

81. *Brown*, 347 U.S. at 493; Lexis search conducted by the author (August 2005).

82. *Brown*, 347 U.S. at 493.

83. *Brown*, 347 U.S. at 494.

84. *Brown*, 347 U.S. at 495.

85. *Brown*, 347 U.S. at 494.

86. See Kluger, *Simple Justice*, 679: "The more he had pondered the question, Warren said, the more he had come to the conclusion that the doctrine of separate-but-equal rested upon the concept of the inferiority of the colored race. He did not see how Plessy and its progeny could be sustained on any other theory—and if the Court were to choose to sustain them, 'we must do it on that basis,' he was recorded by Burton as saying."

87. *Brown v. Board of Education II*, 349 U.S. 294 (1955).

88. *Heart of Atlanta Motel v. United States*, 379 U.S. 241 (1964); *Katzenbach v. McClung*, 379 U.S. 294 (1964).

Conclusion

1. Mark S. Weiner, *Black Trials: Citizenship from the Beginnings of Slavery to the End of Caste* (New York: Alfred A. Knopf, 2004), 323–27.

2. Adda B. Bozeman, *The Future of Law in a Multicultural World* (Princeton: Princeton University Press, 1971).

3. See Weiner, *Black Trials*, 325–72.

4. On political culture, see Gabriel A. Almond and Sidney Verba, *The Civic Culture: Political Attitudes and Democracy in Five Nations* (Princeton: Princeton University Press, 1963); for one overview, see Stephen Welch, *The Concept of Political Culture* (New York: St. Martin's Press, 1993).

Index

About the Author

Mark S. Weiner teaches constitutional law, legal history, and legal ethics at Rutgers School of Law in Newark, New Jersey. He is the author of *Black Trials: Citizenship from the Beginnings of Slavery to the End of Caste*. He holds an A.B. in American Studies from Stanford University, a Ph.D. in American Studies from Yale University, and a J.D. from Yale Law School. He lives in Hamden, Connecticut.